Section Four of

THE STATUTE OF FRAUDS

THE STATUTE OF FRAUDS

Section Four

IN THE LIGHT OF ITS

JUDICIAL INTERPRETATION

BY

JAMES WILLIAMS, LL.M. (N.Z.)
PH.D. (Cantab.)
A Barrister and a Solicitor of
The Supreme Court of New Zealand

CAMBRIDGE
AT THE UNIVERSITY PRESS
1932

CAMBRIDGE
UNIVERSITY PRESS

University Printing House, Cambridge CB2 8BS, United Kingdom

Published in the United States of America by Cambridge University Press, New York

Cambridge University Press is part of the University of Cambridge.

It furthers the University's mission by disseminating knowledge in the pursuit of education, learning and research at the highest international levels of excellence.

www.cambridge.org
Information on this title: www.cambridge.org/9781107673779

First published 1932
First paperback edition 2013

A catalogue record for this publication is available from the British Library

ISBN 978-1-107-67377-9 Paperback

To

MY MOTHER

CONTENTS

Part I

CONTRACTS AFFECTED BY THE STATUTE

Part II

THE WRITING

Part III

OPERATION OF THE STATUTE

PREFATORY NOTE

I DESIRE to express my sincere thanks to Dr Hazeltine for his kindness in supplying the foreword, and for the advice, criticism and encouragement which I have received from him while I have been writing this book. I also wish to thank the Syndics of the University Press for undertaking the publication of the book; and the officials and staff of the Press for their courtesy and assistance.

J. W.

CAMBRIDGE,

August, 1932.

TABLE OF STATUTES OTHER THAN THE STATUTE OF FRAUDS

TABLE OF CASES

FOREWORD

THE Statute of Frauds (29 Car. II, c. 3), with its twenty-five sections, is one of the most comprehensive and important statutes known to the history of English law. With the exception of sections 4 and 23, the whole of this great Statute has been repealed, many of its provisions finding a place in other Acts of the Parliament; and even a part of section 4 has been repealed by the Law of Property Act, 1925, although re-enacted in modified form by that Statute. Section 4 of the Statute of Frauds still remains, however, as an integral part of our legal system; and at the present day it has, in fact, a practical importance not only in England, but also in other countries (notably certain of the British Dominions and of the States of the American Union) which have succeeded to it or adopted its provisions.

On this fourth section of the Statute of Frauds, Dr Williams has written an illuminating treatise; and it is, indeed, the only book in our legal literature which deals exclusively with this part of our Statute law. If it be remembered that, in the course of the two hundred and fifty years which have elapsed since the enactment of the Statute in 1677, a vast mass of case-law has grown up around section 4, the great advantage to the profession in possessing a lucid and orderly commentary on the judicial decisions will be readily seen. By his scholarly analysis of the cases, many of which are of conflicting tendency, as well as by his skill in weaving the principles laid down by the judges into a consistent entity, Dr Williams has greatly lightened the labour alike of courts and practitioners in all the many jurisdictions where section 4 is still a part of the law that is administered.

While primarily a treatise on an aspect of the law of contracts, the present work is at the same time a commentary on other features of our legal system. No better illustration could be given of the inter-relation of all the parts of our law of civil justice. Not only does the literary presentation of the judicial rules relating to this section of the Statute of Frauds involve, in general, a consideration of both common law and equity, but within these two main divisions of our system various topics which have a significance wider than contract, such as agency, evidence, quasi-contract, and the nature of legal documents, must be brought within the scope of the author's study. In setting forth the special legal characteristics of the Statute of Frauds, section 4, in the light of the general principles of law and equity, Dr Williams has achieved a notable success.

Since the main purpose of the author has been to expound the law of to-day, he has naturally arranged his several topics in compliance with a systematical scheme adapted to the subject-matter; and by following this method he has been enabled to present each topic in its proper legal perspective. It is worthy of observation, however, that the case-law now enforced by the courts is the product of an historical development which goes back to the time of Charles II. Many doctrines have been shaped by the courts through a slow constructive process; and some of these doctrines bear the imprint of the changing conditions of English social, economic, and legal life during the last two hundred and fifty years. It is not surprising to find, therefore, that under several of the main headings of the present work the treatment of the subject-matter is essentially historical; and, indeed, the literary treatment of almost any branch of our existing law must of necessity possess, in large measure, an historical character. This characteristic of our legal literature results, in part at least, from the fact that our law is so largely based on judicial precedents and that its principles are so often the result of a long series of distinctions drawn by the judges from age to age. From this point of view, Dr Williams' book is a contribution to English legal history; and, in truth, nowhere else in our legal literature will the reader find the historical development of this branch of our system set out in greater fulness or with equal illumination.

The close relation between law and life, an accepted maxim of historical and theoretical jurisprudence, is exemplified in a striking manner by the growth of the law in regard to the Statute of Frauds. Originating in the social and legal conditions of the age of Charles II, the Statute was intended as an instrument to effect certain definite purposes, more particularly the prevention of fraud as between parties to contracts. In truth, the Statute has always been intimately related to social and economic life; and, while the special conditions of the Caroline age have long since ceased to have practical bearing, the law contained in the fourth section of the Statute and in the interpretive judicial decisions still possesses a character which makes it of importance to many classes of the community, not least to those who are concerned with commercial transactions. It is this social and economic significance of the law expounded by Dr Williams which will awaken an interest in many persons who are not judges or members of the legal profession.

It is not unimportant to observe, furthermore, that this treatise on the Statute of Frauds, written by a practising lawyer who is also in close touch with academic life, is of value as a text-book in schools of law. The improvement of legal education, both academic and professional, is one of the outstanding features of the intellectual life alike of England and the British Empire and of the United States of America during the last half century. In the future work of students and teachers of the law, Dr Williams' book, treating as it does of a vital feature of legal history and of our present-day system, should hold a special place.

As a result of his extensive survey of the judicial interpretation of the Statute of Frauds, section 4, the learned author has shewn us clearly that there has been to a large extent a nullification of the section by the courts; and, moreover, he has demonstrated, with remarkable lucidity and in abundant detail, that "the processes by which the courts have achieved this result have of necessity brought in their train many complexities and over-refined distinctions". In view of this undesirable feature of our existing law, Dr Williams raises the question as to whether the section should not be repealed by the legislature, or, if not repealed, at least extensively modified. He himself favours repeal; and indeed at the present day, both in legal and in commercial circles, this view is generally held. Dr Williams' arguments for repeal, based as they are on an elaborate and scholarly study of all the problems involved, are worthy of the most careful consideration by law reformers.

H. D. HAZELTINE

INTRODUCTION

THE Statute of Frauds,[1] s. 4 of which is considered in this treatise, was stated in its preamble to be an act "For prevention of many fraudulent practices which are commonly endeavoured to be upheld by perjury and subornation of perjury". The Statute therefore purported to remedy certain abuses and mischiefs which at the time of its passing affected the administration of justice; and hence it may be of interest if brief reference be made to the general nature of the Statute, the circumstances which brought about its enactment, and the general lines upon which it proceeded in effecting its purpose.[2]

The Statute of Frauds was a measure of a very extensive character: Thayer[3] described it as "a very extraordinary enactment to have been passed by an English-speaking community in any age, so comprehensive is it and so far-reaching". It contained some twenty-five sections and dealt with such diverse subjects as contract, real property and conveyancing, wills, trusts, administration of deceased estates, creditors' remedies, procedure, and the law of succession. Of the twenty-five sections of the Statute, however, not all related directly to the prevention of fraud and perjury. This, the main purpose of the Statute, was carried out chiefly by those sections which prescribed writing or other adequate evidence as a necessary ingredient in certain transactions. The transactions with which the Statute dealt in

[1] (1677) 29 Car. II, c. 3.

[2] The historical materials utilized in the introduction have been derived chiefly from Holdsworth, *History of English Law*, VI, pp. 379–397, and Thayer, *Preliminary Treatise on Evidence*, chapters vi and x. In the former work the history of the Statute of Frauds is learnedly and exhaustively set forth.

[3] *Preliminary Treatise*, 430.

this manner were certain conveyances of interests in land,[1] wills,[2] trusts[3] and certain contracts.[4]

Probably the most important, certainly the best known, of these provisions "for prevention of Frauds and Perjuryes", were those contained in the sections (4 and 17) relating to contracts. "It is the latter clauses [i.e., those prescribing written or other adequate evidence for certain transactions]," wrote Holdsworth,[5] "which have added important chapters to the branches of law and equity affected by them, by reason of the large number of judicial decisions to which they have given rise. It is these clauses and especially the clauses relating to contracts, which have roused the greatest number of divergent criticisms."

Of the sections relating to contracts, s. 4 provided that five specified classes of contracts should not be enforceable by action unless evidenced by some note or memorandum in writing signed by the party to be charged or his authorized agent. S. 17 provided similarly for contracts for the sale of goods where the price was £10 or more; but it allowed, as an alternative to the writing, the acceptance and actual receipt of the goods, part payment, or the giving of something in earnest.

Why, it may be asked, should it have been considered necessary to prescribe a particular form of evidence in these cases? Is not contract a matter between party and party, and could not the parties be trusted to embody their contracts in a form which would protect them both? The answer to these questions is to be found in a consideration of the method of trial and the imperfectly developed state of the law of evidence at the time when the Statute of Frauds was passed.

Actions on contracts would normally be tried before a jury.

1 29 Car. II, c. 3, ss. 1–3.

2 *Ib.* ss. 5, 6, 19–23. In the *Statutes Revised* (1888), ss. 19–23 are numbered 18–22, respectively.

3 *Ib.* ss. 8, 9.

4 *Ib.* ss. 4, 17 (16 in *Statutes Revised*).

5 *History of English Law*, VI, p. 387.

At the period when the Statute of Frauds was enacted, however, the jury was a most unsatisfactory tribunal. It was still entitled to decide matters on its own knowledge, and therefore might reject the whole of the evidence brought before it.[1] And there was practically no way of obtaining relief, if the jury gave a perverse verdict. As Holdsworth wrote,[2] "the mediaeval method of controlling the jury by writ of attaint was obsolete, the sixteenth and early seventeenth century method of controlling it by fine or imprisonment had been decided in Bushell's Case[3] to be illegal, and the modern device of getting an order for a new trial, when the verdict was against the weight of evidence, was in its infancy". It was indeed with good cause that Powell, J., in 1659, referring to the admissibility of extrinsic evidence to add to a will, remarked:[4] "il n'est safe d'admitter un Jury a tryer l'Intent del Testator".

Not only, however, was the jury a most unsatisfactory tribunal in itself, but the position was made worse by the comparatively undeveloped condition of the law of evidence at that period. Especially did the rules which excluded the testimony of the parties to the action, their husbands or wives and all who had any interest in the outcome of the proceedings, operate to defeat justice and render needlessly difficult the ascertainment of what was said and done between the parties.[5]

The Statute of Frauds effected a substantial improvement in this condition of affairs. First, it prevented questions relating to the several matters with which it dealt, from being left at large to the jury, possibly to be decided by jury's own knowledge or lack of knowledge; henceforth, before a jury could find a verdict in these cases, evidence of the prescribed sort had to be

[1] Thayer, *op. cit.* 429; Holdsworth, *op. cit.* VI, p. 388.
[2] *Ubi supra.*
[3] (1670) Vaugh. 435.
[4] In *Lawrence* v. *Dodwell*, (1659) 1 Lutw. 734, 735; 125 E.R. 384, 385.
[5] Holdsworth, *op. cit.* 388, 389; per Cave, J., in *Evans* v. *Hoare*, [1892] 1 Q.B. 593, 597.

adduced.[1] Secondly, the Statute went some distance towards overcoming the rules which disqualified parties as witnesses, for where a writing was prescribed, it had to be signed by the party or his agent. And thirdly, the Statute provided some certainty amidst the general uncertainty with which the law of evidence as a whole was invested.

Of the twenty-five sections of which the Statute was originally composed, only two, ss. 4 and 23,[2] remain in their original Caroline dress; and the former section lost a limb in the sweeping law reform of 1925.[3] With the exception of these two sections, the whole of the original Statute has been repealed. Some of its provisions have been transferred with but little change to other statutes; others have been replaced by more extensive or more elaborate enactments. Of the two surviving sections, s. 23 relates to the wills of soldiers and mariners, while s. 4 contains the provisions requiring certain contracts to be in writing. It is with s. 4 that this treatise is concerned, and in the following pages s. 4 will (except where the context otherwise requires) be referred to as the Statute, simply.

[1] Thayer, *op. cit.* 430. [2] 22 in the *Statutes Revised.*
[3] Law of Property Act, 1925, s. 207 and Seventh Schedule.

PART I

CONTRACTS AFFECTED BY THE STATUTE

CHAPTER I

CONTRACTS EXPRESSLY COMPRISED WITHIN THE STATUTE

THE Statute[1] provides as follows:

"no Action shall be brought whereby to charge any Executor or Administrator upon any special Promise, to answer Damages out of his own Estate; or whereby to charge the Defendant upon any special Promise to answer for the Debt, Default or Miscarriages of another Person; or to charge any Person upon any Agreement made upon Consideration of Marriage; or upon any Agreement that is not to be performed within the Space of one Year from the making thereof; unless the Agreement upon which such Action shall be brought, or some *Memorandum* or Note thereof, shall be in writing, and signed by the Party to be charged therewith, or some other Person thereunto by him lawfully authorized".

The Statute, therefore, is not of general application, but affects only contracts falling within the several specified classes. In the present chapter it is proposed to consider those contracts expressly comprised within the Statute, and in the chapter following, certain contracts and arrangements to which the Statute has been held to have no application.

(I) *Contract by executor or administrator to answer damages out of his own estate.* An executor or administrator, discharging his

[1] 29 Car. II, c. 3, s. 4. As originally enacted, this section applied also to contracts "to charge any Person...upon any Contract or Sale of Land, Tenements or Hereditaments, or any Interest in or concerning them". This part of the section was repealed by the Law of Property Act, 1925 (15 Geo. V, c. 20, s. 207, & Sched. 7), and in lieu thereof the following enacted (*ib.* s. 40 (1)): "No action may be brought upon any contract for the sale or other disposition of land or any interest in land, unless the agreement upon which such action is brought, or some memorandum or note thereof, is in writing, and signed by the party to be charged or by some other person thereunto by him lawfully authorized". "Land" is defined (*ib.* s. 205). It is to be observed that the new provision differs considerably in its terms from the enactment it replaces, and it may be doubted whether it does not as well differ somewhat in its effect. The question, however, seems more properly to come within the scope of a work on the law of real property, and is not discussed in this treatise.

duties in a legal fashion, is not liable out of his own estate for the obligations of the deceased, but he can assume personal liability for those obligations, or any of them, by contracting to that effect.[1] Such a contract will, in general, come within the provisions of the Statute, and will therefore require to be evidenced by a signed writing in order to be enforceable by action.

It was decided by Lord Hardwicke, L.C., in *Tomlinson* v. *Gill*,[2] that the Statute did not apply to a promise made before the promisor had been appointed an administrator, even though he clearly contemplated at the time when he made the promise that he would be appointed to that office. It is conceived that this decision would apply equally where the promise was made by one who was subsequently granted administration as an executor.

The Statute refers to promises "to answer damages". But it would certainly appear from *Tomlinson* v. *Gill*[2] that Lord Hardwicke thought that a promise to be responsible for the deceased's debts would be comprehended by these words, for although he held that the promise in that case (to answer for the deceased's debts) was out of the Statute, he did not suggest, as a ground of his decision, that the promise related to debts and not to damages. It would seem, therefore, that this clause of the Statute applies generally to promises by executors or administrators to answer for the liabilities of the deceased, whether such liabilities be for liquidated and ascertained sums, or for unliquidated damages.[3] Liabilities for unliquidated damages fall within the very words of the Statute; while liabilities for liquidated and ascertained sums, inasmuch as they are enforceable by way of an action for damages for non-payment, would therefore also be comprised within the terms of the Statute.

In regard to contracts coming under the present head, as well as in regard to other contracts to which the Statute applies, it was at one time thought that the presence of writing was an alternative to the common law requirement of consideration.[4] But this suggestion was emphatically rejected in the case of

[1] Williams, *Executors and Administrators*, 12th ed. II, p. 1164.
[2] (1756) Amb. 330; 27 E.R. 221.
[3] Williams, *op. cit.* II, p. 1164.
[4] *Pillans* v. *Van Mierop*, (1765) 3 Burr. 1663; 97 E.R. 1035.

Rann v. *Hughes*,[1] where it was held by the House of Lords (affirming the decision of the Court of Exchequer Chamber), that the presence of writing in such cases was a condition which had to be satisfied in addition to the common law requirement of consideration.

(II) *Contract to answer for the debt, default or miscarriages of another person*. The question of what contracts do and what do not come under this heading has given rise to much litigation. The Statute refers to the debt, default or miscarriages of *another* person. Hence it was early laid down[2] that before a promise could be affected by the Statute it had to be *collateral*, i.e. it had to be conditional upon the non-discharge of an *original* liability, contractual or tortious, of another.[3] If the promise sued on were itself *original*, i.e. were not so conditional, it did not come within the Statute. This distinction was first drawn in the leading case of *Birkmyr* v. *Darnell*.[4] In that case it was laid down by the Court of King's Bench that,

> "If two come to a shop, and one buys, and the other, to gain him credit, promises the seller, *if he does not pay you, I will*; this is a collateral undertaking, and void without writing, by the Statute of Frauds: but if he says, *Let him have the goods, I will be your paymaster* or *I will see you paid*, this is an undertaking as for himself, and he shall be intended to be the very buyer, and the other to act but as his servant".

The principle of *Birkmyr* v. *Darnell* has been repeatedly accepted and applied in subsequent cases, and the result of these authorities may be summed up by saying that the only contracts included under the present head of the Statute are contracts of guarantee or suretyship.

What constitutes a contract of guarantee or suretyship was

[1] 7 T.R. 350n.; 101 E.R. 1014.

[2] *Birkmyr* v. *Darnell*, (1704) 1 Salk. 27; 91 E.R. 27.

[3] "The true difference", said Lee, C.J., in *Read* v. *Nash*, (1751) 1 Wils. K.B. 305, 306; 95 E.R. 632, "is between an original promise and a collateral promise; the first is out of the Statute, the latter is not when it is to pay the debt of another which was already contracted."

[4] (1704) 1 Salk. 27, 28; 91 E.R. 27. S.C. 6 Mod. 248; 3 Salk. 15; Holt 606; 1 *Smith's Leading Cases*, 13th ed. p. 331.

defined in the following terms by Vaughan Williams, L.J., in *Davys* v. *Buswell*:[1]

"As I understand it, in any case where, in substance and in fact, an obligation has been undertaken by a person to the creditor to pay a debt due from another person, for which that other remains responsible, in the event of his making default, prima facie that is a guarantee, and the case comes within the 4th section of the Statute of Frauds".

The conditions required to be fulfilled by a promise in order that it may constitute a guarantee as thus defined, may be stated as follows:

(i) It must be a promise by a third party to one to whom another is, or will be, indebted, i.e. a creditor, present or prospective; and it must be to answer for the debt or liability (or portion thereof) in respect of which that other is, or will be, so indebted.

(ii) The liability of the third party must be conditional upon default first being made by the debtor in respect of the guaranteed liability.

(iii) The debtor must continue responsible, notwithstanding the promise of the third party.

(iv) The foregoing matters are to be tested by the real intent of the parties, "the substance and fact" of the matter, and not merely by the outward form with which the parties have invested their transaction.

(i) *Promise must be to a creditor, present or prospective.*

"There can be no suretyship", said Lord Selborne in *Lakeman* v. *Mountstephen*,[2] "unless there be a principal debtor, who of course may be constituted in the course of the transaction by matters *ex post facto*, and need not be so at the time, but until there is a principal debtor there can be no suretyship. Nor can a man guarantee anybody else's debt unless there is a debt of some other person to be guaranteed".

Accordingly, it has been repeatedly decided by the courts that a promise, to come within the Statute, must be made to the

[1] [1913] 2 K.B. 47, 54.
[2] (1874) L.R. 7 H.L. 17, 24.

person to whom another is, or will become, liable, and it must be in respect of such liability.

"The Statute", said Parke, B., delivering the judgment of the Court of Exchequer in *Hargreaves* v. *Parsons*,[1] "applies only to promises made to the persons to whom another is already, or is to become, answerable. It must be a promise to be answerable for a debt of, or a default in some duty by that other person towards the promisee."

In *Hargreaves* v. *Parsons*[1] the defendant had assigned to the plaintiff the benefit of certain contracts entered into between himself and a third party. The defendant had, at the same time, undertaken that the third party would perform those contracts, and it was upon this undertaking that the plaintiff sued. The defendant pleaded the Statute, but the Court of Exchequer held that that defence was not available, inasmuch as the third party was under no liability to the plaintiff.

"In this case", said Parke, B.,[2] "Parker [the third party] had not contracted with the plaintiff, nor was it intended that he should; there was no privity between them; the non-performance of Parker's contract with the defendant would be no default towards the plaintiff, and consequently the undertaking by the defendant was no promise to answer for the default or miscarriage of Parker in any debt or duty towards the plaintiff. It was an original promise that a certain thing should be done by a third person."

That the promise, to come within the Statute, must relate to and be in respect of the liability of the debtor to the promisee, was emphasized by Erle, C.J., in his judgment in *Reader* v. *Kingham*.[3] In that case the plaintiff, a bailiff, was about to arrest a debtor on a warrant of contempt for non-payment of a judgment debt, but desisted upon receiving the defendant's undertaking to pay £17 on a given day, or else to surrender the debtor. It was held by the Court of Common Pleas that this undertaking, not being to the original creditor, nor yet being in respect of the original debt, was outside the Statute.

[1] (1844) 13 M. & W. 561, 570; 153 E.R. 235, 238.
[2] *Ib.*
[3] (1862) 13 C.B. (N.S.) 344, 354; 143 E.R. 137, 141.

"But clear I am", said Erle, C.J., "that upon the balance of authority, the promise of the defendant in this case is a collateral promise, and not within the Statute. The debts are totally distinct debts, as well as the debtors. No satisfaction resulted to Malins [the creditor] on account of what passed between Kingham and Reader. Reader was the agent of Malins to accept £17 in satisfaction of the debt and costs in the county court; but he was not his agent to postpone the payment....The payment of the £17, therefore, would not necessarily have been a discharge of Malins's demand, but only a discharge or satisfaction of the contract between Kingham and Reader. The case is clearly not one to which the Statute of Frauds can apply."[1]

It seemed at one time doubtful whether the rule established by the foregoing authorities would become the law; and in *Green* v. *Cresswell*[2] it was held by the Court of King's Bench, disapproving of *Thomas* v. *Cook* (the case in which the rule was first expressly laid down),[3] that a promise made by the defendant to the plaintiff, in respect of the default of a third party who was under no liability to the plaintiff, was nevertheless within the Statute. The effect of the promise in *Green* v. *Cresswell*[2] was stated by Denman, C.J. (who delivered the judgment of the court in that case), to be as follows:

"If you will become bail for Hadley, and Hadley, by not paying or appearing, forfeits his bail bond, I will save you harmless from all the consequences of your becoming bail. If Hadley fails to do what is right towards you, I will do it instead of him".

The contention that this promise was out of the Statute because Hadley's debt was not owed to the bail (the promisee) but to a third person, was thus disposed of by Lord Denman:

"A distinction was also hinted at, from the circumstance of Hadley's debt being due to a third person, and the default therefore incurred towards him, not towards the bail. But here again is the surmise of an intention in the Legislature which none of

[1] See also *Anderson* v. *Hayman*, (1789) 1 H.Bl. 120; 126 E.R. 73; *Thomas* v. *Cook*, (1828) 8 B. & C. 728; 108 E.R. 1213; *Eastwood* v. *Kenyon*, (1840) 11 A. & E. 438, per Lord Denman, C.J., 446; 113 E.R. 482, 485; *Cripps* v. *Hartnoll*, (1863) 4 B. & S. 414; 122 E.R. 514; *Guild* v. *Conrad*, [1894] 2 Q.B. 885; *In re Hoyle*, [1893] 1 Ch. 84, 91.

[2] (1839) 10 A. & E. 453, 459; 113 E.R. 172, 174.

[3] (1828) 8 B. & C. 728; 108 E.R. 1213.

its language bears out; and, besides, may it not be said that the arrested debtor, who obtained his freedom by being bailed, undertakes to his bail to keep them harmless by paying the debt, or surrendering?"

The opinion intimated in this passage, that the guaranteed obligation need not be owed to the person to whom the guarantee is given, was disapproved in *Reader* v. *Kingham*,[1] where the Court of Common Pleas refused to follow *Green* v. *Cresswell*.[2] *Green* v. *Cresswell*[2] had already been described by Pollock, C.B., in *Batson* v. *King*,[3] as not rightly decided, and some years later it was distinguished and not followed by the Court of Exchequer in *Cripps* v. *Hartnoll*.[4] Then, in 1874, the point was raised before Malins, V.-C., in *Wildes* v. *Dudlow*,[5] and that learned judge, after reviewing the authorities, expressed the opinion that *Green* v. *Cresswell*[2] should be considered as overruled, and that the cases established that an indemnity, as distinct from a guarantee, was not within the Statute. After referring to *Green* v. *Cresswell*,[2] Malins, V.-C., said:[5]

"But I am happy to find that, the matter having been most carefully and elaborately considered in the case of *Reader* v. *Kingham*, when the full number of Judges was present, the case of *Green* v. *Cresswell* was overruled....I accordingly decide that where one person induces another to enter into an engagement, by a promise to indemnify him against liability, that is not an agreement within the *Statute of Frauds*, and does not require to be in writing".

Wildes v. *Dudlow*,[5] and the original case on the point, *Thomas* v. *Cook*,[6] were expressly approved and followed by the Court of Appeal in *Guild* v. *Conrad*,[7] as also was *In re Bolton*,[8] in which Chitty, J., had followed these same authorities. *In re Bolton*[8] illustrates quite well the rule under discussion, viz., that the promise, to constitute a guarantee coming within the Statute,

[1] (1862) 13 C.B. (N.S.) 344, per Williams, J., 355; 143 E.R. 137, 141.
[2] (1839) 10 A. & E. 453, 459; 113 E.R. 172, 174.
[3] (1859) 4 H. & N. 739, 740; 157 E.R. 1032, 1033.
[4] (1863) 4 B. & S. 414; 122 E.R. 514.
[5] (1874) L.R. 19 Eq. 198, 201.
[6] (1828) 8 B. & C. 728; 108 E.R. 1213.
[7] [1894] 2 Q.B. 885.
[8] (1892) 8 T.L.R. 668.

must be made to one to whom another is, or will become, liable. In *In re Bolton*,[1] the promise sued on was found by Chitty, J., to be to the effect following:

"In consideration that the solicitors [i.e. the promisees] would procure the bankers to make the loan of £4000 to the company and would personally guarantee to the bankers the repayment of the loan, the testator promised that to the extent of £2000 he would repay the solicitors what they should pay to the bankers under the guarantee". "This", continued the learned judge, "is not a promise to answer for the debt, default, or miscarriage of another, but an original contract between the parties, whereby the testator agreed to pay £2000 in an event which has happened."

It is to be noted, however, that although it is necessary that the guaranteed liability and the guarantee should be owed and made to the same person, it is immaterial that, at the time the promise of guarantee is entered into, the liability guaranteed should be prospective merely. In the argument in *Jones* v. *Cooper*,[2] indeed, it was said that Lord Mansfield, in *Mawbrey* v. *Cunningham*,[3] had decided that a promise made in respect of the liability of a third party towards the promisee, but before such liability had been incurred, was for that reason an original promise, and not within the Statute. But even if this was decided by Lord Mansfield, it was afterwards overruled by the Court of King's Bench in *Jones* v. *Cooper*.[2] In *Jones* v. *Cooper*[2] it was held that the sole question for consideration was whether the liability of the alleged guarantee was original or collateral; and it was decided that in the circumstances of that case, the promise was collateral and within the Statute, although given before the guaranteed liability had been incurred.[4] In *Peckham* v. *Faria*[5] Lord Mansfield stated the effect of *Jones* v. *Cooper* to be as follows:

"that wherever a man is to be called upon, only in the second instance, he is within the Statute; otherwise, where he is to be called upon in the first instance".

[1] (1892) 8 T.L.R. 668. [2] (1774) 1 Cowp. 227; 98 E.R. 1058.
[3] (1773) cited 1 Cowp. 228; 98 E.R. 1058.
[4] See also *Matson* v. *Wharam*, (1787) 2 T.R. 80; 100 E.R. 44.
[5] (1781) 3 Dougl. 13, 15; 99 E.R. 514.

Willes, J., stated the true position very clearly in the course of his judgment in *Mountstephen* v. *Lakeman*.[1]

"Again", he said, "if there was a contract with reference to a liability, not existing at the time, by reason of the debt not being due at the time, but being payable in future, that would come under the word default, and there would be no difficulty about that. So, if there was a contract, 'If *A.B.* will employ you to do work, I promise to become surety for him that he shall pay you'; in that case the promise would clearly come within the statute, because, although there was no liability existing at the time when the promise was made, there was a liability contemplated as the foundation for the promise of the defendant."

Although, however, the guaranteed liability need not be present but may be prospective, it must be real. This is established by the case of *Lakeman* v. *Mountstephen*.[2] In that case the plaintiff had done certain work for a local board on the undertaking of the Chairman of the board to see the work paid for. The plaintiff contended that the Chairman's undertaking constituted an original liability, and it was argued in support of that contention that the Chairman's liability could not be otherwise than original, inasmuch as there had never been any contract between the plaintiff and the board in respect of which the board could have made a default to be answered for by the Chairman. The Court of Queen's Bench declined to accept this contention, and held that the Chairman's promise constituted a guarantee coming within the Statute.

"I think", said Blackburn, J.,[3] "that the statute must be taken to apply to any contract of suretyship where there is an intention of guaranteeing the payment of a debt of another, and to require a writing wherever the contract, according to the intention of the parties, is a contract of suretyship. The enactment was aimed against what the legislature deemed the mischief of allowing a person to be fixed with liability for another by loose and idle talk; and the mischief, as it seems to me, would be just as great

[1] (1871) L.R. 7 Q.B. at p. 202.

[2] (1874) L.R. 7 H.L. 17, affirming the judgment of the Court of Exchequer Chamber, L.R. 7 Q.B. 196, which had reversed the Court of Queen's Bench, L.R. 5 Q.B. 613.

[3] L.R. 5 Q.B. 619.

in a case where there is only a supposed or suspected liability in the original debtor as where there is an actual legal liability existing or afterwards contracted."

When the case was taken to appeal, however, the decision of the Court of Queen's Bench was reversed by the Court of Exchequer Chamber, and this reversal was upheld by the House of Lords. In the Court of Exchequer Chamber, Willes, J., pointed out[1] that the ground upon which the Court of Queen's Bench had based its decision could not be supported, inasmuch as, assuming that the promise sued upon had been made and accepted on the assumption of the local board being liable or becoming liable, it would have been void (independently of the Statute) if that condition were not fulfilled. And in the House of Lords, Lord Selborne emphatically repudiated[2] the suggestion that there could be a contract of guarantee without there being a principal debtor; although he expressly recognized that it was no objection that the principal debtor should be "constituted in the course of the transaction by matters *ex post facto*".

(ii) *The liability of the promisor must be conditional upon default first being made by the debtor in respect of the guaranteed liability.* It has been pointed out above[3] that a promise made to one who is not a creditor, present or prospective, of a third party, amounts only to a promise of indemnity, and need not comply with the requirements of the Statute. And while the extent of such a promise may sometimes be measured by the liability of a third party,[4] or the loss which the promisee may suffer by dealing with a third party,[5] its fixed characteristic is that it is absolute and in no way dependent on the third party's making default towards the promisee. Indeed, *ex hypothesi*, the third party would be under no liability to the promisee in respect of which he could make default. But even where the third party is or becomes liable to the promisee, so that the promisee is a creditor of the third party, it may yet happen that he has become such creditor in reliance on the promise of the promisor to save him

[1] L.R. 7 Q.B. 202. [2] L.R. 7 H.L. 24. [3] Pp. 6, 9, *supra*.
[4] E.g. *Wildes* v. *Dudlow*, (1874) L.R. 19 Eq. 198.
[5] E.g. *In re Bolton*, (1892) 8 T.L.R. 668.

harmless. And it has been decided that such a promise, if it be absolute and not conditional on the third party's making default, will, like a similar promise where the third party is not and is not intended to be under any liability to the promisee, amount to an indemnity merely, and not a guarantee coming within the Statute.[1]

Whether a promise constitutes an indemnity falling outside the Statute because it is not made in respect of a liability owed or to be owed by a third party to the promisee, or whether because, although made in respect of such a liability, it is absolute and not conditional on the third party's defaulting in the discharge of that liability, it will in either case be reducible to the following formula: "If you will enter into this transaction, I promise unconditionally to save you harmless from the consequences of your so doing".

It is the unconditional nature of the promise which distinguishes an indemnity from a guarantee: an indemnity, as it is said, is an *original*[2] promise. Where there is no third party liable to the promisee the matter is put thus:[3] "If *A* undertakes a liability at the request of *B* and upon a promise by *B* to pay to *A* what he pays under the liability, *B*'s promise is not within the Statute of Frauds". The unconditional nature of the promise is not stressed, as there is no liability owed to the promisee upon which it might be conditional. Where, however, the transaction involves a third party's becoming liable to the promisee, then the necessity for the promise to be unconditional is strongly emphasized.

"In my opinion", said Davey, L.J., in *Guild* v. *Conrad*,[4] "there is a plain distinction between a promise to pay the creditor if the principal debtor makes default in payment, and a promise to keep a person who has entered, or is about to enter, into a contract of liability indemnified against that liability independently of the question whether a third person makes default or not."

The foregoing propositions and submissions are supported

[1] *Guild* v. *Conrad*, [1894] 2 Q.B. 885.
[2] Per Chitty, J., in *In re Bolton*, 8 T.L.R. at p. 669.
[3] *Ib.*
[4] [1894] 2 Q.B. at p. 896.

and illustrated by the decision of the Court of Appeal in *Guild* v. *Conrad*.[1] In that case the plaintiff was in correspondence with a Demerara firm and accepted certain of their bills on the undertaking of the defendant to indemnify him up to a named sum, if he would give the Demerara firm credit in this way. This undertaking was in writing, but the sum was afterwards enlarged by verbal agreement. As time went on the Demerara firm got overdrawn, and the plaintiff at length became so reluctant to accept their bills as to refuse them altogether. Thereupon the defendant made a fresh arrangement with the plaintiff in consequence of which the plaintiff accepted certain further bills of the Demerara firm. In the subsequent litigation it was decided that the first promise was in fact conditional on the Demerara firm making default in meeting the bills, and was therefore a guarantee and unenforceable to the extent to which it had been verbally enlarged. With regard to the subsequent arrangement, however, Mathew, J. (whose finding on the point was adopted by the Court of Appeal), held that it comprised an unconditional promise by the defendant to the plaintiff, to save him harmless if he would accept the further bills, and that it was therefore an indemnity and outside the Statute.

"It was not a contract to pay if the foreign firm did not pay", said Mathew, J.,[2] "because there was no expectation at that time that the foreign firm would be able to pay. The contract was to find funds to enable the plaintiff to meet these acceptances."

On this Lindley, L.J., remarked as follows:[3]

"I cannot help thinking that the true result of those interviews was this—that the defendant did promise the plaintiff, that, if he would accept those batches of bills, he, the defendant, would take care that they should be met, and that he himself would provide funds to meet them; and it was on the faith of that promise that the plaintiff accepted those bills. If this is the real contract, and if the learned judge is right in saying that the contract was not a contract to pay if the Demerara firm did not pay, but was a contract to pay in any event, then, in my opinion, the authorities shew that the Statute of Frauds does not apply".

[1] [1894] 2 Q.B. 885. [2] *Ib.* 888. [3] *Ib.* 892.

The general statement of the principle given by Lopes, L.J., in the course of his judgment may also be quoted.

"A promise", said the learned Lord Justice,[1] "to be liable for a debt conditionally on the principal debtor making default is a guarantee, and is a promise to make good the default of another within the statute. On the other hand, a promise to become liable for a debt whenever the person to whom the promise is made should become liable, is not a promise within the Statute of Frauds and need not be in writing."[2]

(iii) *The debtor must continue responsible, notwithstanding the promise of the alleged guarantor.* Inasmuch as a liability, present or prospective, outstanding in some third person, is a necessary element in the constitution of a guarantee, it follows that if the arrangement between the promisor and the promisee involves the extinction of the third party's liability, this arrangement will not amount to a guarantee but will constitute an original undertaking outside the scope of the Statute. Thus in *Goodman* v. *Chase*,[3] the defendant, in consideration that the plaintiff would release from custody a third party whom he had taken under a *ca. sa.*, promised to pay the third party's debt. The third party was thereupon released, and a discharge of the debt thereby effected. It was accordingly held by the Court of King's Bench that the defendant's undertaking was not for "the debt, default or miscarriage of another person", but was in the nature of an original undertaking and outside the Statute.

[1] *Ib.* 895.

[2] See also *Lakeman* v. *Mountstephen*, (1874) L.R. 7 H.L. 17, per Lord Cairns, L.C., 23.

In some of the earlier cases *dicta* are to be found in which it was apparently laid down that the only question was whether the promise of the guarantor had been given in respect of an obligation owed or to be owed by a third party to the promisee. Thus in *Matson* v. *Wharam*, (1787) 2 T.R. 80, 81; 100 E.R. 44, 45, Buller, J., said: "the general line now taken is, that, if the person for whose use the goods are furnished be liable at all, any other promise by a third person to pay that debt must be in writing, otherwise it is void by the Statute of Frauds". But, as *Guild* v. *Conrad* and *Lakeman* v. *Mountstephen* shew, such *dicta* are too wide and must be qualified to exclude promises which, while fulfilling the conditions stated, are nevertheless not conditional on the third party making default in discharging his obligation to the promisee, but absolute and independent of any such condition.

[3] (1818) 1 B. & Ald. 297; 106 E.R. 110.

"The words of the 4th section of the Statute of Frauds", said Abbott, J.,[1] "have always been construed to mean, that the person for whose debt the collateral promise is made must still remain himself liable for the debt."

And Lord Ellenborough, C.J., remarked:[2]

"The promise by the defendant here is not a collateral but an original promise, for which the consideration is the discharge of the debt as between the plaintiff and Chase Junior [the third party, taken on the *ca. sa.*]".[3]

(iv) *The foregoing matters are to be tested by the real intent of the parties, "the substance and fact" of the matter, and not merely by the outward form with which the parties have invested their transaction.* Accordingly,[4] where the agreement was that the defendant, in consideration of receiving a commission, should take from the plaintiff the acceptances of a third party, without recourse against the plaintiff, it was held by the Court of Exchequer Chamber, affirming the judgment of the Court of Common Pleas, that this was in substance, and despite its form, a contract of guarantee, and as such, within the Statute.

"The real question here", said Pollock, C.B.,[5] "is whether the contract declared upon is not substantially a contract that, if Calvert and Co., the buyers of the goods, do not pay for them at the expiration of the month's credit, the defendant will indemnify the plaintiff against their default. In consideration of a discount of 3 per cent., the defendant undertakes to hold the bill without recourse to the plaintiff. That is, in substance, an engagement by which the buyers of the goods are not to be exonerated, but the defendant is to indemnify the seller against their default. That is clearly a contract within the Statute of Frauds."[6]

Whether the promise was intended by the parties to be absolute and unconditional, and therefore an indemnity outside

[1] (1818) 1 B. & Ald. 302; 106 E.R. 112. [2] *Ib.* 303; E.R. 112.

[3] See also *Read* v. *Nash*, (1751) 1 Wils. K.B. 305; 95 E.R. 632; *Butcher* v. *Steuart*, (1843) 11 M. & W. 857; 152 E.R. 1052; and *Bird* v. *Gammon*, (1837) 3 Bing. N.C. 883; 132 E.R. 650. Cf. *Tomlinson* v. *Gell*, (1837) 6 A. & E. 564; 112 E.R. 216.

[4] In *Mallet* v. *Bateman*, (1864) 8 C.B. (N.S.) 530; 143 E.R. 1235; on appeal to the Exchequer Chamber, L.R. 1 C.P. 163.

[5] L.R. 1 C.P. 171.

[6] See also *Harburg India Rubber Comb Co.* v. *Martin*, [1902] 1 K.B. 778.

the Statute, or whether it was intended to be conditional and therefore within the statutory provisions, is a question of fact to be determined upon a consideration of all the circumstances of the case. Thus in *Keate* v. *Temple*[1] the question was whether a lieutenant in the navy had unconditionally, or at all, undertaken to pay for certain clothes supplied to the crew of his ship; and it was laid down that in an action on such an alleged undertaking, the court, in determining what the parties had really intended, would take into consideration not only the expressions used, but the particular situation of the defendant at the time of such alleged undertaking, and the amount of the sum to which he would thereby be made liable.

"There is one consideration", said Eyre, C.J., "independent of everything else, which weighs so strongly with me, that I should wish this evidence to be once more submitted to a jury. The sum recovered is £576. 7*s*. 8*d*. and this against a lieutenant in the navy: a sum so large that it goes a great way towards satisfying my mind that it never could have been in the contemplation of the defendant to make himself liable, or of the slopseller to furnish the goods on his credit, to so large an amount."[2]

It is apparent that the question of fact involved in deciding whether a promise is a guarantee within the Statute, or an indemnity and therefore outside the Statute, will frequently be very difficult to answer. That is well illustrated by the case of *Guild* v. *Conrad*,[3] already referred to.

"The question", remarked Lopes, L.J., in the course of his judgment in that case, "was one which, no doubt, it was difficult to decide. It appears to me that the evidence given at the trial as to the character of the promise is capable of either interpretation; and the question we have to determine is, was the learned judge wrong in putting upon it the interpretation which he did...."

Although promise satisfies foregoing conditions it may yet be out of Statute. A promise satisfying the foregoing conditions will

[1] (1797) 1 B. & P. 158, 159; 126 E.R. 834, 835.
[2] See also *Lakeman* v. *Mountstephen*, (1874) L.R. 7 H.L. 17; especially judgment of Lord Cairns, L.C., pp. 20 *et seq.*
[3] [1894] 2 Q.B. 885, 895.

prima facie fall within the Statute. If, however, it appears from a consideration of all the facts of the case, either (1) that the object intended to be secured by the contract to the promisor in return for his promise is (*a*) the discharge of an encumbrance affecting property belonging to him or in regard to which he possesses a legal right or rights, or (*b*) the transfer to him, by way of purchase, of the promisee's right against the debtor, or (2) that the promise of guarantee is an incidental term in a larger contract to whose main object the guarantee is accessory merely, then such promise will not be within the Statute.

The guarantee, in all of these cases, is regarded as being merely ancillary to the main purpose of the transaction; and the courts, having decided that the Statute applies only where the contract is substantially a contract of guarantee, have therefore held that the Statute does not affect these cases.

"What was the subject-matter of the contract?" said Vaughan Williams, L.J., in *Harburg India Rubber Comb Co.* v. *Martin.*[1] "If the subject-matter of the contract was the purchase of property—the relief of property from a liability, the getting rid of incumbrances, the securing greater diligence in the performance of the duty of a factor, or the introduction of business into a stockbroker's office—in all those cases there was a larger matter which was the object of the contract. That being the object of the contract, the mere fact that as an incident to it—not as the immediate object, but indirectly—the debt of another to a third person will be paid, does not bring the case within the section."

(1) (*a*) *Promise given to secure discharge of encumbrance affecting property belonging to promisor or in regard to which he possesses a legal right.* The first case of this sort in which the Statute was held not to apply was *Williams* v. *Leper*,[2] which came before the Court of King's Bench in 1766. There the plaintiff's tenant, being three quarters in arrear with his rent, and insolvent, conveyed all his effects for the benefit of his creditors, and they employed the defendant as a broker to sell these effects. On the morning of the sale, the plaintiff came to distrain for his rent, but desisted upon receiving the defendant's promise to pay the

[1] [1902] 1 K.B. 778, 786.
[2] (1766) 3 Burr. 1886, 1890; 97 E.R. 1152, 1153.

amount of the arrears. The defendant having failed to perform this promise, the plaintiff commenced proceedings for its enforcement. It was argued for the defendant that the promise was within the Statute, but the majority of the court held that it was an original undertaking by the defendant to buy off the plaintiff's lien, and therefore outside the Statute.

"The plaintiff is in possession of the goods", said Wilmot, J., "having entered with intent to distrain them. Leper was the agent for the creditors. He makes this promise, in order to discharge the goods of this distress. I consider this distress as being actually made. Leper says, 'If you will quit the goods and disencumber the fund, I will pay you'."[1]

As it was expressed in a later case,[2] the defendant had not the discharge of the tenant principally in his contemplation, but the discharge of himself by freeing from the plaintiff's lien the property entrusted to him for sale.[3]

[1] It may sometimes be a question, in a case such as *Williams* v. *Leper* (*supra*), whether the promisor's undertaking was not a promise merely to sell the goods and administer the resulting fund. In *Williams* v. *Leper*, the goods actually produced more than the landlord's demand, and Aston, J., placed his judgment solely upon the ground that the defendant had promised to apply the proceeds of the sale to the satisfaction of the landlord's claim. Moreover, both Lord Mansfield, C.J., and Wilmot, J., adopted this ground as an additional basis upon which to support their judgments, Wilmot, J., saying: "Leper became the bailiff of the landlord: and when he had sold the goods, the money was the landlord's (as far as £45) in his own bailiff's hands. Therefore an action would have lain against Leper, for money had and received to the plaintiff's use". Yates, J., put the case on the ground for which it is cited as an authority in the text, viz. that the defendant had given his promise to obtain the discharge of the plaintiff's lien.

It seems clear, indeed, that cases such as *Williams* v. *Leper* do not require, to sustain them, evidence that the fund or property disencumbered produced more, or was more valuable than, the debt which constituted the encumbrance. Thus in *Bampton* v. *Paulin*, (1827) 4 Bing. 264; 130 E.R. 769, in which *Williams* v. *Leper* was expressly followed, no mention was made of the value of the distress. And in *Fitzgerald* v. *Dressler*, (1859) 7 C.B. (N.S.) 374, 391; 141 E.R. 861, 868, Williams, J., explained *Williams* v. *Leper* in the following terms: "*Williams* v. *Leper*, if looked at closely, was within the statute. The threat to distrain was treated as tantamount to an actual distress. The court got the case out of the statute by saying it was a purchase by the party of a lien upon his own property". See also per Joyce, J., in *Davys* v. *Buswell*, [1913] 2 K.B. 47, 59.

[2] Per Lord Ellenborough, C.J., in *Castling* v. *Aubert*, (1802) 2 East 325, 331; 102 E.R. 393, 395.

[3] See also *Bampton* v. *Paulin*, (1827) 4 Bing. 264; 130 E.R. 769; and *Edwards* v. *Kelly*, (1817) 6 M. & S. 204; 105 E.R. 1219.

In order, however, that the court shall be able to hold that the discharge of the debtor was not the matter principally in the contemplation of the defendant when he made his promise, it must appear either that he was the owner of the property disencumbered or that he possessed a legal right in regard to it. By legal right is meant some right which the law will recognize, as distinct from a merely moral right.[1] In *Williams* v. *Leper*[2] the court regarded the broker as identified in interest with his principals, the creditors.[3] The position was similar in *Castling* v. *Aubert*.[4] In *Fitzgerald* v. *Dressler*,[5] the defendant, who was alleged to have made a promise of guarantee, was the sub-purchaser of a parcel of linseed, and the liability he was alleged to have guaranteed was that of the purchaser to the vendor, who, upon receiving this alleged guarantee, had surrendered possession of the linseed and hence his lien for unpaid purchase money. It was held by the Court of Common Pleas that the defendant's undertaking was not within the Statute.

"At the time the promise was made", said Williams, J., "the defendant was substantially the owner of the linseed in question, which was subject to the lien of the original vendors for the contract price. The effect of the promise was neither more nor less than this, to get rid of the incumbrance, or, in other words, to buy off the plaintiff's lien. That being so, it seems to me that the authorities clearly establish that such a case is not within the statute. The case of *Williams* v. *Leper* proceeded upon this, that the defendant there had an interest in the property: his property was incumbered by the landlord's claim for rent; therefore, the promise was a promise to pay a debt to which that property was subject, and not simply a promise to answer for the debt or default of another, within the meaning of the statute."

[1] See per Stirling, L.J., in *Harburg India Rubber Comb Co.* v. *Martin*, [1902] 1 K.B. 778, 791. No distinction is intended to be drawn in the text between *legal*, as apart from *equitable*, rights. See per Joyce, J., in *Davys* v. *Buswell*, [1913] 2 K.B. 47, 58.

[2] (1766) 3 Burr. 1886; 97 E.R. 1152.

[3] See per Williams, J., in *Fitzgerald* v. *Dressler*, (1859) 7 C.B. (N.S.) 374, 391; 141 E.R. 861, 868; per Stirling, L.J., in *Harburg India Rubber Comb Co.* v. *Martin*, [1902] 1 K.B. 778, 790.

[4] (1802) 2 East 325; 102 E.R. 393.

[5] (1859) 7 C.B. (N.S.) 374, 394; 141 E.R. 861, 869. See also *Thomas* v. *Williams*, (1830) 10 B. & C. 664; 109 E.R. 597.

(*b*) *Promise given to secure transfer, by way of purchase, of promisee's right against debtor.* It would seem apparent from Lord Ellenborough's remarks in *Castling* v. *Aubert*,[1] that he was of opinion that a contract which was in substance merely for the purchase of a debt was not within the Statute, even though an incidental result of such a contract was to secure to the vendor payment of the sum or portion of the sum owing to him by the debtor. "It is rather", he said, "...a purchase of the securities which the plaintiff held in his hands. This is quite beside the mischief provided against by the statute...." And Lawrence, J., stated the position in similar terms, saying: "This is to be considered as a purchase by the defendant of the plaintiff's interest in the policies". These remarks were but *obiter dicta*; but two years later the opinion which they intimated was confirmed as the law by the case of *Anstey* v. *Marden*,[2] decided by the Court of Common Pleas on the express ground that a contract to purchase a debt was not within the Statute.

The facts of *Anstey* v. *Marden*[2] were as follows. The defendant was insolvent, and one Weston offered that if the creditors would assign to him their debts he would pay ten shillings in the pound for them. The plaintiff verbally accepted this offer, but subsequently refused to sign the deed of assignment, and sued the defendant for the full amount of the debt. The plaintiff contended that Weston's promise to him was within the Statute and therefore no satisfaction of his claim, but it was held by the Court of Common Pleas that the Statute had no application to the case.

"I think upon the evidence", said Chambre, J., "it is perfectly clear that this was a contract to purchase the debts of the several creditors, instead of being a contract to pay or discharge the debts owing by Marden. It was of the substance of the agreement that these debts should remain in full force, to be assigned to Weston. When he had purchased them he did not mean to exact them rigorously, but the contract was a contract of purchase, and he had a right to make use of the names of the original creditors to recover the same to the full amount, if Marden had

[1] (1802) 2 East 325, 331; 102 E.R. 393, 395.
[2] (1804) 1 B. & P. (N.R.) 124, 133; 127, E.R. 406, 409

effects to satisfy the debts...we all agree fully upon the point that it is a contract for the purchase of the debts of Marden, which is not prohibited by the Statute of Frauds."[1]

In such cases as *Anstey* v. *Marden*, however, the form of the transaction is not decisive; and the courts sometimes have to consider whether a contract, apparently a contract of sale, is not in truth and in fact a contract of guarantee. In deciding this question, the courts have regard to the substance of the matter rather than to the form in which the transaction has been cast. Vaughan Williams, L.J., in the course of his judgment in *Harburg India Rubber Comb Co.* v. *Martin*,[2] expressed this rule in the following terms: "the form of the promise given by the promisor has never been held to be conclusive of the matter. He may, or he may not, promise in terms to answer for the debt of another; but, whether he does so or not, it is the substance, not the form, which is regarded". Thus in *Mallet* v. *Bateman*,[3] already referred to, the Court of Exchequer Chamber came to the conclusion that in spite of the form of the transaction (a contract to purchase bills "without recourse" against the vendor, who was the drawer), the real arrangement between the parties was that the alleged purchaser should guarantee to the alleged vendor payment by the acceptor of the sums in respect of which the bills were drawn.

Discharge of encumbrance or transfer of right must be secured to promisor by terms of contract itself. Whether it be contended that the contract is out of the Statute as being primarily entered into to disencumber some property of the promisor, or whether because it is substantially for the purchase of a security or debt, it must in either case appear that this object is secured to the promisor by virtue of the terms of the contract itself. Thus in *Harburg India Rubber Comb Co.* v. *Martin*[4] the defendant was a director and a large shareholder in a limited liability company. The plaintiffs obtained a judgment against the company and issued a writ of *fi. fa.*, and thereupon the defendant promised, in

[1] See also per Williams, J., in *Fitzgerald* v. *Dressler*, 7 C.B. (N.S.) 374, 395; 141 E.R. 861, 869.

[2] [1902] 1 K.B. 778, 784.

[3] (1865) L.R. 1 C.P. 163.

[4] [1902] 1 K.B. 778, 787.

consideration of the withdrawal of this writ, to endorse bills at three months and six months for the amount of the judgment. He subsequently failed to carry out this promise, and upon action being brought against him he pleaded the Statute. It was contended that his object in contracting was "to protect his own property"; but the Court of Appeal held that although this may have been the motive which induced him to enter into the contract, it was not the *object of that contract*.

"And the mere fact", said Vaughan Williams, L.J.,[1] "that the defendant had, as he seems to have done, financed the syndicate to a large extent, and that that was his motive for thus coming forward and bargaining for forbearance, cannot make any difference in the object of the contract. That might have been the motive which induced him to make himself answerable for the debt of the syndicate, but it was not the object of the contract. The object was simply to obtain the forbearance of the creditors in respect of the debt."

Unless the contract actually and by its terms secures to the guarantor the discharge of his property or the transfer to him of a debt or security, any forbearance by the promisee which may follow upon the guarantor's giving the guarantee and result in some benefit in regard to the guarantor's property or in regard to the debtor, will merely constitute the motive inducing the guarantor to give the guarantee. But "motive" is not a factor which the court will take into account in these cases.[2] The question for the court's consideration is not "why did the parties contract?" but "for what did they contract?".[3] And the answer to this question depends on the terms of their contract.[4]

(2) *Promise of guarantee incidental term in larger contract.* On analogy with cases in which the Statute has been held to be excluded by reason of the guarantee being merely incidental to the acquisition of property by the guarantor or the discharge of some encumbrance affecting property already his, it has been

[1] [1902] 1 K.B. 787.

[2] Per Cozens-Hardy, L.J., in *Harburg India Rubber Comb Co.* v. *Martin*, [1902] 1 K.B. 778, 792.

[3] Per Vaughan Williams, L.J., *ib.* 786.

[4] See also *Davys* v. *Buswell*, [1913] 2 K.B. 47.

decided that where the promise of guarantee is merely an incidental term in a larger contract, such as a contract of *del credere* agency, the Statute will similarly be excluded. This principle was first established in English law by the decision of the Court of Exchequer in *Couturier* v. *Hastie*.[1] The effect of that and similar cases is very well stated in the following passage from the judgment of Cozens-Hardy, L.J., in *Harburg India Rubber Comb Co.* v. *Martin*:[2]

"The third class consists of those cases which have been called 'del credere cases'. When they are fairly regarded they seem to me to amount only to this: that a contract, e.g. for the employment of a del credere agent, need not be in writing, although it incidentally involves the answering for a debt of another person. In other words, if the court can find that there is a main contract, the object of which is not to answer for the debt of another, that contract is not within s. 4, even though incidentally it may result in a liability to answer for the debt of another".

This principle has not been restricted to cases of *del credere* agency, but would seem to be of general application. It was applied by Bowen, L.J. (sitting as an additional judge of the Queen's Bench Division), and the Court of Appeal, in *Sutton* v. *Grey*,[3] a case in which the defendant had agreed with the plaintiffs, a firm of stockbrokers, that he should introduce clients to them, on the terms that he was to receive half the profits and bear half of the losses.

"It seems to me", said Bowen, L.J.,[4] "that although *Couturier* v. *Hastie*[1] is not exactly in point, it would be perhaps introducing

[1] (1852) 8 Ex. 40, 55; 155 E.R. 1250, 1257. The decision in *Couturier* v. *Hastie* was to a large extent based on the American case of *Wolff* v. *Koppel*, 5 Hill, N.Y. Rep. 458; 8 Ex. 56n. "Suppose", said Cowen, J., in that case, "a factor agrees by parol to sell for cash, but gives credit. His promise is, virtually, that he will pay the amount of the debt he thus makes. Yet, who would say his promise is within the statute? The amount of the argument for the defendant would seem to be, that an agent for making sales, or indeed a collecting agent, cannot, by parol, undertake for extraordinary diligence, because he may thus have the debt of another thrown upon him. But the answer is, that all such contracts have an immediate respect to his own duty or obligation. The debt of another comes incidentally as a measure of damages."

[2] [1902] 1 K.B. 778, 793.

[3] (1893) 69 L.T. 354; on appeal, [1894] 1 Q.B. 285.

[4] 69 L.T. at p. 355.

too fine a distinction if I were to endeavour to distinguish between it and the present case. It is certain that the object of the contract in the present case was that the defendant should introduce responsible persons to the plaintiffs, and the contract included a guarantee that he would indemnify the firm against his not doing so. That, I think, is really a contract which regulates the terms of the agency, and the defendant's liability to answer for the debt of another is only an ulterior consequence of the terms in which the contract is framed."[1]

Guarantee of liability arising ex delicto *included within the Statute.* It is established that the Statute applies to guarantees of liabilities arising *ex delicto* as well as to such as arise *ex contractu*. A liability for a debt presently owed is plainly within the words of the Statute; a liability for a breach of contract or a debt to be incurred in the future is included in the term "default";[2] and a liability for tort, in the term "miscarriages". This last point was decided by the Court of King's Bench, in *Kirkham* v. *Marter*.[3] In that case, a third party had wrongfully caused the

[1] On an analogous principle it has been held that where a partnership has been entered into by parol, the mere fact that one of its terms is that the partnership business shall include, or be exclusively, dealing in land, does not prevent the partnership from being proved, nor preclude the partners from establishing the interests in the land (as being the stock-in-trade of the partnership) which the partnership agreement secures to them respectively. See *Forster* v. *Hall*, (1800) 5 Ves. 308; 31 E.R. 603; *Dale* v. *Hamilton*, (1846) 5 Ha. 369; 67 E.R. 955; *Essex* v. *Essex*, (1855) 20 Beav. 442; 52 E.R. 674. Cf. *Caddick* v. *Skidmore*, (1857) 2 De G. & J. 52; 44 E.R. 907; *Isaacs* v. *Evans*, (1899) 16 T.L.R. 113; and *Gray* v. *Smith*, (1889) 43 Ch.D. 208.

[2] See per Willes, J., in *Mountstephen* v. *Lakeman*, (1871) L.R. 7 Q.B. 196, 202.

[3] (1819) 2 B. & Ald. 613, 616; 106 E.R. 490, 491. *Kirkham* v. *Marter* involved another point, viz. whether an agreement to pay a sum in consideration of the withdrawal or non-commencement of proceedings against a third person is within the Statute. It was held, in *Kirkham* v. *Marter*, distinguishing *Read* v. *Nash*, (1751) 1 Wils. K.B. 305; 95 E.R. 632, that the Statute applied in such a case. The ground upon which *Read* v. *Nash* was distinguished, however, is not convincing: it was said (as also in *Fish* v. *Hutchinson*, (1759) 2 Wils. K.B. 94; 95 E.R. 704) that *Read* v. *Nash* concerned a promise to withdraw an action of tort which had not been tried, and accordingly "It did not appear that the defendant in that action had ever committed the assault, or that he had ever been liable in damages". But that objection would apply to any guarantee where the third party's liability had not first been ascertained by the judgment of a court of law. See notes to *Forth* v. *Stanton*, 1 Wms. Saund., 1871 ed. p. 232. In the *Notes to Saunders' Reports* (p. 231), indeed, it is said that *Kirkham* v. *Marter* on this point must be taken to have overruled

death of the plaintiff's horse. The defendant, in consideration of the plaintiff's not suing the third party, undertook to pay the amount of the damage. It was held that this promise was within the Statute.

"Now the word 'miscarriage'", said Abbott, C.J., "has not the same meaning as the word 'debt' or 'default'; it seems to me to comprehend that species of wrongful act, for the consequences of which the law would make the party civilly responsible. The wrongful riding the horse of another, without his leave and licence, and thereby causing its death, is clearly an act for which the party is responsible in damages; and, therefore, in my judgment, falls within the meaning of the word 'miscarriage'."

The contract of guarantee and consideration. A contract of guarantee, like any other contract, must have a sufficient consideration to support it; and the general rule in contracts under the Statute is that the writing shall state the whole of the contract. Therefore, in general, the consideration for the contract must appear from the writing.[1] This rule, however, caused great inconvenience and much injustice in the case of contracts of guarantee, which, being of very common occurrence in ordinary business transactions, are frequently drawn up by the parties without professional aid. Consequently, and especially where the consideration did not involve the promisee's doing any positive act, as, for example, where the consideration was merely refraining from suing a debtor, it would often not be stated very distinctly in the writing, and not infrequently there would be no reference to it at all.[2]

In their endeavour to do justice in such cases, the courts seem sometimes to have discerned a statement of the consideration in language which would perhaps not normally have been con-

Read v. *Nash*. But perhaps these cases may be reconciled on the ground that in *Read* v. *Nash* the third party's liability (whatever it may have been) was completely discharged by virtue of the subsequent transaction. See *Bird* v. *Gammon*, (1837) 3 Bing. (N.C.) 883, 889; 132 E.R. 650, 653. If in *Kirkham* v. *Marter* the third party's liability were to be regarded as having been extinguished, it is submitted that that decision could not be supported.

[1] *Wain* v. *Warlters*, (1804) 5 East 10; 102 E.R. 972.

[2] See, e.g. *Wain* v. *Warlters* (*supra*); *James* v. *Williams*, (1834) 5 B. & Ad. 1109; 110 E.R. 1103; *Raikes* v. *Todd*, (1838) 8 A. & E. 846; 112 E.R. 1058.

sidered sufficient to sustain the meaning which the courts saw fit to attribute to it. One of the most extreme decisions of this sort was *Bainbridge* v. *Wade*.[1] In that case the writing was in the following terms: "I hereby guarantee the payment of any sum or sums of money due to you from Mr Andrew Little, of Richmond, the amount not to exceed at any time the sum of one hundred pounds". It was held by the Court of Queen's Bench that this sufficiently stated the consideration, which was that the promisee should, in the way of his business, supply goods on credit to Little.

In spite of the lenient attitude of the courts, however, the position was considered unsatisfactory; and in 1856 the Mercantile Law Amendment Act was passed to deal with the matter. By that Act[2] it was provided, *inter alia*,

> "that no special promise made by any person after the passing of this Act to answer for the debt, default or miscarriage of another person, being in writing and signed by the party to be charged therewith or some other person by him thereunto lawfully authorized, shall be deemed invalid to support an action, suit or other proceeding to charge the person by whom such promise shall have been made, by reason only that the consideration for such promise does not appear in writing or by necessary inference from a written document".

Since 1856, therefore, it has been unnecessary, in the case of a contract of guarantee, for the writing to set forth the consideration. It is apparent, however, that where the consideration is in fact stated in the writing, it may well be utilized to explain or ascertain the promise. But it has been held[3] that parol evidence admitted to prove a consideration in pursuance of the Mercantile Law Amendment Act may not also be utilized to supplement any deficiencies which may exist in the writing with regard to the promise. "But a consideration expressed in writing formerly discharged two offices, it sustained the promise

[1] (1850) 16 Q.B. 89; 117 E.R. 808. See also *Boehm* v. *Campbell*, (1819) 8 Taunt. 679; 129 E.R. 548; *Lysaght* v. *Walker*, (1831) 2 Dow & Clark, 211, 227; 6 E.R. 707, 713; *Powers* v. *Fowler*, (1855) 4 El. & Bl. 511; 119 E.R. 187.

[2] 19 & 20 Vict. c. 97, s. 3.

[3] *Holmes* v. *Mitchell*, (1859) 7 C.B. (N.S.) 361; 141 E.R. 856.

and might also explain it. Now, however, parol evidence, though it may supply the consideration, cannot go further, and explain the promise."[1]

(III) *Contracts in consideration of marriage*. The Statute applies only to contracts made upon consideration of marriage, and not to contracts to marry. A contrary decision was, indeed, given by the Court of Common Pleas in *Philpot* v. *Walcot*,[2] decided in 1681; but that case was very soon overruled. In the report of *Harrison* v. *Cage*,[3] tried before the King's Bench in 1698, we read that "Mr Northey said at the Bar, that the statute intended only agreements to pay marriage portions, and that it had often been ruled so by Holt Chief Justice. Quod Holt non negavit". This ruling was followed, some years later, by the Court of Common Pleas in *Cork* v. *Baker*,[4] which finally settled the point.

(IV) *Contracts not to be performed within the space of one year from the making thereof*.[5] This clause of the Statute has been a fertile source of litigation; but for the most part its construction is now well settled. It is submitted that the effect of the cases may be stated in the following propositions:

(i) "The space of one year from the making" of the contract is not exceeded where the contract is to enure for one year commencing on the day immediately following the day on which the contract is made; as where *A*., on Tuesday, contracts to serve *B*. for one year, the service to commence on Wednesday.

(ii) If the period within which the contract is to be performed is not stated in the contract, the contract will not be within the Statute unless it appears that it cannot, according to its terms, be performed within the year.

(iii) If the period within which the contract is to be performed

1 *Holmes* v. *Mitchell*, (1859) 7 C.B. (N.S.) 370; 141 E.R. 859.

2 (1681) Skin. 24; 90 E.R. 13; S.C. *sub nom. Philpot* v. *Wallet*, 3 Lev. 65; 83 E.R. 579.

3 (1698) 1 Ld. Raym. 386, 388; 91 E.R. 1156.

4 (1717) 1 Strange 34; 93 E.R. 367.

5 It has been held that this clause of the Statute may apply to contracts coming within s. 4 of the Sale of Goods Act, 1893. *Prested Miners Co. Ltd.* v. *Garner Ltd.*, [1910] 2 K.B. 776; affirmed by Court of Appeal, [1910] W.N. 276.

is stated in the contract to exceed the year, then although the contract contains a proviso enabling it to be determined within the year, it will nevertheless be within the Statute. And this rule would also appear to apply where the contract (leaving out of consideration any such proviso), although not stating any definite period for its duration, is such that it cannot be performed in accordance with its terms within the year.

(iv) Whether the contract as a whole is for an unstated period or whether it is stated to be for a period exceeding the year, if all that one of the parties is to do is required by the terms of the contract to be done within the year, the contract will not be within the Statute.

(i) *The space of one year from the making thereof*. The only case to present any difficulty in the computation of the period of one year was that where the period was for one year to commence on the day following the making of the contract. Would a contract to enure for that period be one to be performed within one year from the making thereof? This question, after the expression of some contrary opinion,[1] has now been answered in the affirmative by the decision of a Divisional Court and the Court of Appeal in *Smith* v. *Gold Coast and Ashanti Explorers, Ltd.*[2] In that case the plaintiff set up a contract made on December 6, 1901, to serve the defendants for a year certain from December 7, 1901. The Common Serjeant had ruled as a matter of law that this contract was within the Statute and had therefore directed the jury to find for the defendants. It was held by the Divisional Court and the Court of Appeal, however, that although the Statute would apply if the service was to commence on December 8 (i.e. the second day after the making of the contract),[3] yet there was evidence to show that it was intended by the parties to commence on December 7, in which case the Statute would

[1] Willes & Byles, JJ., in *Cawthorne* v. *Cordrey*, (1863) 13 C.B. (N.S.) 406, 407; 143 E.R. 161, expressed an *obiter* opinion that the Statute was excluded in such a case. Lord Esher, in *Britain* v. *Rossiter*, (1879) 11 Q.B.D. 123, 125, commented on this opinion and seemed inclined to concur in it; but Darling, J., in *Dollar* v. *Parkington*, (1901) 84 L.T. 470, had refused to follow it.

[2] [1903] 1 K.B. 285, 288; C.A. *ib.* 538.

[3] *Britain* v. *Rossiter*, (1879) 11 Q.B.D. 123.

(as it was decided) be excluded. A new trial was accordingly ordered. Lord Alverstone, C.J. (who delivered the principal judgment in the Divisional Court), after reviewing the authorities, summed up the position in the following terms: "I think that these cases shew that a contract for a year's service to commence on the day next after the day on which the contract was made is not an agreement which is not to be performed within the space of one year from the making thereof, within the meaning of s. 4".

(ii) *Period within which contract to be performed unstated.* As early as 1694, it was decided by the Court of King's Bench in *Peter* v. *Compton*,[1] that a contract stating no definite time for its performance was not within the Statute unless it appeared that it was incapable of being performed, according to its terms, within the year. Skinner's report of the opinion of the judges runs as follows:

"the Chief Justice [Holt] advised with all the judges, and by the great opinion (for there was diversity of opinion and his own was *e contra*) where the agreement is to be performed upon a contingent, and it does not appear within the agreement that it is to be performed after the year, there a note in writing is not necessary, for the contingent might happen within the year; but where it appears by the whole tenour of the agreement that it is to be performed after the year, there a note is necessary: otherwise not".

This decision has been repeatedly followed, and the principle laid down is firmly established in the law. It was applied in *Fenton* v. *Emblers*[2] to a case in which the contract was to leave money by will. A similar decision was given in *Wells* v. *Horton*;[3] and in *Souch* v. *Strawbridge*[4] it was held that a contract for the maintenance of a child "so long as the defendant should think proper", was not within the Statute. In the course of his judgment in that case, Tindal, C.J., stated the rule to be

"that, where the agreement distinctly shews, upon the face of it,

[1] (1694) Skinner 353; 90 E.R. 157; 1 Sm. L.C. 13th ed. p. 350.

[2] (1762) 3 Burr. 1278; 97 E.R. 831.

[3] (1826) 4 Bing. 40; 130 E.R. 683.

[4] (1846) 2 C.B. 808, 815; 135 E.R. 1161, 1164. See also *Ridley* v. *Ridley*, (1865) 34 Beav. 478; 55 E.R. 720.

that the parties contemplated its performance to extend over a greater space of time than one year, the case is within the Statute, but that, where the contract is such that the whole may be performed within a year, and there is no express stipulation to the contrary, the Statute does not apply".

An example of a case in which, although no definite time was stated for the completion of the contract, yet it appeared that it could not, in accordance with its terms, be performed within the year, is afforded by *Boydell* v. *Drummond*.[1] There the contract was to buy a book to be published in parts. One of the terms of the agreement was as follows: "that one number at least should be published annually; and the proprietors were confident they should be enabled to produce two numbers within the course of every year". It was held by the Court of King's Bench that this was a contract which could not, in accordance with its terms, be performed within the year, and was therefore within the Statute.

"The whole scope of the undertaking", said Lord Ellenborough, C.J., "shews that it was not to be performed within a year; and if, contrary to all physical probability, it could have been performed within that time, yet the whole work could not have been obtruded upon the subscribers at once, so as to have entitled the publishers to demand payment of the whole subscription from them within the year."

The foregoing authorities were approved and applied by the Court of Appeal in *McGregor* v. *McGregor*,[2] in which the contract sued upon was one between a husband and wife whereby it was agreed that they should live apart and that the husband should pay to the wife a weekly sum for maintenance. This was held by the Court of Appeal to be outside the Statute, as being a contract which might, in accordance with the terms agreed upon, be performed within the year. "If the contract can by possibility be performed within the year, the Statute does not apply", said Lindley, L.J.

[1] (1809) 11 East 142, 155; 103 E.R. 958, 963.

[2] (1888) 21 Q.B.D. 424, 431. Overruling *Davy* v. *Shannon*, 4 Ex.D. 81, and *Eley* v. *Positive Assurance Co.* 1 Ex.D. 21 (so far as relating to Statute of Frauds). The rule in *McGregor* v. *McGregor* was recognized by the House of Lords in *Hanau* v. *Ehrlich*, [1912] A.C. 39.

(iii) *Period within which contract to be performed stated in contract to exceed the year, but contract containing proviso for determination within the year.* In view of the general rule that the Statute does not apply to contracts which can by possibility be performed within the year, it might well have been expected that the Statute would have had no application to a contract containing within itself a provision enabling either party to determine it within the year.[1] But side by side with the general rule in question, another rule has developed, by way of exception, as it were, to the general rule. The exception is that where the contract states for its duration a definite period exceeding the year, it will be within the terms of the Statute although there is reserved to the parties a power to determine it within the year. This rule was first applied in *Birch* v. *Liverpool*.[2] In that case there was a contract for the hiring of a coach for five years, but it was contended that by the custom of the trade the contract might have been determined at any time within the five years by the payment of a year's hire. It was held by the Court of King's Bench, however, that even if that were so, the contract would still be within the Statute.

"Assuming", said Bayley, J., "that the custom proved is to be considered as part of the contract, still the contract was in its terms an agreement for five years, determinable by the parties within that period. It was in the very terms of it an agreement not to be performed within a year."

Birch v. *Liverpool* was followed by the Court of Exchequer in *Dobson* v. *Collis*,[3] a case of a contract of service for more than a year, determinable on three months' notice by either party. These cases were accepted by the Lords Justices in Chancery in *In re Pentreguinea Fuel Co.*,[4] and by the Court of Appeal in *Lavalette* v. *Riches*.[5] In *Hanau* v. *Ehrlich*,[6] however, it was

[1] See per Fletcher Moulton, L.J., in *Hanau* v. *Ehrlich*, [1911] 2 K.B. at p. 1068.

[2] (1829) 9 B. & C. 392, 395; 109 E.R. 145, 147.

[3] (1856) 1 H. & N. 81; 156 E.R. 1126.

[4] (1862) 4 De G. F. & J. 541; 45 E.R. 1294. S.C. *sub nom. ex parte Acraman*, 31 L.J. Ch. 741.

[5] (1908) 24 T.L.R. 336.

[6] [1911] 2 K.B. 1056; [1912] A.C. 39.

argued that the foregoing authorities should be overruled as being inconsistent with the rule in *McGregor* v. *McGregor*.[1] But neither A. T. Lawrence, J. (who heard *Hanau* v. *Ehrlich* in the first instance), the Court of Appeal, nor the House of Lords would accede to this argument. The contract sued on in *Hanau* v. *Ehrlich* was a contract of service for a definite period exceeding one year, but subject to determination by six months' notice by either party during that period; and such a contract, it was unanimously decided by all the judges before whom the case came, was within the Statute.

"The one class of cases", said Lord Alverstone, in the House of Lords,[2] "decides that if there is no mention of time, and the time is uncertain, the agreement is not within the statute. The other class of cases decides that if the time mentioned is more than one year, but there is a power to determine, the agreement is within the statute."

It is submitted that the rule in *Hanau* v. *Ehrlich* applies not only to contracts expressly stated to be for more than the year, but also to such as (leaving out of account any proviso for determination) cannot be performed in accordance with their terms, within the year. For example, it cannot be supposed that even if the contract in *Boydell* v. *Drummond*[3] had contained a proviso enabling either party to give three months' notice determining the contract, it would have been any the less within the Statute. As A. T. Lawrence, J., said in *Hanau* v. *Ehrlich*,[4] the effect of cases such as *Dobson* v. *Collis*[5] is to "shew that the existence of a power to determine by notice does not take the contract out of the statute if otherwise in it". And a contract is equally within the Statute whether it is expressly stated to be for more than one year, or whether it appears from its terms that it cannot be performed within the year in accordance with such terms.

This submission receives support from the statement by Lord Loreburn, L.C.,[6] and Fletcher Moulton, L.J.,[7] that the rule in *Hanau* v. *Ehrlich* is to be regarded as an exception to the

[1] *Supra*, pp. 30 *et seq.*
[2] [1912] A.C. at p. 42.
[3] (1809) 11 East 142; 103 E.R. 958.
[4] [1911] 2 K.B. at p. 1060.
[5] (1856) 1 H. & N. 81; 156 E.R. 1126.
[6] [1912] A.C. at p. 41.
[7] [1911] 2 K.B. 1069.

rule in *McGregor* v. *McGregor* (*supra*). But as Lord Wrenbury (Buckley, L.J., as he then was) pointed out,[1] the rule in *McGregor* v. *McGregor* may ultimately be traced back to *Boydell* v. *Drummond*,[2] a case in which the contract was for no definite period, but plainly could not be performed, according to its terms, within the year. The law would seem to be accurately stated by Kennedy, L.J., in *Lavalette* v. *Riches*.[3]

"There must", he said, "be something expressed upon the face of the contract which showed that it contemplated that it would last beyond the year, and if that were so, it was none the less within the Statute because there might be a defeasance within the year."

(iv) *Whether the contract as a whole is for an unstated period or whether it is stated to be for a period exceeding the year, if all that one of the parties is to do is required by the terms of the contract to be done within the year, the contract will not be within the Statute.* This statement is based upon the judgments of Bray and Lord Coleridge, JJ., in *Reeve* v. *Jennings*.[4] Prior to the case of *Reeve* v. *Jennings*,[4] it appeared to be established, by authorities referred to below, that if all that one of the parties to the contract was to do, could, conformably with the terms of the contract, be done within the year, the contract was out of the Statute. But in *Reeve* v. *Jennings*[4] it was held that this rule was restricted to cases where the contract expressly *required* performance by the party within the year; if the contract merely *allowed* of such performance, without *requiring* it, the Statute applied. In *Reeve* v. *Jennings*[4] the plaintiff employed the defendant as a servant in his business. No period was stated for the duration of this contract, which was determinable on a week's notice by either party. One of the terms of the contract was that for thirty-six months after its determination the defendant would not carry on in the neighbourhood a business similar to the plaintiff's. It was contended that this contract was one to be performed within the year, inasmuch as the employer might, conformably with the terms of the agreement, have completely

[1] [1911] 2 K.B. at p. 1072.
[2] (1809) 11 East 142; 103 E.R. 958.
[3] (1908) 24 T.L.R. 336, 338.
[4] [1910] 2 K.B. 522.

performed his side of it within the year. This contention, however, was rejected by the court, and the Statute held to apply.

It is submitted that the restriction placed upon the rule by the decision in *Reeve* v. *Jennings* is not in accordance with previous authorities, and that that decision is erroneous. The first case bearing on the point was *Bracegirdle* v. *Heald*,[1] and there Abbott, J., expressed an *obiter* opinion which certainly did not go beyond the view of the law adopted in *Reeve* v. *Jennings*. Then followed *Donellan* v. *Read*,[2] the first actual decision on the point. In that case a landlord had agreed with his tenant to do certain repairs, the tenant undertaking "to pay him an increased rent of £5 a year during the remainder of the term, to commence from the quarter preceding the completion of the work". The Court of King's Bench held that this was not a contract within the Statute.

"As to the contract not being to be performed within a year", said Littledale, J., who delivered the judgment of the court, "we think that as the contract was entirely executed on one side within a year, and as it was the intention of the parties, founded on a reasonable expectation, that it should be so, the Statute of Frauds does not extend to such a case."

The contract in *Donellan* v. *Read* was one in which the landlord's part might have extended beyond the year: there was no provision requiring it to be performed within the year. This point was raised in the argument. Counsel for the landlord urged:[3] "It is only assumed here that the plaintiff's part was to be executed within a year"; to which Taunton, J., replied: "Unless the contrary is expressly agreed, the statute does not apply, *Fenton* v. *Emblers*".[4]

It would seem, therefore, that *Donellan* v. *Read* and *Reeve* v. *Jennings* were really indistinguishable on their facts. In both cases the whole of one party's side of the contract might have been performed, conformably with the terms of the contract, within the year. In neither was it required to be so performed.

[1] (1818) 1 B. & Ald. 722, 727; 106 E.R. 266, 267.

[2] (1832) 3 B. & Ad. 899, 906; 110 E.R. 330, 333.

[3] *Ib.* 903; E.R. 332.

[4] (1762) 3 Burr. 1278; 97 E.R. 831. *Vide* p. 30 *supra*.

Bray, J., distinguished *Donellan* v. *Read* by saying that it was a case in which the parties *intended* performance on one side to take place within a year. But it would seem that, whenever the contract can, in accordance with its terms, be performed on one side within the year, such performance must be taken to be in accordance with the intention of the parties, for the terms of the contract, it must be presumed, represent that intention.

The next case was *Cherry* v. *Heming*.[1] According to the *Law Journal Report*, Parke, B., *arguendo* stated the effect of *Donellan* v. *Read* as follows:[2] "We read the statute as meaning a contract incapable of being performed on one side or the other within the year".

Shortly afterwards the matter was considered by the Court of Common Pleas in *Smith* v. *Neale*.[3] The contract in that case was described by Willes, J., (delivering the judgment of the court) in the following terms:

"In this case the plaintiff sought to recover damages for non-performance of a contract alleged to have been entered into by the defendant with her, whereby she was to assign a patent which she had obtained for making toys, in trust for an institution called the Ladies' Guild, which was under the management of the defendant, which patent was to be used by the Guild for making toys; and the plaintiff was to have 5 per cent., upon the profits made thereby, and the defendant was to provide for the next payment to be made in respect of the patent; and, if the profits made did not reach a certain sum in the first and sub-

[1] (1849) 4 Ex. 631; 154 E.R. 1367.

[2] 19 L.J. Ex. at p. 65. In his judgment Parke, B., repeated these words, and added that the Statute "did not include cases where the contract was entirely executed on one side". Both Bray and Lord Coleridge, JJ., in *Reeve* v. *Jennings* ([1910] 2 K.B. at p. 529), took exception to this statement; and indeed, it seems clear that the question of whether a contract is one to be performed within a year from the making thereof, is not to be answered by the actual event, but according to the terms of the contract and as at the time the contract is entered into. See per Ellenborough, C.J., in *Boydell* v. *Drummond*, (1809) 11 East 142, 155; 103 E.R. 958, 963. When it was suggested, *arguendo*, in *Smith* v. *Neale*, (1857) 2 C.B. (N.S.) 67, 81; 140 E.R. 337, 343, that *Donellan* v. *Read* had proceeded on the ground that the landlord had actually performed his side of the contract within the year, Cresswell, J., replied: "The contract must, with reference to this point, be good or bad at the time it is made".

[3] (1857) 2 C.B. (N.S.) 67; 140 E.R. 337.

sequent years, the plaintiff should have the right, upon giving one month's notice, and repaying any payments made to keep up the patent, to reclaim it, unless the deficiency in the year was made up within the month: and, in case of the Ladies' Guild not being carried on, the patent was to revert to the plaintiff, subject to her repaying any moneys paid to keep it up"

This contract, therefore, was not required by its terms to be performed by the plaintiff within the year, and the parties plainly contemplated that the plaintiff might after the year have obligations imposed on her under the contract. Yet it was held that the Statute did not apply.

"With respect to the first point [that the contract was within the Statute]", said Willes, J.,[1] "we think it may be disposed of ...by reference to the terms of the agreement, by which all that was to be done by the plaintiff constituting one entire consideration for the defendant's promise was capable of being performed within a year, and that *it does not appear from its terms, which were undoubtedly agreed to in part, that any part of what the plaintiff was to do constituting such consideration, was intended to be postponed until after a year from the time of making the agreement....*"

It is submitted that the italicized words merely mean that the contract in question was not one which expressly, or of necessity apparent from its terms, could not be performed on one side within the year. This seems to be made clear by a remark which fell from Willes, J., in the course of the argument. Crowder, J., asked[2] counsel for the defendant: "What part of this agreement do you say was to be performed by the plaintiff beyond the year?" Counsel answered: "The fourth clause [relative to the plaintiff's right to reclaim the patent in a certain event]". To this Willes, J., replied: "*Not necessarily*. The fifth clause seems the strongest one for you—'that, in the event of the Guild not being carried on, the patent should revert to you, subject to the re-payment of moneys paid to keep it up'".

In *Miles* v. *New Zealand Alford Estate Co.*[3] the alleged con-

[1] *Ib.* 88; E.R. 345. The italics are mine.
[2] *Ib.* 82; E.R. 343. The italics are mine.
[3] (1886) 32 Ch.D. 266, 276.

tract was that in consideration of the defendants' not taking proceedings against a director, he would pay certain moneys over a period of ninety years. It was held by North, J., to be "quite sufficient if the agreement was or might be performed by one side within a year", and he decided that the defendants' obligation was one which could be performed within that time.

This case was approved by the Court of Appeal in *Milsom* v. *Stafford*,[1] a case which was not cited in *Reeve* v. *Jennings*.[2] In *Milsom* v. *Stafford* the contract was for the hire of a gas plant for three years. The owners of the plant contended that their contract was out of the Statute as it was capable of being performed on their side within the year, by their delivering the plant. But the Court of Appeal held that their obligation was a continuous one extending over the three years. Both Smith and Williams, L.JJ., accepted the view that the rule under discussion applied to contracts capable of being performed on one side within the year, and Romer, L.J., concurred. Williams, L.J., said: "The proposition that a contract is not one that is not to be performed within the space of one year if all that is to be done by one party as the consideration for the contract can be done within one year, is perfectly accurate". He then quoted with approval from the judgment delivered by Willes, J., in *Smith* v. *Neale* (*supra*), and proceeded to express his agreement with the decision of North, J., in *Miles* v. *New Zealand Alford Estate Co.*[3]

For the foregoing reasons it is submitted that *Reeve* v. *Jennings*[2] is a wrong decision and that it should not be followed by courts of first instance and would be overruled by a superior court. The true principle, it is suggested, is that if all that one of the parties is to do under the contract may by possibility (conformably with the terms of the contract) be performed within the year, then that contract is out of the Statute. It would seem, however, that the rule in *Hanau* v. *Ehrlich*[4] would apply, so that if performance by both parties is stated to extend beyond the year, then the existence of a defeasance clause enabling one of the parties to bring his performance to an end within the year

[1] (1899) 80 L.T. 590, 591.
[2] [1910] 2 K.B. 522.
[3] (1886) 32 Ch.D. 266.
[4] *Supra*, pp. 32 *et seq.*

will not exclude the Statute. If a defeasance clause enabling the whole contract to be determined within the year does not take that contract out of the Statute, there seems to be no reason why such a clause should have that effect where it can operate with regard to the performance of one party only.[1]

[1] See generally hereon the judgment of Fletcher Moulton, L.J., in *Hanau* v. *Ehrlich*, [1911] 2 K.B. at pp. 1066 *et seq.*

CHAPTER II

CONTRACTS AND ARRANGEMENTS OUTSIDE THE STATUTE

(1) *Sales by the Court.* Notwithstanding the Statute, it has been decided and is now established as the law, that where property is sold by order of the court the Statute has no application. The earliest reported authority for this rule seems to be *Attorney-General* v. *Day*,[1] where Lord Hardwicke, L.C., stated the law as follows:

"But the present is a judicial sale of the estate, which takes it entirely out of the statute; the order of the Court...includes... the carrying the purchase into execution...; amounting to a decree for the conveyance of the estate on one side, and payment of the money on the other; who might be prosecuted for a contempt in not obeying that order. And it is stronger than the common case of purchasers before the *Master*, who are certainly out of the statute: nor should I doubt the carrying into execution against the representative a purchase before the *Master* without subscribing, after confirmation of the *Master's* report, that he was the best purchaser; the judgment of the Court taking it out of the statute".

This principle applies to sales by order of the court under the present practice.[2] It was expressly recognized in the Law of Property Act, 1925.[3]

(2) *Negotiations not resulting in contracts.* The Statute "'is a weapon of defence, not offence', and 'does not make any signed instrument a valid contract by reason of the signature, if it is not such according to the good faith and real intention of the parties'".[4] The question, therefore, may arise, of whether the

[1] (1748) 1 Ves. Sen. 218, 221; 27 E.R. 992, 994; see also *Blagden* v. *Bradbear*, (1806) 12 Ves. 466, 472; 33 E.R. 176, 178; and *Lord* v. *Lord*, (1827) 1 Sim. 503; 57 E.R. 666.

[2] Dart, *Vendors and Purchasers*, 8th ed. II, 988. For practice, see *ib.* 965 *et seq.*

[3] 15 Geo. V, c. 20, s. 40 (1).

[4] Per Lord Selborne, *Hussey* v. *Horne-Payne*, (1879) 4 App. Cas. at p. 323.

written evidence tendered to satisfy the Statute actually proves a concluded contract. This question is really independent of the Statute,[1] but as it is frequently raised in connection with contracts to which the Statute applies, reference is here made to the more important principles.

The question of whether the writing proves a concluded contract has chiefly been discussed in two classes of cases: (i) cases where it is sought to prove a contract from letters; and (ii) cases where the writing has contained a provision for the subsequent execution of a more formal document.

(i) *Cases where it is sought to prove contract from letters.* Where parties are negotiating for a contract, it is well settled that so soon as there emerges from the mist of negotiation a definite offer unequivocally accepted, the position changes from negotiation to contract: thenceforth the parties will be bound, and neither may, without the consent of the other, recede from his bargain. Thus, where the parties have been negotiating by correspondence, it will sometimes happen that one, in the course of the correspondence, makes a definite offer, and this will be accepted by the other. *Prima facie* the matter will then be concluded: negotiation will have ripened into contract, and the parties will be bound.

"'Though, when a contract is contained in letters, the whole correspondence should be looked at, yet if once a definite offer has been made, and it has been accepted without qualification, and it appears that the letters of offer and acceptance contained all the terms agreed on between the parties'—that means, of course, agreed on at the date of the offer and acceptance—'the complete contract thus arrived at cannot be affected by subsequent negotiation. When once it is shewn that there is a complete contract, further negotiations between the parties cannot,

[1] "The real truth", said Kay, J., in *Bristol, Cardiff, and Swansea Aerated Bread Co.* v. *Maggs*, (1890) 44 Ch.D. 616, 622, "is that the Statute was not meant to affect contracts in any way, but only the evidence of them. It does not provide that a memorandum duly signed shall be a contract, but only that no contract concerning land shall be proved by any lower evidence than such a written memorandum. The question whether the two letters relied on in this case were a complete contract, or were only steps in a negotiation, is altogether independent of the *Statute of Frauds*."

without the consent of both, get rid of the contract already arrived at.'"[1]

But where correspondence is relied upon to prove a contract, the court is entitled to look at the whole of that correspondence, and if, from the whole of the correspondence, both prior and subsequent to the letters containing the alleged offer and acceptance, it appears that at the date of such offer and acceptance there were in fact terms still under discussion between the parties on which agreement had not been, and was not subsequently, reached, the alleged contract will be void for want of a complete *consensus ad idem*.

The leading case on this matter is *Hussey* v. *Horne-Payne*.[2] There two letters, *prima facie* proving a concluded contract, were relied upon by the plaintiff. But it appeared, partly from evidence of earlier negotiations (conversations), and partly from subsequent correspondence, that at the time those letters were written, certain terms were still under discussion between the parties; and in fact no agreement with regard to those terms was ever reached. Earl Cairns, L.C., summed up the position, and stated the law, in the following words:

"Now, my Lords, the conclusion I draw from that is this, that we have here the Appellant himself telling us that the two original letters, which, if you took them alone without any knowledge supplied to you of the other facts of the case, might lead you to think that they represented and amounted to a complete and concluded agreement, yet really were not a complete and concluded agreement, that there were to be other terms which at that time had not been agreed upon, that efforts were made afterwards to settle those terms, and that these efforts did not result in a settlement of these other terms. The consequence therefore of the whole is, that it appears to me not only that there is no note in writing, according to the *Statute of Frauds*, of that which was a completed agreement between the parties, but that there was in point of fact no completed agreement between the parties".

[1] Per Lord Cozens-Hardy, M.R., in *Perry* v. *Suffields, Ltd.* [1916] 2 Ch. 187, 191, quoting with approval the headnote to *Bellamy* v. *Debenham*, 45 Ch.D. 481, a decision which he "absolutely accepted".

[2] (1879) 4 App. Cas. 311, 320. See also *Jones* v. *Daniel*, [1894] 2 Ch. 332; *Bellamy* v. *Debenham*, (1890) 45 Ch.D. 481; *May* v. *Thomson*, (1882) 20 Ch.D. 705; and *Morrell* v. *Studd & Millington*, [1913] 2 Ch. 648, 658 *et seq.*

(ii) *Writing containing provision for execution of more formal document.* Where the writing relied upon to prove the contract provides for the execution of a more formal document, it will be a question whether the execution of such formal document is to be a condition precedent to the conclusion of the contract, or whether it is merely to provide for the more effectual evidencing of a contract already entered into. The answer to this question will depend on the intention of the parties to be ascertained from the construction of the writing relied upon and the circumstances of the particular case.

"It appears to be well settled by the authorities", said Parker, J., in *Von Hatzfeldt-Wildenburg* v. *Alexander*,[1] "that if the documents or letters relied on as constituting a contract contemplate the execution of a further contract between the parties, it is a question of construction whether the execution of the further contract is a condition or term of the bargain or whether it is a mere expression of the desire of the parties as to the manner in which the transaction already agreed to will in fact go through. In the former case there is no enforceable contract either because the condition is unfulfilled or because the law does not recognize a contract to enter into a contract. In the latter case there is a binding contract and the reference to the more formal document may be ignored. The fact that the reference to the more formal document is in words which according to their natural construction import a condition is generally if not invariably conclusive against the reference being treated as the expression of a mere desire."

Thus, in *Winn* v. *Bull*[2] the defendant agreed in writing with the plaintiff to take a lease of a house for a certain term and at a certain rent, "subject to the preparation and approval of a formal contract". No other contract was every entered into between the parties. Jessel, M.R., held that the writing relied upon by the plaintiff did not prove a concluded contract.

"Now, in the present case," remarked the Master of the Rolls, "the plaintiff says in effect, 'I agree to grant you a lease on

[1] [1912] 1 Ch. 284, 288. Parker, J., doubts *North* v. *Percival*, [1898] 2 Ch. 128.

[2] (1877) 7 Ch.D. 29, 31. See also *Filby* v. *Hounsell*, [1896] 2 Ch. 737; and *Rossiter* v. *Miller*, (1878) 3 App. Cas. 1124.

certain terms, but subject to something else being approved'. He does not say, 'Nothing more shall be required beyond what I have already mentioned', but 'something else is required', which is not expressed. That being so, the agreement is uncertain in its terms and consequently cannot be sustained."

PART II

THE WRITING

CHAPTER I

THE WRITING

Introductory: whether the Statute applies to contracts by deed. In general a contract the terms of which are in issue in a judicial proceeding may be proved to the court or other tribunal by any evidence of sufficient probative force.[1] The Statute affects this general principle by restricting the kind of evidence which may be offered to prove contracts coming within its terms. It requires, as a condition precedent to the enforcement by action of such contracts, that "the agreement upon which such action shall be brought or some memorandum or note thereof shall be in writing and signed by the party to be charged therewith or some other person thereunto by him lawfully authorized".

Although there is no express decision on the point, it seems reasonably certain that the Statute applies to simple contracts only, and that where the parties have reduced their contract to the form of a deed, it falls outside the section. *Cherry* v. *Heming*,[2] which came before the Court of Exchequer in 1849, appears to be the only case in which the point has been raised; and in that case, the unanimous opinion of the learned Barons was that the Statute had no application to contracts by word. Parke, B., after giving judgment on other grounds, continued:

"...I must own that I think a deed is not within the Statute of Frauds, because, in my opinion, that statute was never meant to apply to the most solemn instrument which the law recognizes".

[1] Wigmore, *Treatise on Evidence*, 2nd ed., I, pp. 152–153, and the authorities there cited. "All facts having rational probative value are admissible unless some specific rule forbids....This principle does not mean that anything that has a probative value is admissible; this would be an entire misconception. The true meaning is that everything having a probative value is *ipso facto* entitled to be assumed to be admissible, and that therefore any rule of policy which may be valid to exclude it is a superadded and abnormal rule." *Op. cit.* 152.

[2] (1849) 4 Ex. 631, 636; 154 E.R. 1367, 1369.

Alderson, B., expressed a similar opinion and Rolfe, B., elaborated the reasons given by Parke, B., saying:

"I am strongly inclined to think that the statute does not extend to deeds, because its requirements would be satisfied by the parties putting their mark to the writing. The object of the statute was to prevent matters of importance from resting on the frail testimony of memory alone. Before the Norman time, signature rendered the instrument authentic. Sealing was introduced because the people in general could not write. Then there arose a distinction between what was sealed and what was not sealed, and that went on until society became more advanced, when the statute ultimately said that certain instruments must be authenticated by signature. That means, that such instruments are not on parol testimony only, and it was not intended to touch those which were already authenticated by a ceremony of a higher nature than a signature or a mark".

Platt, B., concurred in the judgments delivered by the other members of the court.

These observations of the learned Barons were probably *obiter*; but having regard to the exceptional strength of the court, the unanimity of the opinions expressed, and the fact that those opinions have now stood in the reports for over eighty years without being shaken, it seems reasonable to accept *Cherry* v. *Heming* as correctly setting forth the law.[1]

Distinction between written and verbal contracts in regard to the Statute. The Statute implies that an *agreement* may either be written or else evidenced by writing: the words of the Statute being "the *agreement* or *some note or memorandum* there-

[1] See also *Cooch* v. *Goodman*, (1842) 2 Q.B. 580; 114 E.R. 228, and *Aveline* v. *Whisson*, (1842) 12 L.J. C.P. 58. These cases related to s. 1 (now repealed) of the Statute, but s. 1 sufficiently resembled s. 4 to render these cases applicable to the latter section. In *Cooch* v. *Goodman*, (1842) 2 Q.B. 580; 114 E.R. 228, Lord Denman, C.J., discussing the application of s. 1 to a deed of lease, referred to contradictory opinions on the question expressed by Blackstone in his *Commentaries* (ed. Christian, 1809, II, p. 306), and Preston in his edition of *Sheppard's Touchstone*, p. 56, n. 24, but expressed no opinion of his own. In *Aveline* v. *Whisson*, the point was actually decided, Tindal, C.J., disposing of it very briefly. "Is there anything in the point?" he asked. "The Statute of Frauds [i.e. s. 1] does not apply: there is a sealing by the lessee." This case was referred to by Parke, B., in the course of the argument in *Cherry* v. *Heming* (*supra*).

of".[1] *Agreement*, it has been decided, means *contract*;[2] and hence it becomes necessary to consider briefly the distinction between written contracts and those which are not written.

A contractual writing may be

(*a*) both the contract and the evidence of the contract; or

(*b*) the evidence of the contract; or

(*c*) part of the evidence of the contract.

Where the writing is both the contract and the evidence of the contract, the contract may be described as a *written contract*. Where the writing is the evidence of the contract or part of the evidence of the contract or where the contract has been made and evidenced solely by words it may be described as a *verbal contract*.

A written contract is one where the parties by the very act of

[1] This distinction, it is submitted, is justified by the words of the Statute, and it seems to have been judicially recognized in several cases. In *Saunderson* v. *Jackson*, (1800) 2 Bos. & P. 238; 126 E.R. 1257, Lord Eldon, C.J., remarked in the course of his judgment (at p. 239; E.R. p. 1258): "This bill of parcels, *though not the contract itself* [the italics are mine], may amount to a note or memorandum of the contract within the meaning of the statute". In *Williams* v. *Lake*, (1859) 2 E. & E. 349; 121 E.R. 132, the following argument was addressed to the court by counsel (at p. 353; E.R. 133): "Even admitting, however, that a formal agreement must contain the names of the parties to it, the same particularity cannot be required in a memorandum or note of the agreement, between which and the agreement itself the language of the 4th section of the Statute of Frauds implies a distinction". Cockburn, C.J., while he declined to admit the conclusion contended for by counsel yet acknowledged the validity of the distinction on which counsel had based his argument. "I cannot concur", said Cockburn, C.J. (p. 354; E.R. 134), "in Mr Norman's view, that any greater laxity in this respect is permissible in a memorandum of an agreement than in an agreement itself." This distinction was again referred to in *Parton* v. *Crofts*, (1864) 16 C.B. (N.S.) 11, 21; 143 E.R. 1027, 1031, where Erle, C.J., remarked: "I make a distinction between the contract and the memorandum of the contract: the latter may be made long after the terms have been agreed to; and the making of the one is entirely distinct from the other". And see also *Reuss* v. *Picksley*, (1866) L.R. 1 Ex. 342, 353, where Willes, J., in delivering the judgment of the Court of Exchequer Chamber, used the phrase "a regular agreement or memorandum of it". In the Irish case of *Dyas* v. *Stafford*, (1881) 7 L.R. Ir. 590, 599, Chatterton, V.-C., clearly recognized the distinction. "In the case of sales by auction", he said, "the actual agreement is constituted by the bidding on the one part, and acceptance of it by the auctioneer on the other; and the writing necessary to satisfy the requirements of the statute is, therefore, a memorandum or note of the agreement so made."

[2] Pp. 54, 55 *infra*.

bringing about the contractual relation adopt a writing as their contract; from the moment the contract comes into existence its terms are to be found in the writing.[1] A verbal contract, on the other hand, is one the terms of which are not to be found *ab initio* in writing, but must be collected from the words and acts of the parties or partly from their words and acts and partly from writings.[2]

The terms of a verbal contract may subsequently be reduced to writing, either in whole or in part. In that event the result may assume one of two shapes. Either the original contract remains, the writing being merely the evidence of it (this is necessarily so where the terms are only partially reduced into writing); or else the writing becomes the contract (a written contract) and the original contract becomes merged in it.

When all the terms of the original verbal contract appear in the writing, the question of whether this writing amounts only to a memorandum of the original contract or whether, on the other hand, it constitutes a written contract discharging the

[1] This definition would include contracts by deed as well as simple written contracts, but inasmuch as the Statute of Frauds affects only simple contracts, it has not been thought necessary to elaborate the definition in its application to deeds.

A written contract may come into existence in any one of the following ways. First, one party may accept in writing the written offer of the other party; this would seem to be what happened in the case of *Morison* v. *Turnour*, (1811) 18 Ves. 175; 34 E.R. 284.

Secondly, both parties may agree that a writing setting out contractual terms and conditions shall be their contract. For example, two parties who are negotiating about the sale and purchase of a piece of land, instruct a solicitor to prepare an appropriate form of agreement; and after perusing the form so prepared, they agree that it expresses the contract they wish to make and that it shall be their contract. That would constitute a written contract, even though the parties did not sign the instrument.

Thirdly, one party may verbally accept a written offer submitted by the other party. An example of this kind of contract is provided by *Smith* v. *Neale*, (1857) 2 C.B. (N.S.) 67; 140 E.R. 337, where a written proposal, signed by the person to be bound, and accepted by word of mouth by the person to whom it was made, was held to be a sufficient agreement to satisfy the Statute.

[2] Cf. Salmond and Winfield, *Law of Contracts*, 98. Salmond's definition of a written contract is in these words: "A contract in writing, then, is one the terms of which are set out in a contractual instrument; and such an instrument is a document which is accepted by the parties, in the act of making the contract, as containing the authentic expression of its terms".

earlier contract, depends on the intention of the parties. In general that intention will be that the writing is henceforth to be their contract. Such an intention will readily be inferable if the writing is formally drawn up,[1] but not if the writing comes

[1] It is written in *Viner's Abridgement* (Contract G. 18) as follows: "If an agreement made by parol to do any thing be afterwards *reduced into writing* [the italics are mine], the parol agreement is thereby discharged; and if an action be brought for non-performance of this agreement, it must be brought upon the agreement reduced into writing, and not upon the parol agreement, for both cannot stand together, because it appears to be but one agreement, and that shall be taken which is the latter, and reduced to the greater certainty by writing; for *vox emissa volat, litera scripta manet*".

What, then, is the meaning of *reduced into writing*? It is submitted that a contract can be said to be reduced into writing only when it has been put into written form by agreement of the parties with the intention that the writing shall henceforth be their contract, so that their rights and duties will no longer depend on the uncertain basis of oral testimony: *vox emissa volat.* The point has been nicely illustrated in some cases arising out of the Bills of Sale Acts. S. 9 of the Bills of Sale Act, 1878, provided that a document being a bill of sale as defined by that Act should be *void* unless complying with certain conditions. Now, to construe that section as applying to documents which were evidentiary merely and did not constitute contracts, would have been equivalent to saying that the Act avoided *evidence.* But evidence is admissible or inadmissible, not valid or *void.* Hence it was decided that the Act was aimed only at instruments which, as well as evidencing contracts, constituted them. Therefore it was decided that where the alleged bill of sale could be shown to be nothing more than an incidental memorandum, the party could still rely on any precedent verbal contract. Thus in *Newlove* v. *Shrewsbury*, (1888) 21 Q.B.D. 41, it was held by the Court of Appeal that a receipt did not discharge a verbal contract between the parties; and therefore the defendant, relying on the verbal contract, was not defeated by the Bills of Sale Act, 1878. Lord Esher, M.R., said (at p. 43): "The question is, whether there was not an oral transaction entirely independent of this receipt which would entitle the defendant, having the possession of this machine, to retain it as against the plaintiffs. That seems to me to depend on the question whether it can be said that this receipt operated as a reduction into writing of the agreement between the parties with regard to the giving of this security. If the agreement is reduced into writing so that there cannot be any question of a parol agreement independent of the writing, and the writing being a bill of sale is void under the Bills of Sale Acts, then no subsequent possession of the goods can in my opinion give the grantee any right to them; because the parties having reduced their agreement into writing, such writing is the only evidence of the agreement, and, if that is void, then there is nothing to which the possession can be referred". In *Ex parte Parsons*, (1886) 16 Q.B.D. 532, on the other hand, it was held that the writing (a letter addressed by one party to the other, expressly dealing with the subject-matter of the contract, and with nothing else) had discharged the original verbal contract; and hence the provisions of the Bills of Sale Act applied. "Whatever the verbal arrangement between Townsend and Parsons may have been, the terms of it were reduced into writing by the document of the 7th of August. That being so,

into existence incidentally, and without being intended by the parties to have any contractual effect.[1]

A contract is none the less a written contract merely because the law implies certain of its terms, which accordingly are not expressed in the contract or in the writing.[2]

Application of Statute. The Statute, as will be shewn in a later chapter,[3] requires that the whole of the contract shall be evidenced by writing. Therefore, bearing in mind the foregoing distinctions, the application of the Statute to contracts coming within its provisions may be stated as follows. (1) Written contracts, provided they are duly signed, will necessarily satisfy the Statute, for in their case the writing, *ex hypothesi*, is the contract, and therefore there can be no question of whether the contract is properly set forth in that writing.[4] (2) Verbal contracts not evidenced by writing or only partially evidenced by writing will not satisfy the Statute. (3) Verbal contracts wholly evidenced by a properly signed writing will satisfy the Statute. As, however, the writing in such a case is not itself the contract, it will always be a question whether, in fact, it wholly sets forth

we cannot look at anything but the writing; the writing is the sole evidence of the agreement whatever it was."

[1] Cases to illustrate this part of the proposition can readily be found. Thus it would have been impossible to contend that the witness's proof which did duty as a memorandum in *Daniels* v. *Trefusis*, [1914] 1 Ch. 788, was the contract, although it contained all the terms thereof. See also *Gibson* v. *Holland*, (1865) L.R. 1 C.P. 1, where a memorandum was constructed from letters passing between the defendant and his agent; and *In re Hoyle*, [1893] 1 Ch. 84.

[2] See Salmond and Winfield, *Law of Contracts*, p. 106.

An open contract for the sale of land is generally a written contract; yet many terms are implied in it beyond the agreement to buy and sell set out in the writing. And see *Hoadly* v. *McLaine*, (1834) 10 Bing. 482, 487; 131 E.R. 982, 984. That was a contract for the sale of goods, where, no price being fixed, the law implied a term that a reasonable price was to be paid. "What is implied by law", said Tindal, C.J., "is as strong to bind the parties as if it were under their hand. This is a contract which is silent as to price, and the parties therefore leave it to the law to ascertain what the commodity contracted for is reasonably worth."

[3] Part II, chapter ii, p. 54, *infra*.

[4] This point is well illustrated by *Mackenzie* v. *Coulson*, (1869) L.R. 8 Eq. 368, 375. That was a suit for the rectification of an insurance policy, on the ground that it mistakenly set forth the contract between the parties. James, V.-C., however, held that the policy was the contract and hence refused relief, for the policy could not be regarded as erroneously setting forth its own terms.

the contract, or whether, on the other hand, it merely states part of the contract.

The principal matters for consideration in the following chapters, therefore, will be first, what must be set forth in the writing in order that it may be said to evidence the whole of the contract;[1] secondly, the form of the writing;[2] and thirdly the signature required,[3] including signature by an agent,[4] and the application of a single signature to two or more documents.[5]

[1] Part II, chapters ii and iii.
[2] Part II, chapter iv.
[3] Part II, chapter v.
[4] Part II, chapter vi.
[5] Part II, chapter vii.

CHAPTER II

CONTENTS OF THE MEMORANDUM

WHERE the writing is merely the evidence of the contract, it is necessary to consider precisely how much of the contract the writing must prove and with what degree of particularity the various terms of the contract must be set forth.

The Statute refers to the writing in these cases as a *note or memorandum*; it will be convenient to adopt the term *memorandum* for and to restrict it to the writing evidencing verbal contracts.

To satisfy the express words of the Statute the memorandum must be a memorandum *of the agreement*. The Statute refers both to the *promise* and the *agreement*; and the courts, inferring from the use of these two words in the same section that a distinction was intended, have held that *agreement* is the larger term and comprises both the *promise* and the consideration therefor.[1] But a promise taken together with its consideration

[1] From at least as early as 1721 it has been laid down by the courts that a memorandum must set forth the whole of the contract—both the promise and the consideration therefor. In that year Lord Macclesfield, L.C., in *Seagood* v. *Neale*, 1 Strange 426; 93 E.R. 613 (also in Prec. Ch. 560; 24 E.R. 251 *sub nom. Seagood* v. *Neale and Leonard*; and also in 2 Eq. Ca. Abr. 49; 22 E.R. 42) dismissed a bill for specific performance on the ground that the memorandum relied on was defective "because the agreement does not appear in it".

The distinction between the promise and the contract is expressly drawn by Ellenborough, C.J., in *Wain* v. *Warlters*, (1804) 5 East 10, 16; 102 E.R. 972, 975; 1 Sm. L.C. 13th ed. 358. In the course of his judgment Lord Ellenborough remarked: "The clause in question in the Statute of Frauds has the word agreement....And the question is, whether that word is to be understood in the loose incorrect sense in which it may sometimes be used, as synonymous to promise or undertaking, or in its more proper and correct sense, as signifying a mutual contract on consideration between two or more parties? The latter appears to me to be the legal construction of the word, to which we are bound to give its proper effect...The obligatory part is indeed the promise, which will account for the word promise being used in the first part of the clause, but still in order to charge the party making it, the Statute proceeds to require that the agreement, by which must be understood the agreement in respect of which the promise was made, must be reduced into writing. And indeed it seems necessary for effectuating the object of the

is a contract. It may therefore be inferred from the authorities cited in the last note that *agreement* as used in the Statute means *contract*. Hence to satisfy the Statute the memorandum must set forth the contract; it must be a memorandum *of the contract*.

If a memorandum is to be described as "of the contract" it must be possible to discover from that memorandum what the contract is; it would not suffice that the memorandum disclosed a part of the contract, or even the chief parts of it. In these cases, the proper description of the memorandum would be "of some parts of the contract", or "of the chief parts of the contract". But to satisfy the Statute the memorandum must set forth *all* of the contract; and as a contract exists only in its various terms, the memorandum must therefore disclose all the terms of the contract.[1]

Statute that the consideration should be set down in writing as well as the promise...". See also *Stadt* v. *Lill*, (1808) 9 East 348; 103 E.R. 605. In *Jenkins* v. *Reynolds*, (1821) 3 Brod. & B. 14, 19; 129 E.R. 1187, 1189, Dallas, C.J., re-stated the principle laid down in *Wain* v. *Warlters*, and in 1855 that principle was once more expressly affirmed in *Powers* v. *Fowler*, 4 E. & E. 511, 517; 119 E.R. 187, 189. Coleridge, J., one of the judges who decided this last-mentioned case, thus stated the law: "The memorandum of agreement must in itself disclose all the requisites of a contract. You may have recourse to all the circumstances admissible to apply the agreement; but the signed memorandum must in itself contain the whole requisites in writing".

[1] Per Eldon, L.C., in *Coles* v. *Trecothick*, 9 Ves. 234, 250; 32 E.R. 592, 599: "Though the agreement is not signed, if that letter contains all the terms, and describes the consideration and all the circumstances, so that by the contents of the letter it can be connected and identified with the agreement, that letter...is a writing signed". And in *Rose* v. *Cunynghame*, (1805) 11 Ves. 550, 555; 32 E.R. 1202, 1203, the same Lord Chancellor remarked of another letter: "It amounts to no more than that there was a parol agreement upon some terms; admitting that; but leaving altogether to parol evidence to say, what the terms were".

In *Peirce* v. *Corf*, (1874) L.R. 9 Q.B. 210, 214, Blackburn, J., states in express words the proposition contended for in the text: "But in order to make a valid contract, the document the auctioneer signs on behalf of the buyer must contain *all the terms of the contract*". (The italics are mine.) And this was the opinion of Sir Edward Fry: see Fry, *Specific Performance of Contracts*, 6th ed. pp. 242, 243: "...it is obvious that the mischief [to prevent which the Statute had been passed] is avoided wherever there exists, under the hand of the party sought to be charged, a written statement containing, either expressly or by necessary inference, all the terms of the contract...". See also *Archer* v. *Baynes*, (1850) 5 Ex. 625, 629; 155 E.R. 274, 276, where Alderson, B., delivering the judgment of himself, Rolfe, and Platt, BB., said: "No doubt, if the letter of the plaintiff of the 3rd of October, and of the defendant in answer, taken together, contained a sufficient contract, namely, one that

But although the memorandum must disclose all the terms of the contract, every individual term need not be stated expressly and at length. A term is sufficiently disclosed if it can be discovered by reasonable inference[1] from the terms expressly set forth and the general nature of the contract, assisted by parol evidence of an explanatory nature admitted in accordance with the principle stated below.[2]

Language has sometimes been used by judges which would seem to indicate that they considered that a memorandum need only disclose the "essential" or "material" terms of the contract. But contract is a matter of the intention of the parties: what is material or essential must therefore be determined by reference to that intention; and it may well be asked by what test the court is to decide this delicate matter.[3] No help in answering this question can be found in the cases. And it is significant that in no case has the court ever refused relief on the expressed ground that a memorandum failed to set forth a *material or essential* term; nor, conversely, can any case be found in which the court has actually decided that although a memor-

would express *all its terms*, they would constitute a memorandum in writing within the statute....They do not express *all the terms* of the contract...". (The italics are mine.) In *Blore* v. *Sutton*, (1817) 3 Mer. 237, 246; 36 E.R. 91, 94, Grant, M.R., speaking of an alleged memorandum of an agreement for a lease, said: "It merely specifies the rent, and the number of years. It does not even specify the commencement of the lease. By the parol evidence, indeed, it is said, that it was to be from the expiration of a subsisting lease. But then the *whole* [italics mine] agreement is not in writing".

Note that a memorandum of a contract of guarantee need not now set out the consideration for the guarantee. See p. 27 *supra*.

[1] Per Lord Cranworth, L.C., in *Caddick* v. *Skidmore*, (1857) 2 De G. & J. 52, 55; 44 E.R. 907, 908: "And although the court has struggled to bring within the description of a signed agreement any instrument, however informal, which does in truth disclose what the terms of the contract were, it has never repealed the Statute of Frauds by holding a writing to be within its meaning which has not that effect, i.e. which does not *by plain words or reasonable inference disclose what was the contract of the parties*". (The italics are mine.)

[2] See p. 59 *infra*.

[3] Per Parke, B., in *Marshall* v. *Lynn*, (1840) 6 M. & W. 109, 117; 151 E.R. 342, 345: "I must also observe, that it seems to me to be unnecessary to inquire what are the essential parts of the contract, and what not, and that every part of the contract, in regard to which the parties are stipulating, must be taken to be material...".

andum did not disclose all the terms of the contract, those omitted terms were immaterial or non-essential; and therefore that the memorandum was sufficient for the purpose of the Statute.

Special reference may be made to two cases containing *dicta* which suggest that a distinction should be drawn between "essential" and "non-essential" terms. In *Jenkins* v. *Reynolds*,[1] Dallas, C.J., remarked:

"If therefore, agreement means more than promise, the agreement itself, or some note or memorandum of it must appear; by memorandum, I mean, not the whole detail of what has been agreed on, but such a note as to render oral testimony unnecessary, towards proving what is of the essence of the contract".

But it is submitted that the learned Chief Justice did not mean that to discover the whole contract, recourse might be had to parol evidence to prove those terms which were *non-essential*; but rather that he considered that the whole detail of the arrangement between the parties need not be expressly stated so long as it might be gathered from the memorandum by necessary inference without recourse to parol evidence. The real point raised in this case was whether a memorandum which set forth the promise alone without expressing the consideration therefor, was yet enough to satisfy the Statute; and the court merely followed *Wain* v. *Warlters*[2] in deciding that the consideration, as well as the promise, must appear in the memorandum. As Park, J., said:[3] "All that was essential to be proved before [the Statute was enacted] by oral testimony, must now appear on the face of the writing".

The second case is *Gray* v. *Smith*.[4] The question there was whether certain rough heads of an agreement were a sufficient memorandum. Cotton, L.J., who delivered the principal judgment, said: "When a memorandum is intended to be worked out by a more formal document it is not necessary that every

[1] (1821), 3 Brod. & B. 14, 20; 129 E.R. 1187, 1190.
[2] 5 East 10.
[3] 3 Brod. & B. at p. 21; E.R. 1190.
[4] (1889) 43 Ch.D. 208, 219.

stipulation which would be contained in the latter document should be indicated, but the memorandum must contain all the essential terms of the agreement". But the ground upon which Cotton, L.J., actually rested his judgment was that where a term in a contract is implied by law neither the contract when there is a written contract nor the memorandum in the case of a verbal contract need expressly state that term.[1]

The memorandum, therefore, must disclose either by plain words or reasonable inference all the terms of the contract. Whether in the particular case a term can be collected by *reasonable inference* is often a question of very considerable difficulty. It is not enough that the memorandum is *consistent with the existence* of the term sought to be inferred; or that it is *probable* that the parties intended to include such a term in their contract. There must be reasonable certainty both as to the fact of the term and as to its contents.[2]

Such an inference may be drawn from the nature of the transaction itself as it appears from the terms set out in the memorandum; in which case the inferred term is usually said to be *implied*.[3] Or the court may consider that the general circumstances discoverable from the memorandum, together with those facts of which it will take judicial notice (if, in the particular case, there are any), afford a sufficient ground upon which to base such an inference.[4]

[1] It is curious that the term round which the argument centred in *Gray* v. *Smith* (*supra*), so far from being non-essential, was of such fundamental importance in a contract of that kind as to be implied by the law.

Dicta of the sort discussed in the text may sometimes be explained to mean that before even a *prima facie* case of contract can be made out certain essential elements discoverable in all valid contracts must be proved to the court. See Anson, *Law of Contract*, 17th ed. p. 9. The following *dictum* of Cockburn, C.J., in *Williams* v. *Lake*, (1859) 2 E. & E. 349, 354; 121 E.R. 132, 134, may perhaps be accounted for in this way: "But it [the memorandum] must still contain all the essentials of an agreement, and therefore, *inter alia*, the names of both parties". It is essential that there should be two or more parties before there can be a contract; and it is suggested that the *dictum* of Cockburn, C.J., means nothing more than that.

[2] See per Hill, J., advising the House of Lords in *Fitzmaurice* v. *Bayley*, (1860) 9 H.L.C. 79, 93; 11 E.R. 657, 663, quoted *infra*, p. 66.

[3] See, for example, *Gray* v. *Smith*, (1889) 43 Ch.D. 208.

[4] See *Commins* v. *Scott*, (1875) L.R. 20 Eq. 11, a decision of Jessel, M.R., for a very good example of this method.

Although in general parol evidence is not admissible to aid a defective memorandum (such inadmissibility being due partly to the common law rule excluding parol evidence to add to, vary, or contradict documents, and partly to the operation of the Statute),[1] the courts nevertheless will admit parol evidence to *explain* a memorandum or the words or phraseology thereof. But the admission of such evidence is subject to very stringent rules and limitations, the general effect of which may, it is submitted, be stated with approximate accuracy as follows: that this evidence must be confined to explanation: so soon as it passes from explaining the memorandum to adding new terms or varying those already written it becomes inadmissible.[2]

The explanatory evidence rule and the reasonable inference rule which have just been considered, can, and frequently do,

[1] See Part III, chapter i, p. 147 *infra*.

[2] Wigram, *Extrinsic Evidence*, 5th ed. p. 8: "Any evidence is admissible, which, in its nature and effect, simply explains what the testator *has* written; but no evidence can be admissible, which, in its nature or effect, is applicable to the purpose of shewing merely what he *intended* to have written".

The general conditions governing the admission of oral evidence to explain a memorandum or other document are very clearly and succinctly stated in Stephen, *Digest of the Law of Evidence*, 11th ed. p. 102, article 91. The following cases arising out of contracts within the Statute of Frauds afford further illustrations of the rules stated by Stephen.

In *Bateman* v. *Phillips*, (1812) 15 East 272, 274; 104 E.R. 847, 848, an action had been brought on a guarantee in these terms: "Sir, the bearer David Williams has a sum of money to receive from a client of mine some day next week, and I trust you will give him indulgence till that day when I undertake to see you paid". Parol evidence was admitted to shew who was the client referred to, and that the sum of money was a debt subsisting at the time. Ellenborough, C.J., remarked: "The parol evidence received did not go to extend the terms of the agreement in writing; it only went to shew that the letter was addressed to him as the attorney for the plaintiff, and not as the principal and creditor of Williams....The parol evidence does not enlarge any term of the letter...".

Harrison v. *Barton*, (1860), 1 J. & H. 287; 70 E.R. 756, a decision of Page-Wood, V.-C., may also be referred to. The headnote of this case states the effect of the decision thus: "On a purchase by two persons contributing equally to the cost of it, parol evidence of surrounding circumstances and of subsequent dealings is, notwithstanding the Statute of Frauds, admissible to prove an intention to hold in severalty. But, *semble*, parol evidence of statements of intention is not admissible".

In *McMurray* v. *Spicer*, (1868) L.R. 5 Eq. 527, the question was whether "the mill property, including cottages in Esher village" described the subject-matter of the contract with sufficient certainty to enable the court to perform the contract, and it was contended that parol evidence to help out this de-

operate together to elucidate a memorandum the full meaning of which does not at first appear.[1] Hence, although all the terms of the contract are not *prima facie* apparent from a perusal of such memorandum, it may yet be a sufficient memorandum for any one of the following reasons:

(1) because the terms not *prima facie* apparent can be implied from the nature of the transaction, or gathered by reasonable inference from the express provisions of the memorandum and the facts of which the court will take judicial notice; or

(2) because those terms appear when parol evidence is admitted to explain the memorandum;[2] or

(3) because those terms can be supplied by reasonable inference from the express provisions of the memorandum and the facts of which the court will take judicial notice, after parol evidence has been admitted to explain the memorandum.[1]

If all the terms of the contract do not appear after a memorandum has been aided by evidence in explanation and all reasonable inferences have been drawn, then that memorandum will be defective and useless for the purposes of the Statute of Frauds.[3]

scription was inadmissible. But Malins, V.-C., allowed parol evidence to identify the property, including evidence of the subsequent conduct of the parties.

See also *Sheers* v. *Thimbleby*, (1897) 76 L.T. 709.

The position was neatly summed up by Lord Blackburn in *Rossiter* v. *Miller*, (1878) 3 App. Cas. 1124, 1153, as follows: "And though the construction by which it is held that there can be no memorandum of the agreement unless the writing shews who the parties are, is now inveterate, it is not necessary that they should be named. It is enough if the parties are sufficiently described to fix who they are without receiving any evidence of that character which Sir James Wigram in his Treatise [*Extrinsic Evidence*, 5th ed. p. 10] calls evidence 'to prove' intention as an independent fact. In the present case, without receiving any more evidence, there is ample to shew that the plaintiffs were those designated by the description of 'the proprietors'".

[1] *McMurray* v. *Spicer*, (1868) L.R. 5 Eq. 527. *Ogilvie* v. *Foljambe*, (1817) 3 Mer. 53; 36 E.R. 21. *Newell* v. *Radford*, (1867) L.R. 3 C.P. 52.

[2] *Wilson* v. *Hart*, (1817) 7 Taunt. 295; 129 E.R. 118. *Shortrede* v. *Cheek*, (1834) 1 A. & E. 57; 110 E.R. 1129. *Catling* v. *King*, (1877) 5 Ch.D. 660.

[3] It has been decided, however, that where the memorandum omits a term exclusively in the plaintiff's favour, the plaintiff may, if he sees fit, waive performance by the defendant of that term, and it will not then be open to the defendant to object that the Statute has not been complied with. *Morrell* v. *Studd & Millington*, [1913] 2 Ch. 648, 660; *North* v. *Loomes*, [1919] 1 Ch. 378, 386. Cf. *Von Hatzfeldt-Wildenburg* v. *Alexander*, [1912] 1 Ch. 284, 290.

CHAPTER III

DEFECTS COMMONLY APPEARING IN THE MEMORANDUM

MEMORANDA failing to satisfy the Statute on account of the defective manner in which they state the contract seem in large measure to range themselves under one or other of several broad headings. Such memoranda may be bad by reason of:

(1) defective nomination of the parties to the contract; or

(2) inadequate statement of the consideration for the contract; or

(3) uncertainty in stating the time from which the contract is to operate; or

(4) inadequate or equivocal description of the subject-matter of the contract.

(1) *Defective nomination of the parties to the contract.* The memorandum must shew who are the parties to the contract. "Independently of any authority", said Blackburn, J., in *Williams* v. *Lake*,[1] "I should have said that no document can be an agreement, or a memorandum of one, which does not shew on its face who the parties making the agreement are."

Numerous examples of memoranda which have been held defective for non-compliance with this rule can be found in the books. One of the earlier cases was *Champion* v. *Plummer*,[2] a decision of the Court of Common Pleas, Mansfield, C.J., delivering the principal judgment. This case was referred to and followed by Blackburn, J., in his judgment in *Williams* v. *Lake*.[3] A similar decision was given by the Lords Justices in 1857 in the case of *Skelton* v. *Cole*.[4] Subsequent cases have confirmed and in some respects elaborated the rule. In *Vandenbergh* v.

[1] (1859) 2 E. & E. 349, 354; 121 E.R. 132, 134.

[2] (1805) 1 Bos. & Pul. (N.R.) 252; 127 E.R. 458. The headnote is not quite accurate; it confuses nomination of parties with signature by the parties.

[3] 2 E. & E. 349; 121 E.R. 132.

[4] 1 De G. & J. 587; 44 E.R. 850; see also *Williams* v. *Jordan*, (1877) 6 Ch.D. 517 (Jessel, M.R.); and *Coombs* v. *Wilkes*, [1891] 3 Ch. 77.

Spooner,[1] the Court of Exchequer (consisting of Pollock, C.B., Martin, Bramwell and Channell, BB.) held that the name of a party appearing on the memorandum without anything more was not enough to satisfy the Statute: the memorandum must go further and shew that the person so named is a party; and it must disclose his relation (as, e.g. vendor, purchaser, lessor, lessee and the like), with regard to the other contracting party or parties. The decision of Horridge, J., in *Dewar* v. *Mintoft*[2] (where *Vandenbergh* v. *Spooner* does not seem to have been cited) was to the same effect.

"I think", said that learned judge, "the memorandum must state both who was vendor and who was purchaser, and I do not think that in the present case the character filled by Mr Mintoft appears on the memorandum itself, and in my judgment therefore such memorandum is insufficient."[3]

[1] (1866) L.R. 1 Ex. 317.

[2] [1912] 2 K.B. 373, 385.

[3] *Vandenbergh* v. *Spooner*, L.R. 1 Ex. 317, and *Dewar* v. *Mintoft*, [1912] 2 K.B. 373, have not passed without criticism. In *Newell* v. *Radford*, (1867) L.R. 3 C.P. 52, 54, before the Court of Common Pleas (Bovill, C.J., Willes, Byles and Keating, JJ.), Willes, J., said: "I own I have considerable difficulty in understanding that case [*Vandenbergh* v. *Spooner*], but if I do so rightly it amounts to this, that a written agreement '*A* agrees to buy *B*'s horse for £10', is not sufficient to satisfy the Statute of Frauds, because it cannot be inferred by reasonable intendment that *B* is the seller. I cannot help observing that that seems to be an extreme case". But although great weight would attach to this observation of Willes, J., if it had accurately stated the effect of *Vandenbergh* v. *Spooner*, it is submitted that the facts in that case could not be reduced to the formula given by that learned judge. *Vandenbergh* v. *Spooner* reduced to terms of horses was this: "*A* agrees to buy the horse purchased by *B*, now grazing at *X*, for £10". "*B*'s horse" implies that *B* is the present owner of the horse; but "the horse purchased by *B*" has no such signification.

In the recent case of *Cohen* v. *Roche*, [1927] 1 K.B. 169, McCardie, J., also expressed doubts as to the correctness of the decision in *Vandenbergh* v. *Spooner*, and refused to follow *Dewar* v. *Mintoft*. But *Cohen* v. *Roche* is distinguishable from both *Vandenbergh* v. *Spooner* and *Dewar* v. *Mintoft* because in *Cohen* v. *Roche* the purchaser's name was written in the memorandum (an auctioneer's book) by an auctioneer during the course of the auction, in the place in which it is usual for the names of purchasers at an auction to be written; and this circumstance afforded a sufficient basis for the inference that the person so named was the purchaser of the lot opposite which his name had been written. See the report at p. 177.

In spite, therefore, of Willes, J.'s observations, and the doubts expressed by McCardie, J., it is submitted that *Vandenbergh* v. *Spooner* and *Dewar* v. *Mintoft* are still good law.

The general principle under discussion was much considered and developed in a series of judgments delivered by Jessel, M.R., in the cases of *Sale* v. *Lambert*,[1] *Potter* v. *Duffield*,[2] *Commins* v. *Scott*[3] and *Catling* v. *King*.[4] In all of these cases the question was whether a general word or description sufficiently identified a party to constitute a memorandum complying with the statutory requirements; and in *Sale* v. *Lambert*, *Commins* v. *Scott* and *Catling* v. *King* it was held that such a general word or description was sufficient. In each of these last-mentioned cases, however, the memorandum contained, as well as the general word or description, evidence of some circumstance which so qualified and defined that general word or description as to render the identification of the party in question as reasonably certain as if he had been named. The only verbal evidence, therefore, needed by the court in these cases was evidence of identification, to shew that the parties possessed the characteristics of those persons described as parties in the memoranda. Such evidence neither added to nor varied the memoranda: its function was purely explanatory and it clearly satisfied the test laid down by Lord Blackburn in *Rossiter* v. *Miller*[5] when considering whether "the proprietors" was a sufficient description. "It is enough", he said, "if the parties are sufficiently described to fix who they are without receiving any evidence of that character which Sir James Wigram in his Treatise[6] calls evidence 'to prove intention as an independent fact'."[7]

In *Sale* v. *Lambert*[1] the general word was *proprietor*: the circumstance discoverable from the memorandum was that the person described as *proprietor* was the owner of certain property, the subject-matter of the sale; and the word *proprietor* being now qualified in this manner becomes a perfectly definite description, "really more precise than the name of the man in many cases would be".[8] *Catling* v. *King*[4] was a similar case. In

[1] (1874) L.R. 18 Eq. 1.
[2] (1874) L.R. 18 Eq. 4.
[3] (1875) L.R. 20 Eq. 11.
[4] (1877) 5 Ch.D. 660.
[5] (1878) 3 App. Cas. 1124, 1153.
[6] Wigram, *Extrinsic Evidence*, 5th ed. Intr. Obs. p. 10.
[7] See also per Lord Denman, C.J., in *Trueman* v. *Loder*, (1840) 11 A. & E. 589, 594; 113 E.R. 538, 541. Cf. p. 59 *supra*.
[8] Per Jessel, M.R., in *Catling* v. *King* (1877) 5 Ch.D. 660, 664.

Commins v. *Scott*[1] the general word was *vendor*, generally an inadequate description; but there it was so defined and limited by particular circumstances stated in the memorandum that it became a sufficient description for the purpose of the Statute. On the other hand, in *Potter* v. *Duffield*[2] the word *vendor* without the help of any such defining circumstances was held insufficient.

It is to be noticed that the circumstances that the *vendor* is disposing of described and identified realty or personalty does not produce that limiting effect which the same circumstance produces when it is the proprietor who sells. Anyone—a mortgagee, trustee, proprietor, even a person without title—may be a vendor; and the apparent qualification and definition in such a case is therefore unreal.[3]

This development of the rule and the distinction drawn by Sir George Jessel in *Sale* v. *Lambert*[4] and *Potter* v. *Duffield*[2] did not pass without criticism, especially from the common law judges, and in *Thomas* v. *Brown*,[5] Mellor, J., said:

[1] (1875) L.R. 20 Eq. 11. [2] (1874) L.R. 18 Eq. 4.

[3] See also *Rossiter* v. *Miller*, (1878) 3 App. Cas. 1124, 1140, where Lord Cairns, L.C., puts the matter thus: "In point of fact, my Lords, the question is, is there that certainty which is described in the legal maxim, *id certum est quod certum reddi potest*. If I enter into a contract on behalf of my client, on behalf of my principal, on behalf of my friend, on behalf of those whom it may concern, in all those cases there is no such statement, and I apprehend that in none of those cases would the note satisfy the requirements of the Statute of Frauds. But if I, being really an agent, enter into a contract to sell Blackacre, of which I am not proprietor, or to sell the house No. 1, Portland Place, on behalf of the owner of that house, there, I apprehend, is a statement of matter of fact, as to which there can be perfect certainty, and none of the dangers struck at by the Statute of Frauds arise...".

In *Jarrett* v. *Hunter*, (1886) 34 Ch.D. 182, 184, Kay, J., stated his view of the law in the following words: "If the vendor is described in the contract as 'proprietor', 'owner', 'mortgagee', or the like, the description is sufficient, although he is not named; but if he is described as 'vendor', or as 'client', or 'friend', of a named agent that is not sufficient". And the learned judge then proceeded to cite *Rossiter* v. *Miller* (*cit. supra*), *Sale* v. *Lambert* (L.R. 18 Eq. 1) and *Potter* v. *Duffield* (L.R. 18 Eq. 4). But although this statement is roughly correct, it is but an empirical way of expressing the law. Generally, of course, *proprietor* will be a good description as it will be defined by the circumstance that the proprietor owns a property described in the memorandum; and conversely, *vendor* will not, as a rule, suffice. But as *Commins* v. *Scott*, (1875) L.R. 20 Eq. 11, shows, *vendor* will be a good description if accompanied by a statement of circumstances which so define it that the person who is the vendor may be identified with reasonable certainty.

[4] L.R. 18 Eq. 1. [5] (1876) 1 Q.B.D. 714, 720.

"Now comparing this decision [*Sale* v. *Lambert*] with the later one, *Potter* v. *Duffield*, where the same learned judge held that the description 'vendor' was insufficient, I have some difficulty in assenting to it. I think, however, that we ought to hold ourselves bound by the last of these two cases, holding that the word 'vendor' is insufficient, though, as far as my judgment goes, I can see no distinction between the nature of the memorandum in either case".

And Quain, J., expressed[1] a similar opinion. But in the next year after *Thomas* v. *Brown* had been decided, a similar question came before the Court of Appeal (of which Jessel, M.R., was a member) in *Catling* v. *King*[2] and the principle of *Sale* v. *Lambert* and *Potter* v. *Duffield* was applied by that court in solving the problem. Any doubts which may have remained after this decision of the Court of Appeal were finally set at rest by the decision of the House of Lords in *Rossiter* v. *Miller*[3] and especially by the judgment of Lord Cairns, L.C., in that case.

On much the same principle, where an agent has contracted in his own name on behalf of his principal, verbal evidence is admitted to establish the identity of the principal with the agent whose name appears in the memorandum. Such a case was *Trueman* v. *Loder*,[4] and there Lord Denman, C.J., expressed the rule in a very instructive way. He said:

"Among the ingenious arguments pressed by the defendant's counsel, there was one which it may be fit to notice; the supposition that parol evidence was introduced to vary the contract, shewing it not to have been made by Higginbotham, whose name is inserted in it, but by the defendant, who gave him the authority. Parol evidence is always necessary to shew that the party sued is the person making the contract and bound by it. Whether he does so in his own name or in that of another,

[1] *Ib.* 723. [2] (1877) 5 Ch.D. 660.

[3] (1878) 3 App. Cas. 1124, 1140.

In *Carr* v. *Lynch*, [1900] 1 Ch. 613, Farwell, J., expressly following *Sale* v. *Lambert* and *Potter* v. *Duffield*, held that "you having this day paid me the sum of £50" was a sufficient description; and in *Stokes* v. *Whicher*, [1920] 1 Ch. 411, the present Lord Russell of Killowen (then Russell, J.) held that the word "I", being defined by the circumstance that the party in question had paid a deposit, was enough to satisfy the Statute.

[4] (1840) 11 A. & E. 589, 594; 113 E.R. 539, 541.

or in a feigned name, and whether the contract be signed by his own hand or by that of an agent, are inquiries not different in their nature from the question who is the person who has just ordered goods in a shop. If he is sued for the price, and his identity made out, the contract is not varied by appearing to have been made by him in a name not his own".

(2) *Inadequate statement of the consideration for the contract.* The general principle that the consideration must be stated in the memorandum was very clearly laid down in *Wain* v. *Warlters.*[1] A numerous class of cases is to be found where a memorandum has been held to be defective on account of the inadequate statement of the consideration sued upon. It is enough, however, that the consideration should appear by reasonable inference in accordance with the rule stated in Chapter II.[2]

(3) *Uncertainty in time from which contract is to operate.* In cases of contracts involving the performance by one or both parties of certain acts for a period of time, memoranda have sometimes been held insufficient owing to the inadequate statement in such memoranda of the time of commencement of the period. The principal authority here is *Fitzmaurice* v. *Bayley*,[3] in which an action had been brought to enforce an alleged agreement of lease. Hill, J., advising the House of Lords, said:

"It is clear that an agreement for a lease not specifying a definite term cannot be enforced, nor can it be connected by parol evidence with an advertisement in which the duration of the term is expressed, *Clinan* v. *Cooke.*[4] Neither is it sufficient that there exists a probability that the Plaintiff intended to let the

[1] (1804) 5 East 10; 102 E.R. 972; 1 Sm. L.C., 13th ed. 358. And see the other cases cited in note on p. 54. Note that as regards contracts of guarantee the principle stated in the text was abrogated by the Mercantile Law Amendment Act, 1856. See p. 27 *supra.*

[2] P. 56 *supra.* See also *Powers* v. *Fowler*, (1855) 4 E. & B. 511; 119 E.R. 187.

In this connection *Steele* v. *Hoe*, (1849) 14 Q.B. 431; 117 E.R. 168, is interesting. There the court applied the maxim of construction *ut res magis valeat quam pereat* in order to infer a present consideration to support a contract of guarantee.

[3] (1860) 9 H.L.C. 78, 93; 11 E.R. 657, 663.

[4] 1 Sch. & Lefr. 22.

stable in Gore Lane for the term commensurate with the remainder of the lease of Hamilton House. Such probability would not be enough to satisfy the Statute of Frauds".[1]

It is doubtless enough in cases of this kind that the time of commencement shall be discoverable by reasonable inference in accordance with the general principle.[2] Fry, J., adopted this method in *Jaques* v. *Millar*,[3] though in view of the decision of the Court of Appeal in *Marshall* v. *Berridge*,[4] it must be taken that the inference which he drew in that case was not warranted by the memorandum before him.

(4) *Inadequate or equivocal description of the subject-matter of the contract.* Although the parties may clearly appear from the memorandum and the consideration and similar matters be sufficiently stated, it may yet happen that the subject-matter of the contract has received no attention or has been but vaguely and indefinitely described. In *Shardlow* v. *Cotterell*,[5] a suit brought to enforce a contract for the sale of realty, Jessel, M.R., in the Court of Appeal thus explained the degree of particularity required in the description of the subject-matter of a contract. "What, then, is a sufficient description in writing? No one can say beforehand. You cannot have a description in writing which will shut out all controversy as to parcels, even with the help of a map. I have known a most bitter and long continued litigation in a case where both sides had most beautiful maps, the contest being between two neighbouring proprietors as to the ownership of a ditch. No description can be framed that will prevent all

[1] One of the earliest cases of a memorandum being held defective on this ground was *Blore* v. *Sutton*, (1817) 3 Mer. 237; 36 E.R. 91, where Grant, M.R., had to consider a suit for the specific performance of an agreement of lease. See also *Nesham* v. *Selby*, (1872) L.R. 7 Ch. 406. In *Elliott* v. *Roberts*, (1912) 28 T.L.R. 436, Lush, J., applied the rule to a contract for personal service.

[2] P. 56 *supra*.

[3] (1877) 6 Ch.D. 153.

[4] (1881) 19 Ch.D. 233. *Jaques* v. *Millar* would seem to have been a faulty application of the principle of benevolent interpretation to advance the intention of the parties. "They [the parties] have described the instrument as a memorandum of agreement, and I must therefore construe it as an agreement if I can", said Fry, J., at p. 155. The objection to the application of the principle in this particular case was that what that intention might be did not appear from the memorandum.

[5] (1881) 20 Ch.D. 90, 93.

dispute, and the framers of the Statute of Frauds knew very well that they could not prevent perjury altogether, but could only go some way towards it; and it was considered that to require a note in writing was a useful check. It could be nothing more: it could not entirely prevent perjury, for parties may suborn witnesses to swear to the existence, destruction, and contents of a memorandum which never in fact existed. Looking at the Statute in that light, what is a sufficient description? I consider that any two specific terms are enough to point out sufficiently what is sold. For instance, 'the estate of *A.B.* in the County of *C.*', or 'the estate of *A.B.* which was devised to him by *C.D.*', would be sufficiently specific. If so, why should not 'the property which *A.B.* bought of *C.D.* on the 29th of March, 1880', be a sufficient description? If it is so in a will why not in a contract?"

The principle to be gathered from *Shardlow* v. *Cotterell*[1] and other cases of the same type may, it is submitted, be expressed as follows:

(1) A quite general description of the subject-matter of the contract such as "a house", "a field" and the like, is little better than a blank in the memorandum. If there were a blank verbal evidence to supply what should have been inserted would be uncontrolled; and to admit it would infringe the principle that all the terms of a contract coming within the Statute must be in writing. And even though the blank be filled up with some general word or description yet the position is but little different.

(2) But the general word or description may be so defined or qualified by some limiting circumstance either expressly stated in the memorandum or inferable in accordance with the general principle,[2] that a definite subject-matter can be identified by the court without any further description, and merely by admitting explanatory verbal evidence to connect the subject-matter with the defined and limited general word or description. In that case the danger of perjury struck at by the Statute is removed, so far as may be, and the Statutory requirements are satisfied.

[1] (1881) 20 Ch.D. 90, 93.

[2] See p. 56 *supra*.

On this principle the courts have been satisfied with such descriptions as "Mr Ogilvie's house",[1] "the intended new public-house at Putney",[2] "the mill property, including cottages in Esher village",[3] "the property in Cable Street",[4] "my house";[5] and there are many more examples of a similar character to be found in the reports.

[1] *Ogilvie* v. *Foljambe*, (1817) 3 Mer. 53; 36 E.R. 21.
[2] *Wood* v. *Scarth*, (1855) 2 K. & J. 33; 69 E.R. 682.
[3] *McMurray* v. *Spicer*, (1868) L.R. 5 Eq. 527.
[4] *Bleakley* v. *Smith*, (1840) 11 Sim. 150; 59 E.R. 831.
[5] *Cowley* v. *Watts*, 17 Jur. 172.

CHAPTER IV

THE FORM OF THE WRITING

IT is necessary next to consider the form, if any, in which a writing must be cast; this question is of equal importance whether the contract is a written contract or a verbal contract evidenced by writing, and for the most part the same rules apply to both kinds of contract.

The Statute requires no more than that all the terms of the contract should be expressed in the writing or discoverable from the writing in accordance with the rules set out in the last two preceding chapters.

From this general principle the following rules may be deduced:

(1) The precise literary shape which the writing may assume is quite immaterial; affidavits, recitals in deeds and wills, invoices, receipts, letters, pleadings, books belonging to a contracting party, witnesses' proofs—all have on occasion served as memoranda to save contracts from the results of non-compliance with the Statute.

(2) The time when a memorandum comes into existence is in general irrelevant.

There is an important exception to this rule, viz. that a memorandum which first comes into existence after the action has been commenced will not support that particular action.

(3) It is not necessary that a writing should have been made with the conscious purpose in view that it should be used as a writing under the Statute, or to support or evidence the contract.

(4) There is no necessity for a writing to be on one sheet or on connected sheets of paper; it may be and indeed frequently is composed of several separate documents; nor is there any necessity for these documents to have come into existence at the same time or to have been all prepared by the same party.

The question of several documents making between them one writing is, however, generally found in practice to be closely bound up with the question of whether these separate documents are all sufficiently authenticated by the signature of the party to be charged or of his agent. It will therefore be convenient to postpone the discussion of several documents making a writing, until after the Statutory requirement of signature has been considered.[1]

(1) *Unnecessary for writing to be in any particular form.* That no special formality was required by the Statute in regard to the writing seems always to have been recognized by the courts. In *Moor* v. *Hart*,[2] a Chancery suit brought some six years after the passing of the Statute, the court (probably Sir Francis North, L.K., afterwards Earl of Guilford) held that certain letters were a sufficient memorandum of the contract and decreed a specific performance accordingly. This decision was followed shortly afterwards in *Wauchford* v. *Fotherley*;[3] and since that time many varied forms of writings have come before the courts. Reference may be made to the following cases, out of the many in the books:

(*a*) *Daniels* v. *Trefusis*.[4] Here the defendant had prepared two statements of the evidence which he could give on behalf of the plaintiff in an action against a third person; and the plaintiff subsequently proceeding against the defendant, Sargant, J., held these statements to be a sufficient memorandum to satisfy the Statute.

(*b*) *Lucas* v. *Dixon*.[5] In this case it was treated by the Court of Appeal as settled law that an affidavit could be a sufficient memorandum.

(*c*) *In re Hoyle*.[6] Here a recital of a contract by a testator in his will was held to be a sufficient memorandum.

The extreme latitude of the requirements of the Statute in regard to form is well expressed by Lindley, L.J., in the course of his judgment in the last-mentioned case.

"The respondents", he remarked, "say that a will is not a memorandum such as is required by the statute. Why should it not be held to be so? The object of the statute was to prevent

[1] Part II, chapter vii, p. 127, *infra*.
[2] 2 Chan. Rep. 284; 21 E.R. 680.
[3] (1694) 2 Freeman 201; 22 E.R. 1159.
[4] [1914] 1 Ch. 788.
[5] (1889) 22 Q.B.D. 357.
[6] [1893] 1 Ch. 84, 98.

fraud and perjury by taking away the right to sue on certain agreements if only established by verbal evidence. The policy of the enactment is well explained in *Welford* v. *Beazely*,[1] and *Barkworth* v. *Young*,[2] and the idea of agreement need not be present to the mind of the person signing. An affidavit made with quite a different object was in that case held to be a sufficient note or memorandum, and so have various other documents. A will is a formal document, and why should it not be sufficient? It is true that the recitals in paragraph 14 of the will are inserted only for the purpose of explaining the directions which the testator was about to give; but the language is plain—'inasmuch as I have guaranteed the said J. A. D. Shipley and the said respective firms against loss in respect of the same debts'. This is a memorandum amply sufficient to take the case out of the *Statute of Frauds* if apart from the memorandum it is within it, which I am disposed to think it is not."

But although the general principle is that so long as a writing contains all the terms of the contract and is duly signed it will satisfy the Statute, no matter what form that writing may take, yet in certain special types of case some difficulty has been met with in applying this rule. Such difficulties seem to have occurred chiefly in the following kinds of cases:

(i) Cases where it has been endeavoured to use a *pleading* as a memorandum.

(ii) Cases where a *letter denying liability* has been tendered as a memorandum.

(i) *Pleading used as memorandum.* In *Jackson* v. *Oglander*[3] an unsuccessful attempt was made to induce the court to hold that a defendant's answer could constitute a sufficient memorandum of the agreement upon which the action had been brought. It is, indeed, very difficult to imagine how this action could possibly have been thought to have had a chance of succeeding, at least so far as its success was dependent on the existence of a memorandum satisfying the Statute. The answer could not form a sufficient memorandum for at least two reasons; first because it had not been in existence before the commencement of the

[1] 3 Atk. 503.
[2] 4 Drew. 1.
[3] (1865) 2 H. & M. 465; 71 E.R. 544.

action;[1] and secondly because it pleaded the Statute and claimed the benefit of it.[2]

A defendant may, indeed, admit the agreement sued upon and refrain from pleading the Statute, in which event the plaintiff will succeed in his action; but that does not imply that under such circumstances the answer or statement of defence containing the admission is held to be a memorandum. At the present time this result would seem to depend on the effect of the Rules of the Supreme Court, Ord. XIX, rr. 15 and 20. Under the old practice the reason commonly ascribed for the rule was that, the Statute being designed to check fraud and perjury, where there was an admission on the pleadings all danger of such fraud or perjury was removed and therefore the case was taken out of the Statute.[3]

Grindell v. *Bass*[4] affords an example of a case where a pleading successfully filled the rôle of memorandum. There Grindell sought to enforce against Bass specific performance of a contract for the sale of a house. Bass by his defence pleaded that he had already contracted verbally to sell the house to Earle, whereupon Grindell joined Earle as a defendant, and Earle, relying on Bass's defence as a memorandum, counterclaimed for a declaration that he was entitled to the house free from any claim by Grindell. Bass's defence had set out all the terms of the parol contract with Earle, and Russell, J., held that it was a sufficient memorandum to support Earle's counterclaim.

(ii) *Letter denying liability tendered as a memorandum.* It sometimes happens that the memorandum relied upon as satisfying the Statute is a letter in which the writer endeavours to repudiate all liability under the contract. Such a letter may contain either (*a*) an admission (express or implied) of the fact of the contract together with all the terms thereof, the writer, however, contending that he is free from liability because of something which has been done or omitted subsequently to the making of

[1] See p. 77 *infra*.
[2] See Part III, chapter ix, p. 275 *infra*.
[3] See the cases cited to s. 755 of *Story's Equity Jurisprudence*, 2nd English ed., p. 498. See also p. 276 *infra*.
[4] [1920] 2 Ch. 487.

the contract; or (*b*) a denial (express or by implication) that a contract was ever entered into.

A letter of the first kind will be a good memorandum, despite the denial or repudiation of liability which it contains. It may indeed be that the subsequent acts or omissions discharge the defendant; but this is a matter for proof and argument and does not affect the question of whether the letter is a sufficient memorandum. This was first laid down in *Bailey* v. *Sweeting*,[1] a decision of the Court of Common Pleas (Erle, C.J., Williams, Willes and Keating, JJ.). Previously to this case professional opinion seems to have inclined to the view that such a letter could not amount to a sufficient memorandum of the contract; and Lord Blackburn, in his work *On the Contract of Sale*,[2] suggested that the law on this point was that a subsequent acknowledgment in writing did not have the effect of satisfying the Statute, if that acknowledgment were accompanied by a repudiation of the defendant's liability under the contract. The authority principally relied on for this proposition was *Rondeau* v. *Wyatt*,[3] but this case really turned on the question of whether a party could admit in his pleadings the fact of the contract and yet take advantage of the Statute, and had no bearing on such a question as that which arose in *Bailey* v. *Sweeting*.[1]

The following passage from the judgment delivered by Erle, C.J., in *Bailey* v. *Sweeting*[4] indicates very clearly the essential reasons for that decision.

"In that state of the authorities [i.e. there being no case in point] we are remitted to the Statute of Frauds itself: and upon reference to its language we think the defendant's letter does amount to a sufficient memorandum in writing and makes the contract good. The purpose of the Statute was, to prevent fraud and perjury. Now, the danger of perjury in this case is effectually prevented by the letter of the defendant; for, he distinctly admits that he made the contract and at the price alleged. I do not consider that the defendant intended to deny his liability by reason of the absence or insufficiency of the contract: but

[1] (1861) 9 C.B. (N.S.) 843; 142 E.R. 332.

[2] 1st ed., p. 66, quoted 9 C.B. (N.S.) 847; 142 E.R. 334. See per Erle, C.J., *ib.* 858; E.R. 338.

[3] (1792) 2 H.Bl. 63; 126 E.R. 430.

[4] 9 C.B. (N.S.) 858; E.R. 338.

that the only question which he intended to raise was, whether he or the plaintiffs should settle with the carriers for the damage done to the goods. I think that constitutes a material distinction between the present case and those cited, in which the defendant, admitting the contract, has rested his defence on the non-compliance with the Statute."

This statement of the law shews clearly that the letter must contain an express or implied recognition of the fact that a contract was actually entered into; it must further set forth all the terms of that contract either expressly or by necessary implication or by reference to other documents in accordance with the rules regulating the use of several documents to form a writing; and the repudiation of liability which such a letter contains must therefore either be expressed generally so that it does not shake the certainty of the letter with regard to the matters already mentioned, or must be referable to the performance of the contract or some other matter subsequent to the making of the contract.

Bailey v. *Sweeting* was followed some five years later in *Wilkinson* v. *Evans*,[1] also before the Common Pleas, the court on this occasion being Erle, C.J., Byles, Keating, and Montague Smith, JJ. Shortly after *Wilkinson* v. *Evans* a similar point came before the Court of Exchequer Chamber in *Buxton* v. *Rust*,[2] and again *Bailey* v. *Sweeting* was followed. The most recent case is *Thirkell* v. *Cambi*,[3] where the Court of Appeal once more affirmed the general principle.[4]

It will generally happen that a letter tendered in evidence as a memorandum under the Statute will have been written by the defendant to the plaintiff; but this need not necessarily be so, and as long as the letter in question complies with the general requirements of the Statute it is quite immaterial to whom it is addressed. The matter would really appear to be too clear for

[1] (1866) L.R. 1 C.P. 407.
[2] (1871) L.R. 7 Ex. 1.
[3] [1919] 2 K.B. 590.
[4] All of the cases cited in the text were decided on s. 17 of the Statute of Frauds; but the similarity in wording of this section and s. 4 would seem to render these cases equally applicable to contracts under the latter section. In *In re Hoyle*, [1893] 1 Ch. 84, 99, Bowen, L.J., referred to both *Gibson* v. *Holland*, (1865) L.R. 1 C.P. 1, and *Wilkinson* v. *Evans*, *ib.* 407, in reference to a contract of guarantee.

argument, but cases have come before the courts in which memoranda have been attacked on the ground that, being letters, they have been addressed to some person other than the plaintiff. *Gibson* v. *Holland*[1] was such a case. There the memorandum to which objection was taken was a letter written by the defendant to his own agent: and in giving judgment holding that this fact constituted no objection to the validity of the letter as a memorandum, Erle, C.J., stated the law in these words:

"The object of the Statute of Frauds was, the prevention of perjury in the setting up of contracts by parol evidence, which is easily fabricated. With this view it requires the contract to be proved by the production of some note or memorandum in writing. Now, a note or memorandum is equally corroborative, whether it passes between the parties to the contract themselves, or between one of them and his own agent. Indeed, one would incline to think that a statement made by the party to his own agent would be the more satisfactory evidence of the two".

Willes, J., as he was wont to do, summed up the matter very neatly, saying:[2]

"This section uses a word which seems to afford a key to its construction; it requires that there shall be, not any particular kind of memorandum, but '*some* note or memorandum of the bargain'".[3]

(2) *When must the writing be in existence?* Inasmuch as the Statute merely regulates the kind of evidence which may be admitted in proof of certain kinds of contracts,[4] it might have been expected that the Statutory requirements would be satisfied if evidence of the prescribed kind were adduced at the trial; and that inquiries as to when that evidence first came into existence

[1] (1865) L.R. 1 C.P. 1, 5.

[2] *Ib.* p. 8.

[3] *Gibson* v. *Holland* was on s. 17 of the Statute but it would appear to be equally an authority on the interpretation of s. 4. See note 4, p. 75 *supra*.

In *Welford* v. *Beazely*, (1747) 3 Atk. 503; 26 E.R. 1090, the following *dictum* fell from the Lord Chancellor (Lord Hardwicke): "There have been cases where a letter written to a man's own agent, and setting forth the terms of an agreement as concluded by him, has been deemed to be a signing within the statute". The Lord Chancellor was in this case concerned with a suit on a contract made in consideration of marriage. See also *Rose* v. *Cunynghame*, (1805) 11 Ves. 550; 32 E.R. 1202.

[4] See pp. 194, 198 *infra*.

would be irrelevant. But in this respect the position of contracts under the Statute is anomalous and it has been repeatedly decided by the courts that the writing must have been in existence before the commencement of the action. In recent cases, however, this rule has been relaxed to the extent that a party who is joined in the action after its commencement, may rely upon any writing which is in existence at the time he is so joined.

The rule under discussion seems to have its basis in, and to be justified by, the words of the Statute, whereby it is enacted that

> "no action shall be brought...unless the agreement upon which such action shall be brought or some memorandum or note thereof shall be in writing and signed by the party to be charged therewith or some other person thereunto by him lawfully authorized".

That is to say, the existence of a writing is made a condition precedent to the bringing of an action.

The leading case on the point is *Lucas* v. *Dixon*.[1] There the Court of Appeal had to consider whether an affidavit made and sworn after the commencement of the action could yet constitute a sufficient memorandum of the contract to sustain that same action. The court, in holding that the affidavit was not a sufficient memorandum, based its opinion partly on the apparent meaning of the words used in the Statute; and partly on the practice of Courts of Equity in allowing a bill which shewed on the face of it that the conditions of the Statute had not been complied with, to be demurred to, whereby they indicated that they considered that such apparent non-compliance could not be cured by evidence.

In the case of contracts coming within s. 17, the rule that in general the writing should be in existence before the action was commenced had been adopted by the courts many years earlier;[2] but in this respect the two sections were not sufficiently alike in their wording to enable the authorities on s. 17 to be regarded as decisive in respect to the interpretation of s. 4.

[1] (1889) 22 Q.B.D. 357.
[2] *Bill* v. *Bament*, (1841) 9 M. & W. 36; 152 E.R. 16.

In the recent case of *Farr, Smith and Co. Ltd.* v. *Messers Ltd.*[1] the general rule was carried a stage further, Wright, J., holding that it was sufficient if the memorandum came into existence before the party relying upon that memorandum became joined in the action. A contract had been made between Farr and Smith, a partnership firm, of the one part and the defendants of the other part. Messrs Farr and Smith subsequently transferred their business (including the contract in question) to the newly incorporated company of Farr, Smith and Co. Ltd., and by a verbal novation this limited company thenceforward became subject to the liabilities under that contract and entitled to its benefits. Subsequently Farr and Smith brought an action on the original contract and the defendants pleaded the novation. Thereupon the action was reconstituted by the substitution of Farr, Smith and Co. Ltd., for the original plaintiffs, Farr and Smith; and Wright, J., held that the defence admitting the novation, having been in existence at the time when Farr, Smith and Co. Ltd. became party to the action, could be relied upon by them, despite the rule in *Lucas* v. *Dixon*.[2]

In view of the last-mentioned decision, it would now seem that the rule laid down in *Lucas* v. *Dixon*[2] should be re-stated in a modified form, viz., in order that a memorandum of a contract may satisfy the Statute, such memorandum must be in existence when the party relying on it becomes a party to the action; in general, that will be when the action is commenced, but in exceptional cases, such as *Farr, Smith and Co. Ltd.* v. *Messers Ltd.*, it will be later.

It was at one time thought that in the case of contracts made in consideration of marriage, the writing had to be in existence before the celebration of the marriage. Farwell, J., adopted this principle in deciding *In re Holland*[3] in 1901. But when that case

[1] [1928] 1 K.B. 387.

[2] (1889) 22 Q.B.D. 357.

In 1920 Russell, J., in *Grindell* v. *Bass*, [1920] 2 Ch. 487, had held a statement of defence a sufficient memorandum under circumstances not unlike those in *Farr, Smith and Co. Ltd.* v. *Messers Ltd.* But *Lucas* v. *Dixon* does not appear to have been cited.

[3] [1901] 2 Ch. 145.

went up to the Court of Appeal,[1] that court emphatically denied that these contracts constituted any such exception to the general rule, and reversed the decision of Farwell, J., accordingly. Vaughan Williams, L.J., thus expounded the law:

"The Statute of Frauds does not deal with the validity of the agreement: *Maddison* v. *Alderson*;[2] it deals only with the evidence to prove the agreement, the Statute requiring that the agreement shall be evidenced by a writing signed by the party thereto against whom the action is sought to be enforced. There is no difference, so far as I know, between an agreement in consideration of marriage and any other agreement within the 4th section of the Statute of Frauds".

(3) *Writing need not be made for purpose of satisfying the Statute.* A document fulfilling the general requirements of the Statute will be a valid memorandum no matter for what purpose it was prepared. The Statute itself makes no reference to the purpose of the party in preparing the memorandum and the courts have carefully refrained from laying down any fettering principle on the matter. If authority be sought to support this proposition one need only refer to the cases in which letters repudiating liability have been held sufficient memoranda; or to cases, such as *Gibson* v. *Holland*[3], where letters passing between a defendant and his own agent have supported an action on the contract. In *Daniels* v. *Trefusis*[4] Sargant, J., used a happy phrase in reference to memoranda which had been held sufficient to satisfy the Statute, although prepared for very different purposes: he described the legal metamorphosis as "the unintentional by-product of satisfying the Statute of Frauds". The passage quoted above[5] from the judgment of Lindley, L.J., in *In re Hoyle*[6] sets forth clearly both the principle above-stated and the reasons therefor.

In one or two cases, it is true, *dicta* are to be found which might seem to imply that under certain circumstances the purpose with which a memorandum has been made is a relevant fact to consider in deciding whether such a memorandum will

[1] [1902] 2 Ch. 360, 375.
[2] 8 App. Cas. 467.
[3] (1865) L.R. 1 C.P. 1.
[4] [1914] 1 Ch. 788, 799.
[5] P. 71 *supra*.
[6] [1893] 1 Ch. 84.

satisfy the Statute. In *Cooke* v. *Tombs*,[1] Macdonald, C.B., said:

"...it is evident that the particular was at first made out and delivered, not as evidence of any agreement, for no agreement had then been made, but merely as a list or catalogue of the matters for sale, to enable the purchaser to form a proper estimate of their value: as this was the original nature of the particular, nothing which has happened since could possibly alter it; it was delivered into Clarke's hands for the same purpose, as an enumeration of the things under sale, to serve as instructions to him in making out the description of them in the conveyance. The signing this particular could have no other effect than to give it authenticity as a true list of the items then offered for sale".

But although the learned Chief Baron referred at such length to the purpose for which the particular had been prepared, that was not the crux of the matter; the particular, it would appear from the report, did not contain the terms of the contract; and this was the true ground of that decision. This is made clear by the next paragraph of the judgment.

"Besides, this was delivered in as the foundation for a sale for £24,000. The sale which took place was for £22,000; as the price has been altered, so the parcels to be sold, and other particulars of the sale, may have been changed; and this catalogue can be no evidence of the terms of the second contract, or even of its existence."

But despite such *dicta* as that in the case just referred to, it seems quite certain that the general principle stands unimpeached; and that a paper writing duly signed and containing all the terms of an agreement will be a sufficient memorandum no matter for what purpose it was originally prepared.[2]

[1] (1794) 2 Anst. 420, 424; 145 E.R. 922, 924.

[2] If, indeed, the memorandum is prepared with a fraudulent purpose, the case will be different: fraud is always a relevant factor to consider in determining whether a contract is good. See Anson, *Law of Contract*, 17th ed. 207.

CHAPTER V

THE SIGNATURE

THE Statute requires that the written contract or the memorandum of the contract, as the case may be, shall be *signed* by the party to be charged or his agent thereunto by him lawfully authorized.

To sign, in its normal signification in connection with documents, means "to attest or confirm by adding one's signature; to affix one's name to (a document, etc.)"; and *signature* means "the name (or special mark) of a person written with his or her own hand as an authentication of some document or writing".[1] Among both lawyers and laymen *signature* normally implies that the signatory shall personally write his name or make his mark and that such name or mark shall be *added* to the document, i.e. shall be placed either at the end or at the beginning or perhaps in the margin, but in any case standing out from the text. And it is an implication of the word that the signatory shall have so signed with the conscious purpose of authenticating the document in the character which it bore when he signed it.

The decisions on the Statute have fixed the word *signed* therein used with a meaning very different from its normal meaning. In *Durrell* v. *Evans*[2] the Court of Exchequer Chamber held to be *signed* a writing (a contract note, with the names of the parties written in to indicate who was vendor and who was purchaser, simply) which Crompton, J., described as containing "nothing which could ordinarily be called a signature". In *Schneider* v. *Norris*[3] the Court of King's Bench decided that a printed name at the top of a bill of parcels was a good signature; and many similar cases are to be found in the reports.[4]

[1] *New English Dictionary* (Oxford), *sub nom.* "sign", and "signature".
[2] (1862) 1 H. & C. 174, 186; 158 E.R. 848, 853.
[3] (1814) 2 M. & S. 286; 105 E.R. 388.
[4] In *Halley* v. *O'Brien*, [1920] 1 I.R. 330, 339, O'Connor, L.J., thus expounded the normal meaning of *signature*: "When we speak of 'signing' or 'signature' we usually think of the person's name, signed by himself in the

A signature (giving the word its ordinary meaning) inscribed on a document serves the following purposes:

(1) It indicates that the signatory *by the very act of inscribing his name* admits the authenticity of the document in question. In its particular reference to contracts under the Statute, this means that the signatory, by inscribing his name on the writing, manifests an intention that the writing shall be treated as a true exposition of the contract.[1]

(2) Being placed at the foot or more rarely at the head of the document, and outside the text, it performs this function with regard to the whole of the document.

Authenticated signature fiction. A party may, of course, shew quite convincingly by means other than signing that he recognizes a writing as a true exposition of his contract. But the Statute says he must sign. Where, however, there has existed a writing setting forth the whole contract, and the party to be charged has clearly shewn by his conduct that he recognizes that writing to be a correct exposition of his contract, the courts have been loath to allow such party to shelter under the Statute;[2] and

form he generally uses, as a clue or mark of his identity. That is the meaning of the term when we ask, 'Is that Mr H.'s signature?' Further, we usually associate 'signed' and 'signature' with a name subscribed or put at the end of a document. But these are not the sole meanings of 'signature' at all. One of the meanings, and, for the purpose of this case, the appropriate meaning, is 'the name of a person, or something used as representing his name, affixed or appended to a writing or the like, either by himself or his deputy as a verification, authentication or assent': *Century Dictionary*".

It is submitted that the dictionary definition given by the learned Lord Justice really takes the matter very little beyond the definition given in his earlier sentences; and that to endeavour to bring such a case as *Halley* v. *O'Brien* within the ordinary dictionary meaning of *signed* is unjustifiable and unnecessary. The true position, it is submitted, is that little by little the courts have in this particular departed from the strict meaning of *signed* as used in the Statute, until they have attributed to that word a meaning so extensive as to be artificial.

[1] *Stroud's Judicial Dict.* 2nd ed., *sub nom.* "Signed: signature": "Speaking generally, a Signature is the writing, or otherwise affixing, a person's name, or a mark to represent his name, by himself or by his authority (*R.* v. *Kent. Jus.* 42 L.J.M.C. 112; L.R. 8 Q.B. 305), with the intention of authenticating a document as being that of, or as binding on, the person whose name or mark is so written or affixed".

[2] As Maule, J., remarked in *Hubert* v. *Treherne*, (1842) 3 Man. & G. at p. 755; 133 E.R. at p. 1343, "Since the statute the courts, anxious to relieve parties against injustice, have not unfrequently stretched the language of the act".

to meet such cases they have gradually developed what may be called the *authenticated signature fiction*. Provided the writing contains the name or initials of the party, the courts are willing to hold that it is duly signed; but they must first be satisfied that the party has shewn that he recognizes the writing as truly expressing the contract. They then quite fictitiously restrict this general recognition to the name or initials and say that the party by recognizing or *authenticating* his name or initials thereby converts such name or initials into a signature, and this signature authenticates the writing. In this manner justice is done without open violation of the words of the Statute.[1] But although the courts have succeeded in enabling the first-mentioned function of a signature to be discharged by other means than a regular signing they have at all times been tender of the forms, and accordingly, even where there is no real signature, they continue to insist on the name (or initials) being in such a position in the writing that were it a genuine signature it would authenticate and apply to the whole of the writing.

History of authenticated signature fiction. The development of the authenticated signature fiction can readily be traced in the decided cases. Until *Stokes* v. *Moore*,[2] decided in the Court of Exchequer in 1786, it does not seem to have been suggested that a writing not bearing a signature as usually understood could yet be sufficiently signed within the meaning of the Statute. The earliest case on the question of signature in general would seem to have been *Bawdes* v. *Amhurst*,[3] where Lord Cowper, L.C., appeared to think that nothing short of a regular signature would suffice. Shortly after came *Hawkins* v. *Holmes*.[4] There the defendant had altered "with his own hand" a draft conveyance, and it was contended that this amounted to a sufficient signing. But Lord Macclesfield, L.C., would have none of this argument and said:

[1] This statement of the fiction is based on the language of the judges in *Schneider* v. *Norris*, (1814) 2 M. & S. 286; 105 E.R. 388. See passages from the judgments, quoted in text *infra* pp. 85, 86.

[2] (1786) 1 Cox 219; 29 E.R. 1137.

[3] (1715) Prec. Ch. 402; 24 E.R. 180.

[4] (1721) 1 P. Wms. 770, 771; 24 E.R. 606, 607.

"Unless in some particular cases where there has been an execution of the contract by entering upon and improving the premises, the party's signing the agreement is absolutely necessary for the compleating of it; and to put a different construction upon the Act, would be to repeal it...".

Then in 1786 came *Stokes* v. *Moore*.[1] In that case the defendant had written out a memorandum of the contract in his own handwriting, and in the text of this memorandum occurred the defendant's name in the third person. Skyner, C.B., held that the *name* of the defendant did not in the particular case amount to an acknowledgment by him that the agreement was his agreement, and it therefore failed to satisfy the Statute. But the learned Judge took no objection to the validity of the name as a signature because it happened not to be written at the end of the document in the usual way.

Eyre, B., however, expressly said that the position of the *name* was immaterial, provided it was inserted so as to give authenticity to the whole instrument; and then he immediately proceeded to qualify this statement.

' It is perhaps difficult", he continued,[2] "except in the case of a letter with a postscript, to find an instance where a name inserted in the middle of a writing can well have that effect; and there the name being generally found in a particular place by the common usage of mankind, it may very probably have the effect of a legal signature, and extend to the whole; but I do not understand how a name inserted in the body of an instrument, and *applicable to particular purposes*, can amount to such an authentication as is required by the statute."

It seems fairly certain, therefore, that even in *Stokes* v. *Moore* the court scarcely contemplated that the Statute would be satisfied by anything less than an ordinary signature. The opinion of the court on that occasion does not seem to have gone beyond this: that the Statute would be equally satisfied with a signature placed at the head or in the margin of a memorandum, as well as one placed at the foot in the usual way; that it is difficult to see how a name in the body of an instrument could

[1] (1786) 1 Cox 219; 29 E.R. 1137.

[2] *Ib.* at p. 223; E.R. 1139.

be a signature, except perhaps in the case put of a letter and its postscript; and that certainly a name inserted in the body of an instrument for particular purposes (as, for example, to identify a party) could not amount to a signature.

In 1794, however, Sir James Eyre, now Chief Justice of the Common Pleas, held in *Knight* v. *Crockford*[1] at *Nisi Prius*, that a memorandum written by the defendant in his own hand and commencing "I, James Crockford" was sufficiently signed. Then came *Saunderson* v. *Jackson*[2] before the Court of Common Pleas, in which it was held that a bill of parcels with the defendant's name printed at the head was signed within the meaning of the Statute. It is difficult to determine from the report, however, whether the court did not rely upon a signature contained in a letter referring to the bill of parcels rather than upon the printed name. But some fourteen years later the Court of King's Bench (Lord Ellenborough, C.J., Le Blanc, Bayley and Dampier, JJ.) expressly decided in *Schneider* v. *Norris*[3] that such a printed name could be a sufficient signature.

The reasons for the decision in *Schneider* v. *Norris* were stated by Lord Ellenborough in the following words:[4]

"I cannot but think that a construction, which went the length of holding that in no case a printing or any other form of signature could be substituted in lieu of writing would be going a great way, considering how many instances may occur in which the parties contracting are unable to sign....But here there is a signing by the party to be charged by words recognizing the printed name as much as if he had subscribed his mark to it, which is strictly the meaning of signing, and by that the party has incorporated and avowed the thing printed to be his; and it is the same in substance, as if he had written Norris and Co. with his own hand. He has by his handwriting in effect said, I acknowledge what I have written to be for the purpose of exhibiting my recognition of the written contract".

The last sentence quoted from Lord Ellenborough's judgment indicates the real ground of the decision. The defendant, by

[1] (1794) 1 Esp. 190; 170 E.R. 324.
[2] (1800) 2 B. & P. 238; 126 E.R. 1257.
[3] (1814) 2 M. & S. 286; 105 E.R. 388.
[4] *Ib.* 288; E.R. 388.

filling up the bill of parcels, shewed that he recognized that bill as an authentic expression of the contract. Dampier, J., expressed this very clearly:[1]

"Here there is the handwriting of the party to be charged to the bill of parcels, which authenticates it as a memorandum of the bargain; the defendant has ratified the sale to Schneider and Co. by inserting their name as buyer to a paper in which he recognizes himself as seller".

It seems tolerably clear that the defendent in *Schneider* v. *Norris* was not particularly concerned about his printed name, as such, and had no thought of its being a signature; but he certainly did act in such a manner as to shew that he recognized the complete bill of parcels to be a correct exposition of his contract. Nevertheless, this recognition, no matter how convincing, was not a signing. To do lip-service to the form of the Statute, therefore, Lord Ellenborough applied this recognition to the printed name; and held that it converted that name into a signature sufficient to satisfy the Statute. But actually it was not the alleged signature which authenticated the writing; it was the defendant's action in drawing up that writing. It is submitted that to talk of signature under these circumstances is merely to preserve the outer shell of the Statutory formality, while allowing the essential objects to effect which the form was imposed to be achieved by other methods.

The inadequacy of a mere name without more to shew that the writing is authentic was very clearly stated by Tindal, C.J., in *Hubert* v. *Treherne*.[2] There a memorandum was alleged to be constituted by unsigned articles of agreement, purporting to be made by certain persons whose names were stated at the commencement of such articles. Tindal, C.J., referring to the question of signature, said:

"I am not satisfied that there is in this case any signature at all. The names of the parties necessarily appear in the body of the instrument which would not otherwise be intelligible. To hold

[1] (1814) 2 M. & S. 290; 105 E.R. 389.
[2] (1842) 3 Man. & G. 743, 753; 133 E.R. 1338, 1342.

that the mere introduction of the names of the parties was sufficient, would be almost to repeal the statute".

This seems to be the crux of the matter. In a case such as *Schneider* v. *Norris* the names of the parties necessarily appear in the body of the writing; and therefore to say that such names can have any authenticating effect is mere pretence. In cases of this sort there is invariably some adequate recognition of the writing by the alleged signatory whereby he indicates that he considers such writing to be an accurate exposition of his contract; but that is very different from his giving this indication by inscribing his signature. The plaintiffs failed in *Hubert* v. *Treherne* because the court held that there was no evidence of such recognition. "*Saunderson* v. *Jackson*[1]", said Tindal, C.J., "depends for its authority more upon the subsequent recognition than upon the printed names. In this case there is no sufficient original signature, and no subsequent recognition."[2]

Subsequent cases have recognized the principle upon which *Schneider* v. *Norris* was decided and have confirmed it as the law. In *Evans* v. *Hoare*[3] Denman, J., expressed the following opinion:

"If the party sued has authorized an agent to lay before the party suing a document *containing his name in full* as that of the party with whom the contract is to be made, so as to announce to the other party that they are offering him certain terms if he will agree to them in writing, and he thereupon signs, I think that there is a sufficient 'agreement or memorandum thereof, signed by a party authorized thereunto' within s. 4 of the Statute of Frauds".

Here all pretence of a regular signature is dropped: there is nothing but the plain statement that a document containing the

[1] 2 B. & P. 238.

[2] See also *Johnson* v. *Dodgson*, (1837) 2 M. & W. 653; 150 E.R. 918.

[3] [1892] 1 Q.B. 593, 596. In the same case Cave, J., remarked (597): "In the present case it is true that the name of the defendants occurs in the agreement; but it is suggested on behalf of the defendants that it was only put in to shew who the persons were to whom the letter was addressed. The answer is that there is the name, and it was inserted by the defendants' agent in a contract which was undoubtedly intended by the defendants to be binding on the plaintiff; and, therefore, the fact that it is only in the form of an address is immaterial". And see also the judgment of Blackburn, J., in *Durrell* v. *Evans*, (1862) 1 H. & C. 174, 190; 158 E.R. 848, 854.

defendant's name and recognized by him is *signed* for the purposes of the Statute.

The matter was last before the courts in 1926 when McCardie, J., in *Cohen* v. *Roche*[1] stated in the following words his view of the Statutory requirements:

"It is, of course, clear that a printed name in the body of an instrument, in order to operate as a signature, must be authenticated by the person to be charged: see per Buckley, J., in *Hucklesby* v. *Hook*.[2] In the case now before me there was ample authentication in that the defendant himself wrote down in his auctioneer's book the price realized by lot 145, and also entered the names of the purchasers. He thus recognized the bargain and his own printed signature".

It is to be observed that the old fiction that the party authenticates his name, thereby transforming it into a signature, still finds a place in the language of the judges.[3]

Nature of the recognition required to support fiction. The recognition of the writing as a proper exposition of the contract seems always in the reported cases to have been evidenced by acts done contemporaneously with the drawing up or completing of the writing; but it is submitted that subsequent acts would be equally efficacious; and it is suggested as not impossible that such recognition might be sufficiently indicated by a party's spoken words.

(1) *Contemporaneous acts*. *Schneider* v. *Norris*[4] is an example: the defendant exhibited his recognition of the writing by the very act of drawing it up. A similar case was *Propert* v. *Parker*.[5]

(2) *Subsequent acts*. There appears to be no case in which a

[1] [1927] 1 K.B. 169 at p. 176.

[2] (1900) 82 L.T. 117.

[3] O'Connor, L.J., in *Halley* v. *O'Brien*, [1920] 1 I.R. 330, used similar language. "When the memorandum was filled up and given to the purchaser to sign, it was authenticated by the name of the vendor, then in it, quite as effectively as if it were put in afterwards."

[4] (1814) 2 M. & S. 286; 105 E.R. 388.

[5] (1830) 1 Russ. & M. 625; 39 E.R. 240. See also *Johnson* v. *Dodgson*, (1837) 2 M. & W. 653; 150 E.R. 918; *Durrell* v. *Evans*, (1862) 1 H. & C. 174; 158 E.R. 848; *Cohen* v. *Roche*, [1927] 1 K.B. 169 and *Halley* v. *O'Brien*, [1920] 1 I.R. 330.

writing has been held to be signed where the acts of recognition have occurred subsequently to the drawing up of that writing, unless *Evans* v. *Hoare*[1] may be regarded as such a case. In that case the defendant's agent drew up the writing, but the court appears not to have relied so much on this fact as evidence of recognition as on the subsequent act of the defendant's agent in submitting the writing for the plaintiff's signature. In *Hubert* v. *Treherne*[2] Tindal, C.J., seemed to think that subsequent recognition would do. "In this case", he said, "there is no sufficient original signature and there is no subsequent recognition." Irrespective of these authorities, however, there would seem to be no logical reason why subsequent acts of recognition should not be equally as efficacious as contemporaneous acts in averting the consequences of non-compliance with the Statute.

(3) *Spoken words*. Here there is no authority. If in *Evans* v. *Hoare*[1] the plaintiff had written out the memorandum and the defendant had thereupon said: "That is the contract between us", it would seem a little difficult to suppose that the courts would have held that memorandum not to be sufficiently signed to satisfy the Statute.[3]

Application of fiction where genuine signature exists. The authenticated signature fiction sometimes applies even when the writing bears a real signature. No authority beyond the Statute need be adduced for the proposition that where the party to be charged regularly signs a completed writing setting forth the whole of the contract, the Statutory requirements as to signature are *prima facie* satisfied. But even in the case of a writing bearing a subscribed autograph of the party's name complications may be introduced. After such signature has been subscribed, the

[1] [1892] 1 Q.B. 595.

[2] (1842) 3 Man. & G. 743; 133 E.R. 1338.

[3] Possibly *Stewart* v. *Eddowes*, (1874) L.R. 9 C.P. 311 and *Koenigsblatt* v. *Sweet*, [1923] 2 Ch. 314, may be adduced in support of the proposition suggested in the text. See per Lord Sterndale, M.R., in the latter case, pp. 324 *et seq*. Certainly this was a case where a genuine signature had been subscribed; but subsequently the document was altered, and thus so far as the alterations went, the case seems little different from the case of a memorandum having no real signature inscribed on it. See text, *infra*.

document may be altered; or it may not have been a complete record of the contract at the time of signing and may subsequently be completed.

It seems apparent that an ordinary signature can only perform the functions described above,[1] in regard to the document in the state it is in at the moment at which that signature is subscribed. Where alterations are introduced subsequently to the signing of the document, the position of these alterations with regard to authentication by the signature seems to be exactly the same as that of those documents containing in the text the name of the party to be charged, but not otherwise signed. In both kinds of case, the name or signature, of its own intrinsic force, possesses no sufficient authenticating power; and in both kinds of case, therefore, the law has found a way out of the difficulty by the fiction of the authenticated signature.

The recent decision of the Court of Appeal in *Koenigsblatt* v. *Sweet*[2] illustrates the position stated in the last preceding paragraph. In that case Sweet had signed a memorandum of a contract to sell certain land to Koenigsblatt and his wife; at the time of signing the date for the completion of the contract and the date of the document were not filled in, blanks being left. When the solicitors met to exchange copies, Koenigsblatt's solicitor asked that the agreements be altered by striking out Mrs Koenigsblatt's name and making consequential alterations: Sweet's solicitor concurred and did so; and the blanks were also filled in. Subsequently Sweet defended an action for specific performance on the ground that the document which was produced was not the document as he had signed it; and hence that there was no memorandum of the contract. The Court of Appeal overruled this contention on the ground that Sweet had subsequently approved of the alterations and ratified the act of his solicitor in making them.

"Therefore", said Lord Sterndale, M.R., "when he said to his agent, Mr Roe, that he approved of the alterations as they appeared not only in the part signed by Koenigsblatt, which he had before him, but in the one signed by him, which he knew

[1] See p. 82 *supra*.

[2] [1923] 2 Ch. 314, 327.

to be in Koenigsblatt's possession, he recognized his signature as attached to the document containing those alterations."

The principle at the basis of this decision, it is submitted, is that the alterations to the signed document were made with the defendant's authority, precedent with regard to the blanks, subsequent with regard to the deletion of Mrs Koenigsblatt's name. By the very act, therefore, of authorizing such alterations the defendant adopted the document, so altered, as an authentic memorandum of the contract. His recognition of the document in this way had precisely that general authenticating effect which an autograph signature has when subscribed to a document which has first been duly completed.

The case of *Bluck* v. *Gompertz*[1] which came before the Court of Exchequer Chamber in 1852 was in some respects similar to *Koenigsblatt* v. *Sweet*. In *Bluck* v. *Gompertz* the position was complicated by a question of interpretation. After deciding that the interpretation of the memorandum was such as to make it expressive of all the terms of the contract, the judgment of the court (delivered by Pollock, C.B.) proceeded in these words:

"It may, however, be inferred, from the fact of the defendant himself writing the memorandum across for the plaintiff to sign, not only that he agreed that the bill for £150, previously substituted instead of one for £146 by the plaintiff, should stand in the place of that for £146, and impliedly, that the defendant should be responsible for it; but also that he admitted that the original contract was, that he should procure to be accepted, and see paid any bill for the amount of the invoice of the second parcel of wine, and that the invoice was £150, so that there would be proof of the contract alleged in the declaration in writing. If so, it may be inferred, from the fact of the second memorandum being written on the same paper by the defendant, that it was meant to be authenticated by the old signature, so as to constitute a memorandum of the defendant's agreement in writing signed by the defendant. If so, the Statute of Frauds has been complied with...".

In deference to tradition and the Statute, Pollock, C.B., speaks of the alterations being authenticated by the old signature; but

[1] (1852) 7 Ex. 862, 868; 155 E.R. 1199, 1202.

in actual fact these alterations were authenticated by the act of the defendant in writing the additional words on the same paper, thereby shewing that he recognized those additional words as part of his contract.

Position of the signature and the authenticated signature fiction. It has already been mentioned[1] that an ordinary signature performs two important functions: it constitutes an admission by the signatory of the authenticity of the document; and from its position on the document it discharges this function with regard to the *whole* document. It might have been expected that upon the courts ceasing to insist on a signature capable of discharging the first function, they would have ceased also to pay any attention to the second function. But, however far the law may have departed from the strict meaning of the word *signed* as used in the Statute, yet the fiction of a genuine signature remains and consequently the name which serves for a signature must be so placed that were it capable of authenticating the document it would authenticate the whole of it.

It was only when the courts began to consider whether a name in the text of the document could serve the purpose of a signature that attention became directed to this function discharged by an ordinary signature. Accordingly, in the very case[2] in which was first debated the possibility of a sufficient signature being constituted by a name written in the body of the instrument, the point was raised that a signature, by its position in the document, indicated that it applied to the whole of that document, and that if a name in the text of the document could be a signature it would have to discharge the same function. The result produced by this argument was quite anomalous. Whenever there was no real signature, but only an empty name having no authenticating effect, then the courts were loud in their insistence on that name being so placed as to "authenticate the whole document".

Accordingly, when some three years after *Schneider* v. *Norris*[3]

[1] P. 82 *supra*.
[2] *Stokes* v. *Moore*, (1786) 1 Cox 219; 29 E.R. 1137.
[3] (1814) 2 M. & S. 286; 105 E.R. 388.

had been decided, the case of *Ogilvie* v. *Foljambe*,[1] involving considerations of this kind, came before Grant, M.R., that learned judge affirmed with renewed emphasis the principle of *Stokes* v. *Moore*,[2] saying that a signature must govern the entire document; and fifty years later Lord Westbury in his speech to the House of Lords in *Caton* v. *Caton*[3] adopted Sir William Grant's words as a correct statement of the law. His Lordship said:

"Probably the phrases 'authentic' and 'authenticity' are not quite felicitous, but their meaning is plainly this, that the signature must be so placed as to shew that it was intended to relate and refer to, and that in fact it does relate and refer to, every part of the instrument. The language of Sir William Grant in *Ogilvie* v. *Foljambe*, is (as his method was) much more felicitous. He says it must govern every part of the instrument. It must shew that every part of the instrument emanates from the individual so signing, and that the signature was intended to have that effect. It follows, therefore, that if a signature be found in an instrument incidentally only, or having relation and reference only to a portion of the instrument, the signature cannot have that legal effect and force which it must have in order to comply with the statute, and to give authenticity to the whole of the memorandum".

The reference made by Lord Westbury to *intention* seems to be unnecessary. In cases of this description, where there is no real signature at all, but only the pretence of one, it seems idle to talk of the name which is called a signature being placed on the document to fulfil an intention on the part of the alleged signatory to authenticate that document. The most accurate way of expressing the principle which *Caton* v. *Caton* and similar cases exemplify is, it is submitted, as follows: that the name which is to do duty as the signature must be placed in such a position in the writing that, were it possessed of any intrinsic authenticating force, it would authenticate or govern the whole of that writing.

In *Caton* v. *Caton*[4] the memorandum commenced thus: "In

[1] (1817) 3 Mer. 53; 36 E.R. 21.
[2] (1786) 1 Cox 219; 29 E.R. 1137.
[3] (1867) L.R. 2 H.L. 127, 143.
[4] L.R. 2 H.L. 127.

the event of a marriage between the under-mentioned parties the following conditions, as a basis for a marriage settlement, are mutually agreed upon". Then followed several sentences, each substantially in this form: "*C.* to do so and so; *H.* to have so and so", *C.*, the party to be charged, being sometimes represented by his initials and once by his surname. No real signature was inscribed on the document and the House of Lords were unanimous in holding that the initials and name were insufficient to constitute a signature, as they referred exclusively to the particular clauses in which they occurred and therefore could not be regarded as governing the memorandum in its entirety.

In *Johnson* v. *Dodgson*[1] there was a memorandum commencing as follows: "Leeds, 19th October, 1836. Sold John Dodgson...". The Court of Common Pleas held that the name *John Dodgson* constituted a sufficient signature, Lord Abinger, C.B., remarking: "And the cases have decided that, although the signature be in the beginning or middle of the instrument, it is as binding as if at the foot of it...". In view, however, of *Caton* v. *Caton*, this statement cannot be regarded as accurate; but the decision itself, it is submitted, may be supported on the ground that the memorandum shewed that *John Dodgson* was the purchaser of the goods; everything else in the memorandum referred to the sale of these goods; and hence the name *John Dodgson* could be regarded as governing every part of the memorandum. In regard to the memorandum in *Stokes* v. *Moore*,[2] on the other hand, no similar process of reasoning was applicable. The memorandum in *Stokes* v. *Moore* was in the following terms:

"The lease renewed, Mrs Stokes to pay the King's tax, also to pay Moore £24 a year, half-yearly. Mrs Stokes to keep the house in good tenantable repair, and to paint the whole outside and wash-house of the house twice in oil in May, 1787, the second painting in like manner in May, 1792, under penalty of £100 sterling: lease paid for by Stokes".

It would have been impossible to say that the name *Moore*, in

[1] (1837) 2 M. & W. 653, 659; 150 E.R. 918, 921.
[2] (1786) 1 Cox 219; 29 E.R. 1137.

this memorandum, related to the latter portion, which referred exclusively to Mrs Stokes and her obligations.

In the Irish case of *Dyas* v. *Stafford*[1] a memorandum in the form of particulars and conditions of sale was tendered as evidence of a contract of sale, and Chatterton, V.-C., held that the auctioneer's name, appearing on the back of the particulars in a sentence announcing the sale, was a sufficient signature. This decision would seem to accord with the principle established by the decisions in other cases of a similar nature; but when *Dyas* v. *Stafford* came before the Court of Appeal,[2] not only did that court reverse the Vice-Chancellor on the ground that there was no concluded contract, but Law, C., and Fitzgibbon, L.J., expressly said that the auctioneer's name merely authenticated the sentence in which it occurred.

In *Cohen* v. *Roche*[3] the facts, so far as concerned the question of signature, were substantially the same as those in *Dyas* v. *Stafford*. McCardie, J., held that the memorandum was duly signed, and expressly followed the Vice-Chancellor's decision in the Irish case; but he does not seem to have been referred to the report of that case as decided in the Court of Appeal. Perhaps it may be said of *Cohen* v. *Roche*, however, that McCardie, J., really based his opinion on the English authorities, and cited *Dyas* v. *Stafford* by way of illustration merely.

The last case to which reference must be made is *Halley* v. *O'Brien*,[4] another Irish case. There also a memorandum endorsed on particulars and conditions of sale and unsigned was tendered in support of a contract under the Statute and both Powell, J.,[5] and the Court of Appeal held that the memorandum was signed for the purpose of the Statute. In its essential facts this case somewhat resembled *Johnson* v. *Dodgson*.[6]

It is a striking feature of all the foregoing cases where a name in the text has been held to constitute a good signature, that that

1 (1881) 7 L.R. Ir. 590.
2 (1882) 9 L.R. Ir. 520.
3 [1927] 1 K.B. 169.
4 [1920] 1 I.R. 330.
5 *Ib.* 149.
6 2 M. & W. 653; 150 E.R. 918.

name has always occurred at the beginning of the document;[1] and that the statement made by the sentence in which the name has occurred has been one setting out the background upon which the details of the contractual picture are to be drawn. This seems to be what is meant by the judges when they say that the name must be so placed as to *govern* the whole of the writing.[2]

Intention in regard to the Statutory requirement of signature. A question which requires some consideration is the part played by the "intention" of the parties in this matter of signature. And here the cases fall into two broad classes. (*a*) First of all, a party in signing a writing may do so with the conscious intention of satisfying the requirements of the Statute; or without being conscious of the Statute he may yet desire to authenticate a writing as a correct exposition of all the terms of a contract; or he may merely intend to sign a document without adverting to the possibility of its having any contractual effect. (*b*) And secondly, a party may intend his name or mark to be a signature or its equivalent or he may have no such intention.

(*a*) *Intention of satisfying Statute.* The presence or absence of an intention to satisfy the Statute is entirely irrelevant. When

[1] In cases such as *Halley* v. *O'Brien*, [1920] 1 I.R. 330, it is true that the memorandum is placed after the particulars and conditions of sale, so that at first sight it would appear that a name occurring at the beginning of the memorandum is yet really placed in the middle of the whole writing. But it is submitted that the writing which satisfies the Statute is the endorsed memorandum, the particulars and conditions being regarded as incorporated in that memorandum by reference.

[2] It was laid down in *Caton* v. *Caton*, (1867) L.R. 2 H.L. 127, 139, that a name cannot be considered to govern the whole of the writing merely because all the various parts of that writing refer to the name. The reference, it was said, must be from the name to the writing. "It was argued", said Lord Chelmsford, L.C., "that the introductory words, 'in the event of a marriage between the under-named parties', gave to the name of Mr Caton, however afterwards appearing, the same force and effect as if he had written his own and Mrs Henley's name at the beginning of the memorandum, instead of the words, 'the under-named parties'. But these words of reference cannot, in my opinion, have any effect upon the question. The name of the party, and its application to the whole of the instrument, can alone satisfy the requisites of a signature. In the memorandum in question, Mr Caton's name is incidentally introduced with reference to a particular purpose, or as a matter of description, and as this mention of his name would clearly be insufficient in itself, it cannot have any new effect given to it by the introductory words of the memorandum."

a party is considered by the law to have signed a writing evidencing a contract under the Statute, his intention when he does so is quite beside the point. In this connection reference need only be made to the cases where incidental letters, letters denying or repudiating any contractual liability, pleadings, affidavits, and such documents have been held to be sufficiently signed writings.[1] In many of such cases it is apparent that the last thing the parties could have had in mind was the production of a writing satisfying the Statute; often this was the very result they intended most to avoid.[2]

(*b*) *Intention that name shall be signature*. The intention of a party that his name, appearing in a document, should be a signature, is chiefly spoken of in those cases where the question is whether a document, not signed in the normal way, is yet sufficiently signed to satisfy the Statute. Where a party has subscribed his name, or being illiterate has made his mark at the foot of a document, the signature or mark speaks for itself. It is only where the signature consists of a name in the text of the writing or where alterations have been introduced in a document previously signed, that the courts proceed to talk of intention in this sense.

For example, in *Caton* v. *Caton*,[3] Lord Westbury remarked in the course of his judgment: "It [i.e. the signature] must shew that every part of the instrument emanates from the individual so signing, and that the signature was intended to have that effect". In *Hubert* v. *Treherne*[4] judgment was given in favour of a defendant on the ground that a memorandum not bearing a subscribed signature was not otherwise sufficiently signed, and Tindal, C.J., referring to this aspect of the case, remarked: "The

[1] See p. 71 *supra*.

[2] "It is also undoubted law", said A. L. Smith, L.J., delivering the judgment of the Court of Appeal in *John Griffiths Cycle Corporation Ltd.* v. *Humber & Co., Ltd.*, [1899] 2 Q.B. 414, 418, "that a signature to a document which contains the terms of a contract is available for the purpose of satisfying s. 4 of the Statute, though put *alio intuitu* and not in order to attest or verify the contract: *Jones* v. *Victoria Dock Co.* (2 Q.B.D. 314)." See also *Coles* v. *Trecothick*, (1804) 9 Ves. 234; 32 E.R. 592; and per Sargant, J., in *Daniels* v. *Trefusis*, [1914] 1 Ch. 788, 799.

[3] (1867) L.R. 2 H.L. 127, 143.

[4] (1842) 3 Man. & G. 743; 133 E.R. 1338 at p. 754; E.R. 1342.

words [as witness our hands] evidently shew that the names of the contracting parties were meant to be subscribed, and that it was not intended that the insertion of the names in the body of the instrument should operate by way of signature". Is it then to be inferred from these and similar *dicta* that before finally deciding whether or not a signature is sufficient to satisfy the Statute the law strictly inquires whether the suggested signature was in fact intended to be a signature? Or, on the other hand, is the law content to call that a signature (for the purposes of the Statute) which satisfies certain purely objective tests taking no account of the intention of the alleged signatory?

The latter alternative, it is submitted, is the correct one. In spite of such *dicta* as those quoted in the last paragraph, it would seem impossible to point to a case where the courts have definitely held that a writing bearing the name of the party to be charged, and otherwise complying with the general requirements of the Statute as to signature, is yet insufficient to satisfy the Statute because the party did not *intend* such name to be a signature. The truth of the position was long ago recognized by Lord Eldon, C.J., who in referring to a case in which a name at the commencement of the text of a memorandum had been held to be a sufficient signature, said:[1] "And yet it is impossible not to see that the insertion of the name at the beginning was not intended to be a signature, and that the paper was meant to be incomplete until it was further signed". Reference may also be made to the words of Blackburn, J., in *Durrell* v. *Evans*:[2]

"In *Johnson* v. *Dodgson*[3] the memorandum was retained by the defendant in his own possession, but as it contained his name, and was intended to be a note of the contract, it was held binding on him, although the fact of his keeping it was a clear indication

[1] *Saunderson* v. *Jackson*, (1800) 2 Bos. & P. 238, 239; 126 E.R. 1257, 1258. The case to which Lord Eldon was referring was *Knight* v. *Crockford*, 1 Esp. N.P. Cas. 190, where it had been decided "that if a man draw up an agreement in his own handwriting, beginning 'I, *A.B.* agree, &c.' and leave a place for a signature at the bottom, but never sign it, it may be considered as a note or memorandum in writing within the statute".

[2] (1862) 1 H. & C. 174, 191; 158 E.R. 848, 855.

[3] 2 M. & W. 653.

that he never intended it as a voucher of his being bound, but only to bind the other party".[1]

Clearly the important thing, in the view of Blackburn, J., was that the party intended the note to be an accurate statement of the contract. But the learned judge made no reference to any intention that the name should be regarded as a signature.

In actual fact, this talk of intention seems to be nothing more than the authenticated signature fiction in another dress. A name appears in the text of a writing—that name lacks authenticating force; that is to say, it was not intended for a signature at all, but only to identify one of the contracting parties. When, therefore, the law attributes to that name an authenticating power which in reality it never had or could have, it is the same thing as attributing to the party to be charged an intention that the name should be a signature. Just as the tradition of a signature which must of itself authenticate has left its traces on the language of the courts, so likewise do references to the necessity for the signature to be intended as such appear from time to time in judgments dealing with cases under the Statute. This, it is suggested, is the true explanation of such *dicta* as those quoted above.

Summary. It is submitted that the position to which the decisions have carried the law may be stated in the following propositions:

(1) Signature, for the purpose of the Statute, bears a technical meaning which is wider than its usual or ordinary meaning.[2]

(2) The Statutory requirement of signature is satisfied by the name (or initials[3]) of the party to be charged appearing in any part of the document tendered as a writing evidencing the contract; provided

(*a*) that such name (or initials) must be so placed in the document as to apply to the whole of the document or at least to the whole of the contractual writing contained in the document;[4] and provided further

[1] And see per Denman, J., in *Evans* v. *Hoare*, (1892) 1 Q.B. 593, 596.
[2] See p. 81 *supra*.
[3] *Caton* v. *Caton*, (1867) L.R. 2 H.L. 127, 143, per Lord Westbury.
[4] See pp. 92–96 *supra*.

(*b*) that if such name (or initials) is not an autograph (which may be made by pen, pencil, typewriter, rubber-stamp or other suitable instrument[1]) or if being an autograph it is placed on the document before the same has been completed as a writing evidencing the contract or is merely part of the text,[2] then before that writing can satisfy the Statute such name (or initials) must be expressly or impliedly *authenticated* by the party to be charged; that is to say such party must expressly or impliedly indicate that he recognizes the writing so containing his name (or initials) as being an authentic expression of the contract.[3]

[1] See *Stroud's Judicial Dictionary*, 2nd ed. III, p. 1882, *sub nom.* "signed'.

[2] See pp. 89–92 *supra*.

[3] See pp. 86–89 *supra*.

CHAPTER VI

AGENCY IN RELATION TO THE STATUTORY REQUIREMENT OF SIGNATURE

THE signature required by the Statute may be supplied either by the party to be charged or by "some other person thereunto by him lawfully authorized".

"The statute", said Best, C.J., in *Maclean* v. *Dunn*,[1] "only requires some note or memorandum in writing, to be signed by the party to be charged, or his agent thereunto lawfully authorized; leaving us to the rules of common law, as to the mode in which the agent is to receive his authority."

It therefore becomes necessary to consider the law of agency in its relation to the Statutory requirement of signature.

It has been pointed out above[2] that a writing may be regarded as satisfying the Statutory requirement, either because it bears on its face a signature properly so-called, or because it contains in its text a name which, by virtue of the authenticated signature fiction, is deemed to be a signature. In considering the question of agency in relation to the signature required by the Statute, it seems appropriate to maintain this distinction, and to discuss the matter (A) first in regard to cases where there is a regular signature, and (B) secondly in regard to cases where there is no such signature but merely the defendant's name in some part of the writing. Moreover, several cases have occurred in which the question has been debated of whether a solicitor is his client's agent for the purpose of the Statute, and the determination in particular cases of the precise limits of the solicitor's authority in this connection has not always been free from difficulty. A section is therefore added on (C) the authority of a solicitor to sign writings on his client's behalf.

[1] (1828) 4 Bing. 722, 727; 130 E.R. 947, 949.
[2] See pp. 82, 83 *supra*.

(A) *Agency where there is a regular signature*

In determining whether the Statute has been satisfied by a writing bearing a regular signature supplied by some third person, three questions appear to call for consideration, viz.:

I. Was that person of capacity to act as an agent?
II. Was he authorized to sign?
III. Did he sign in the appropriate form (if any)?

I. *The capacity of the agent.* The rules determining the legal capacity necessary in a person to enable him to act as an agent are part of the general law of agency, and fall outside the scope of this treatise. One point, however, may be mentioned: it seems clearly to be established that one of the parties to a contract cannot act as the agent of the other for the purpose of signing a writing binding that other under the Statute; the agent must be a third person.[1] Of course a third person may well be the agent of both parties,[2] but it has been said that the courts will not presume such an agency from the relative situation of the parties save in the exceptional case of an auctioneer.[3] An auctioneer is

[1] *Sharman* v. *Brandt*, (1871) L.R. 6 Q.B. 720. This was a case in which a broker, having signed a contract note as selling for an undisclosed principal, sued personally on the contract. It was held by the Court of Exchequer Chamber that the broker's signature did not bind the defendant. "I am also clearly of opinion", said Martin, B. (at p. 723), "that the note was not a memorandum signed as required by the statute; one of the parties cannot be the agent of the other for the purpose of signing the contract." See also *Farebrother* v. *Simmons*, (1822) 5 B. & Ald. 333; 106 E.R. 1213.

It is to be noted, however, that Lord Blackburn, in his *Contract of Sale*, 3rd ed. p. 76, expressed disapproval of these authorities. "It has indeed been decided", he remarked (*loc. cit.*), "that one party cannot be an agent for the other, but this is very doubtful law. It is quite right and proper that such an unusual thing as intrusting the other side with authority should be clearly proved; but if it be clearly proved, there is nothing either in the section or in reason to make it void."

[2] *Thompson* v. *Gardiner*, (1876) 1 C.P.D. 777. This was a case where a broker, primarily employed by the plaintiff (the seller), made and signed an entry of the contract in his book; and he also signed the sold note. It was held by the Court of Common Pleas that the circumstances of the case warranted an implication that the broker was authorized to sign on behalf of the defendant (the buyer). See also *Parton* v. *Crofts*, (1864) 16 C.B. (N.S.) 11; 143 E.R. 1027; and *Bird* v. *Boulter*, (1833) 4 B. & Ad. 443; 110 E.R. 522.

[3] "At first sight", said Pollock, B., in *Murphy* v. *Boese*, (1875) L.R. 10 Ex. 126, 130, "it would seem odd that one who is in a position somewhat adverse to the other should be his representative and agent. But no doubt

almost always expressly authorized to sign a contract on the vendor's behalf, and the law presumes that he has authority to sign for the purchaser.[1]

II. *The authority of the agent.* It is necessary to consider first, the nature of the authority; and secondly, the methods by which it can be acquired.

The nature of the authority. The nature and extent of the authority required to be possessed by an agent under the Statute are indicated by the Statutory description of him—"some other person thereunto lawfully authorized"; that is to say, the agent must be authorized to sign the writing, but he need not be authorized to *sign for the purpose of satisfying the Statute.* "It seems to me", said Sargant, J., in *Daniels* v. *Trefusis*,[2] "that the unintentional by-product of satisfying the Statute of Frauds may be produced as completely by a note or memorandum signed by an agent of the party as by a note or memorandum signed by the party himself, provided, of course, that the agent had authority to sign the particular note or memorandum."

Methods by which authority can be acquired: the appointment of the agent. No special formalities are required in the appointment of the agent. The Statute merely says that the agent must be "lawfully authorized", but, as Best, C.J., remarked,[3] it is

such a thing may happen, as in the instance which has very properly been cited of the auctioneer's clerk signing as agent of both parties. In Lord St Leonard's work on *Vendors and Purchasers*, 14th ed. p. 147, he explains the principle upon which the auctioneer can bind both vendor and purchaser by his signature, citing *Earl of Glengal* v. *Barnard*, 1 Keen 769, and *Emmerson* v. *Heelis*, 2 Taunt. 38, and stating that the implied agency of an auctioneer is not extended to other cases." Thus, although the position of a broker very closely resembles that of an auctioneer, the law has steadfastly refused to presume an authority on the part of a broker to sign a writing on the purchaser's behalf. Where the existence of such authority is a relevant circumstance, it must be proved in the ordinary way. "The authorities are conclusive", said Brett, J., in *Thompson* v. *Gardiner*, (1876) 1 C.P.D. 777, 779, "to shew that the broker acting for one of the contracting parties, making a contract for the other, is not authorized to bind both. But the broker who makes a contract for one may be authorized by that person to make and sign a memorandum of the contract." In that case the court was satisfied *on the evidence* that the broker, although primarily employed by the vendor, was authorized to sign for the purchaser.

[1] Generally as to the authority possessed by an auctioneer to sign writings under the Statute, see p. 105, *infra*.

[2] [1914] 1 Ch. 788, 799.

[3] (1828) 4 Bing. 722, 727; 130 E.R. 947, 949.

left to the rules of the common law to determine the manner in which the agent is to receive his authority. The agent may therefore (1) receive his authority from an express appointment; or (2) his authority may be implied by the law from the particular circumstances of the case; or (3) be presumed from the situation of the parties; or (4) it may result from subsequent ratification by the principal.[1]

(1) *Express appointment.* Such an appointment may be by parol. As long ago as 1804, Lord Eldon said,[2] "It is clearly settled now, that an agent need not be authorized in writing". In *Clinan* v. *Cooke*[3] Lord Redesdale put the matter thus:

"It is insisted, that whenever an authority is given to another to enter into a contract of this description [relating to lands], it must be in writing. There is no foundation for this position: the words of the Statute of Frauds do not import any such thing, and there are decided cases to the contrary".

(2) *Authority implied by law.* The law will imply an authority from one person to another if the circumstances of the case and the conduct of parties are of such a nature as to warrant the implication. In *Daniels* v. *Trefusis*,[4] where the question was as to the authority of a solicitor to write and sign certain letters, Sargant, J., in the course of his judgment, remarked:

"It was agreed between counsel that these answers admitted a general authority on the part of Messrs Taylor and Co....but did not admit any special authority (apart from the preceding general authority) to write particular letters. It is, however, of course competent to me to deduce any such authority as to any particular letters from the surrounding circumstances".

In *Daniels* v. *Trefusis* it was held that the proved circumstances were sufficient to justify such an implication of authority, and accordingly the defence of the Statute failed.[5]

[1] Bowstead, *Law of Agency*, 8th ed. p. 16.

[2] In *Coles* v. *Trecothick*, (1804) 9 Ves. 234, 250; 32 E.R. 592, 598. See also per Selwyn, L.J., in *Heard* v. *Pilley*, (1869) L.R. 4 Ch. 548, 551.

[3] (1802) 1 Sch. & Lef. 22, 31.

[4] [1914] 1 Ch. 788, 797.

[5] For another example of implied authority see *Bird* v. *Boulter*, (1833) 4 B. & Ad. 443; 110 E.R. 522, where an auctioneer's clerk was held in the particular circumstances of the case to have been authorized to sign a writing on behalf of a purchaser at the sale. See this case discussed, below, pp. 115 *et seq*.

A case in which the court declined to make such an implication was *Graham* v. *Musson*,[1] decided by the Common Pleas in 1839. The evidence in that case shewed that one Dyson, the plaintiff's traveller, had struck a bargain with the defendant for the sale to him of some sugar. The defendant thereupon asked Dyson to enter a note of the bargain in the defendant's book; and this Dyson did, the defendant being present throughout. The note was in the following words: "Of North & Co., thirty mats maurs, at 71*s*.,—cash two months. Fenning's wharf. August 19, 1836. Joseph Dyson". It was argued for the plaintiff that the facts warranted the implication that Dyson was the agent of the defendant *qua* signing the note, but the court (Tindal, C.J., Vaughan, Coltman and Erskine, JJ.) held that there was no evidence to support such an implication. Dyson had merely signed his own name; and that was a negative circumstance unless it were first shewn in some way that he had been authorized to sign on behalf of the defendant. Had he signed the defendant's name without the defendant protesting, the case would have been different.

"The only reason", said Bramwell, B., in *Mews* v. *Carr*,[2] "why I make any remark is, that the observations of the court in *Graham* v. *Musson* may not be misunderstood. There the court said, that if the traveller had signed the defendant's name, and he had not expressed any dissent, that would have been a recognition of agency."

(3) *Authority presumed from the situation of the parties. Auctioneer as agent.* Presumption of authority from the situation of the parties occurs chiefly in the case of auctioneer and purchaser. An auctioneer is primarily the agent of the vendor: not infrequently his appointment by the vendor is made in a written instrument; and his agency necessarily includes an authority to sign on the vendor's behalf a binding contract of sale. "It was always clear", wrote Lord St Leonards, "that an auctioneer, appointed by a vendor, was a good agent for *him* within the

[1] (1839) 5 Bing. (N.C.) 603; 132 E.R. 1232.
[2] (1856) 1 H. & N. 484, 488; 156 E.R. 1292, 1293.

Statute."[1] For a long time, however, the law was by no means certain of the precise nature of the auctioneer's relation with the purchaser. And even when it had at last decided that in a limited degree the auctioneer was the purchaser's agent, there still remained for consideration the extent of the authority (if any) to be presumed in the auctioneer's clerk.

History. One of the earliest cases in which the Statute was considered in its application to sales by auction was *Simon* v. *Metivier or Motivos*,[2] a case arising out of an auction sale of drugs at a price exceeding £10. A double argument was submitted to the court: first,

> "That the auctioneer was agent to the buyer *pro tempore*; that his [the buyer's] giving in his name was an authority to the auctioneer to set down the contract";

and secondly, as an alternative argument,

> "That the intent of the Statute of Frauds was, to suppress private fraudulent contracts supported by perjury. [But there is] no such inconvenience in sales by auction, which are transacted in the face of such numbers, that a man cannot, by false evidence, be made a purchaser whether he will or not".[3]

The court (Mansfield, C.J., Wilmot, Yates and Aston, JJ.) determined the case on the ground that if the contract were

[1] Sugden (Lord St Leonards), *Vendors and Purchasers*, 14th ed. p. 147. It is a very general practice (at least in cases involving property of any considerable value) for the auctioneer to receive from the vendor an express written authority, not only to sell the property but also to sign all writings necessary to effectuate the sale. See the form of authorization given in *The Encyclopaedia of Forms and Precedents*, 2nd ed. II, p. 292; and also the form (by deed) in *Bateman on Auctions*, 9th ed. p. 526. Moreover, in cases where there are formal conditions of sale, the memorandum endorsed on such conditions usually shews that the auctioneer is expressly authorized to sign: see the form in *Key and Elphinstone's Precedents in Conveyancing*, 12th ed. part I, I, p. 264. And in any event, the vendor, by employing the auctioneer to sell the property, would necessarily seem to authorize him to sign all requisite writings. "An auctioneer is an agent having power from the seller to sell, and having therefore incidentally authority from him to sign the contract." Blackburn, *Contract of Sale*, 3rd ed. p. 78. And as against a purchaser, an owner of property may be estopped by his conduct from denying the authority of an auctioneer to sell the property and to sign a writing evidencing the sale. See *Pickard* v. *Sears*, (1837) 6 A. & E. 469; 112 E.R. 179.

[2] (1766) 1 Black. W. 599; 96 E.R. 347.

[3] *Ex arg*. Norton and Wallace, p. 600; E.R. 347.

within the Statute, then the Statutory requirements had been satisfied; but Mansfield, C.J., Wilmot and Yates, JJ., inclined to adopt the second argument above quoted, and expressed the opinion that auctions in general were not within the Statute.

The question was next raised before Eyre, C.J. (sitting at *Nisi Prius*), in *Stansfield* v. *Johnson*,[1] a case involving a sale of land. The learned Chief Justice there held that auction sales of land were within the Statute, but that the principle on which *Simon* v. *Metivier*[2] was decided, viz. that the auctioneer was the agent of both vendor and purchaser for the purpose of making a binding note of the sale, was restricted to auction sales of goods, under s. 17 of the Statute of Frauds.[3]

Simon v. *Metivier*[2] and *Stansfield* v. *Johnson*[1] left the law in a very uncertain and very unsatisfactory position; and in 1804 Lord Eldon, L.C., in the course of his judgment in *Coles* v. *Trecothick*[4] made particular reference to the difficulties presented by these two cases.

"Much perplexity", said the Lord Chancellor, "has also arisen by the case of auctions; for in *Simon* v. *Metivier* it was held, as to goods, that the auctioneer taking down the name was a signing within the Statute; and it is very singular, that after, and without disturbing, that [i.e. the decision in *Simon* v. *Metivier*] it was held at *Nisi Prius* by the Lord Chief Justice Eyre, that it would not do as to land. Why not? The form of the two clauses [ss. 4 and 17] is not the same: but the terms as to the memorandum in writing are exactly the same. That case was followed, certainly without much argument or discussion upon the Bench, according to the Report, in *Walker* v. *Constable*.[5] Unless some distinction can be pointed out, the law is very inconvenient as to sales by auction: particularly, if the auctioneer is to be considered the agent of one only."

[1] (1794) 1 Esp. 101; 170 E.R. 293.

[2] (1766) 1 Black. W. 599; 96 E.R. 347.

[3] The opinion that *Simon* v. *Metivier* was restricted to auction sales of chattels was again expressed by Eyre, C.J., in *Walker* v. *Constable*, (1798) 2 Esp. 659; 170 E.R. 488; in the Common Pleas, 1 B. & P. 306; 126 E.R. 919. *Stansfield* v. *Johnson*, 1 Esp. 101; 170 E.R. 293, was followed by Grant, M.R., in *Buckmaster* v. *Harrop*, (1802) 7 Ves. 341, 345; 32 E.R. 139, 140.

[4] (1804) 9 Ves. 234, 249; 32 E.R. 592, 598.

[5] 1 B. & P. 306; 126 E.R. 919.

It was not long before *Simon* v. *Metivier*[1] was again the subject of judicial comment; and in *Blagden* v. *Bradbear*,[2] a case involving an auction sale of land, Grant, M.R., expressed a definite opinion that there was nothing in the Statute to exclude its application to sales by auction.

"As to the doctrine", said the learned judge, "that the Statute of Frauds does not apply to sales by auction, there is no decision; for though in *Simon* v. *Metivier*[1] the Judges did express their opinion, the ground of their decision was, that the memorandum of the auctioneer answered the requisitions of the Statute. The words of the Statute are large enough to comprehend every contract, by whatsoever preliminary means, whether verbal communication, or bidding at an auction, it may have been brought about; and it is not clear to me, that sales by auction are out of the mischief, against which the Statute meant to guard. From the public nature of a sale by auction it does not follow, that what passes there must be matter of certainty; so far from it, that I never saw more contradictory swearing than in those cases, where attempts were made to introduce evidence of what was said and done during the course of the sale....I should therefore hesitate to say, the policy of the Statute does not extend to such sales. Still more should I hesitate to say, the words of the Statute according to the true construction do not include sales by auction."

In the same year as *Blagden* v. *Bradbear*, the Court of King's Bench in *Hinde* v. *Whitehouse*,[3] a case arising out of an auction sale of goods, expressly refused to follow the opinions expressed in *Simon* v. *Metivier* that such sales were out of the Statute.

"With all deference to those opinions", said Lord Ellenborough, C.J., "I do not at present feel any sufficient reason for dispensing with the express requisition of a memorandum in writing in a statute applying to all sales of goods above the value of £10, without exception, merely because the quantum of parol evidence in the case of an auction is likely to render the danger of perjury less considerable."

[1] (1766) 1 Black. W. 599; 96 E.R. 347.
[2] (1806) 12 Ves. 466, 471; 33 E.R. 176, 178.
[3] (1806) 7 East 558, 568; 103 E.R. 216, 220.

These last-mentioned cases[1] seem finally to have established the unsoundness of the opinions expressed in *Simon* v. *Metivier*,[2] that contracts entered into at auction sales were outside the scope of the Statute. And whatever doubts may still have remained as to the authority of the auctioneer to sign a writing on the purchaser's behalf were finally set at rest by the decision of the Court of Common Pleas in *Emmerson* v. *Heelis*,[3] a case which arose out of the sale of an interest in land. Lord Mansfield, C.J., who delivered the judgment of the court, expressed very lucidly the basis of the auctioneer's authority in this behalf.

"Now this memorandum", he said, "is more particular than most memorandums of sale are; and upon it the auctioneer writes down the purchaser's name. By what authority does he write down the purchaser's name? By the authority of the purchaser. These persons bid, and announce their biddings, loudly and particularly enough to be heard by the auctioneer. For what purpose do they do this? That he may write down their names opposite to the lots; therefore he writes the name by the authority of the purchaser, and he is an agent for the purchaser: and it does seem, therefore, that this is a contract signed by an agent for the purchaser, and consequently is binding."

Modern law. So much for the history of the auctioneer's authority to sign a writing on the purchaser's behalf. It is submitted that the modern law on this matter may be stated as follows:

(i) By reason of the nature of the transaction of sale by auction an auctioneer is presumed to be the agent of the highest bidder,[4] to sign on the highest bidder's behalf a binding note of the contract; but this authority is of but brief duration and lapses unless it is exercised either at the sale or so soon thereafter that it can be said that the making or completing of the writing by

[1] *Blagden* v. *Bradbear*, (1806) 12 Ves. 466; 33 E.R. 176; and *Hinde* v. *Whitehouse*, (1806) 7 East 558; 103 E.R. 216. See also the opinion expressed by Erskine, L.C., when *Buckmaster* v. *Harrop* came before him on appeal; (1807) 13 Ves. 456, 472; 33 E.R. 365, 370, 371.

[2] (1766) 1 Black. W. 599; 96 E.R. 347.

[3] (1809) 2 Taunt. 38, 47; 127 E.R. 989, 993.

[4] "...he has authority from the highest bidder to sign the catalogue on his behalf...." Per Blackburn, J., in *Peirce* v. *Corf*, (1874) L.R. 9 Q.B. 210, 214.

the auctioneer is substantially part of the transaction of the sale.

(ii) This authority is personal to the auctioneer and there is no such presumption in the case of the auctioneer's clerk.

(i) (*a*) *The nature of the transaction of sale by auction.* The passage (cited above)[1] from the judgment of Lord Mansfield, C.J., in *Emmerson* v. *Heelis*[2] states very clearly the reasons underlying this presumption. In *Earl of Glengal* v. *Barnard*,[3] Lord Langdale, M.R., expounded the principle of *Emmerson* v. *Heelis* in the following terms:

"The nature of the proceeding by auction—", he said, "the bidding for the purpose of making the purchase—the necessity of making a statement of the bidding—the direction to the auctioneer to write down the bidding, which is perhaps involved in the very process of bidding, and some other circumstances afford intelligible ground for the decision in *Emmerson* v. *Heelis*, and the approbation which has since been bestowed upon it".

(*b*) *A binding note of the contract.* Apparently any sort of a writing will do so long as it sets out all the terms of the contract. In *Peirce* v. *Corf*[4] Blackburn, J., inclined to the view that the auctioneer should sign on the catalogue which is usually annexed to the conditions of sale:

"I have already said that the usage of sales by auction which we must take notice of is, that the auctioneer is the person who has authority to sign, and generally he does wisely if he signs upon the catalogue. I am not prepared to say, if the auctioneer had a ledger or book in which the conditions were copied out, and he signed that ledger, that that, without other evidence, might be said to be a sufficient contract, although he had not signed the catalogue".

But there seems to be no justification for any such restriction to be found in the other cases on the subject; and in *Dyas* v.

[1] P. 109 *supra*.
[2] (1809) 2 Taunt. 38, 47; 127 E.R. 989, 993.
[3] (1836) 1 Keen 769, 788; 48 E.R. 503, 511.
[4] (1874) L.R. 9 Q.B. 210, 214.

Stafford[1] Chatterton, V.-C., expressly stated the law to be otherwise.

"He [the auctioneer] has authority", said the learned Vice-Chancellor, "in his character of agent for each party to sign a note of the contract of sale for each; and this may be either by way of entry in the auctioneer's book or catalogue of sales, or by a memorandum in writing, separate from such book or catalogue."

(*c*) *Substantially part of the transaction of the sale.* The presumed authority of an auctioneer to sign a writing on behalf of the highest bidder arises out of the nature of the transaction of the sale and must be exercised at such a time as in substance to be part of the transaction. One of the earliest references to this point is contained in the judgment of Erskine, L.C., in *Buckmaster* v. *Harrop*.[2] In that case the auctioneer was one of the vendors, and apparently did not make his entry of the bidding at the time of the sale; and objection was taken on that account.

"The only evidence", said the Lord Chancellor, "that I can receive, is the written memorandum itself, unless it is lost; and it must be a cotemporary memorandum, especially in this case: as the auctioneer, being himself the vendor, though only as a trustee, could not in strictness be the agent of the purchaser."

That leaves *cotemporary* to be measured. In *Mews* v. *Carr*[3] it was said by Pollock, C.B., "No doubt an auctioneer is agent for both seller and buyer, so as to bind them by his signature; but the moment the sale is over, the same principle does not apply"; and Bramwell, B., in the same case, said: "as soon as the sale is over, the reason for the rule fails". These *dicta* would seem to put the position clearly enough; but there are two points to be observed in regard to *Mews* v. *Carr*. First, it was not a sale by auction at all; and secondly, the sales took place and the signa-

[1] (1881) 7 L.R. Ir. 590 at p. 599. This case was reversed by the Irish Court of Appeal, but the *dictum* cited from the Vice-Chancellor's judgment does not appear to have been affected. The case on appeal is reported in 9 L.R. Ir. 520.

See also *Bell* v. *Balls*, [1897] 1 Ch. 663. In this case, Stirling, J., elaborately reviewed the authorities, but no reference is to be found in his judgment to any such restriction as that suggested in the *dictum* of Blackburn, J.

[2] (1807) 13 Ves. 456, 472; 33 E.R. 365, 371.

[3] (1856) 1 H. & N. 484, 488; 156 E.R. 1292, 1293.

tures were written in the catalogue, in one instance a day after the auction had been held; and in the other two instances three or four days after the auction. The opinions expressed by the judges on this point were therefore clearly *obiter*.

In this condition of the authorities, Stirling, J., in *Bell* v. *Balls*[1] had to consider a case where the property had been sold by auction and a week later the auctioneer, purporting to act as agent for the purchaser, had signed a writing. The learned judge, in giving his reasons for holding that the auctioneer had by this time ceased to be authorized to sign the purchaser's name, thus expounded Lord Erskine's *dictum*:

"By a cotemporary memorandum I understand one made at the time and as part of the transaction of sale. If in the present case the auctioneer had proceeded to sign a memorandum immediately on the conclusion of the auction I should have been slow to hold that to be beyond his power...".

That statement of the law was somewhat more liberal than the opinions expressed by Pollock, C.B., and Bramwell, B., in *Mews* v. *Carr*, but just as much open to the objection that it was *obiter dictum* as were the views of the two Exchequer judges.

The question was last before the courts in the Irish case of *M'Meekin* v. *Stevenson*,[2] in which Ross, J., held, in view of special circumstances, that a writing signed by an auctioneer on the morning following the sale was good to bind the purchaser. The learned judge, after reading the above-quoted passage from the judgment of Pollock, C.B., in *Mews* v. *Carr*, continued as follows:

"The real test is whether the memorandum was made in substance at the time and as part of the transaction of sale. The circumstances of the case must be considered, and common sense applied. The sale of the chattels occupied a considerable time, and the auction lasted long into the winter evening. Was it reasonable to expect the auctioneer who was entrusted with the entire sale by the vendor to postpone his signature till next morning, when he had an opportunity of going through all the items to make sure that there was no mistake? In these circumstances I think his signing should be regarded as cotemporaneous and

[1] [1897] 1 Ch. 663, 672.

[2] [1917] 1 I.R. 348, 354.

part of the transaction of sale. There is no case deciding that the signature must be made on the day of the sale".

If *M'Meekin* v. *Stevenson* is to be regarded as a safe guide in this somewhat difficult part of the law, the proposition that the act of the auctioneer in signing the writing should be substantially contemporaneous with the transaction of sale might perhaps be better stated thus: that the act of the auctioneer in signing the writing should form, in substance, *one continuous transaction* with the auction sale.[1]

(ii) *The auctioneer's clerk.* A considerable measure of attention has from time to time been directed at the auctioneer's clerk and his authority to sign writings under the Statute. It will be convenient to consider (*a*) first, what authority the clerk possesses to sign on behalf of a vendor; and (*b*) secondly, his authority to sign for a purchaser.

(*a*) *The clerk's authority to sign for a vendor.* The general principle expressed in the maxim *delegatus non potest delegare* would prevent the auctioneer's clerk from deriving an authority through his master to sign for the vendor. It seems to be the better opinion, however, that the vendor, in employing the auctioneer, must be presumed at the same time to confer a collateral authority on the auctioneer's clerk.

"The auctioneer", said Chatterton, V.-C., in *Dyas* v. *Stafford*,[2] "being himself an agent, cannot delegate his authority, and his clerk cannot by any act of his be constituted an agent of the

[1] An alternative view suggested by the language of Ross, J., is that the auctioneer should be allowed a *reasonable* time after the actual selling of the property, in which to complete the writing. The limitation of a reasonable time was also suggested by Stirling, J., during the argument in *Bell* v. *Balls*, [1897] 1 Ch. 663. Counsel had contended that the agency of an auctioneer to sign on behalf of a purchaser ceased at the end of the sale, whereupon Stirling, J., interjected (p. 667): "Would not he have a reasonable time to fill up the document?"

[2] (1881) 7 L.R. Ir. 590, 600. This case was reversed by the Irish Court of Appeal on other grounds: 9 L.R. Ir. 520.

"It is not necessary", said Taunton, J., in *Bird* v. *Boulter*, (1833) 4 B. & Ad. 442, 448; 110 E.R. 522, 524, "to suppose that the vendor rested a particular confidence in the auctioneer for the purpose of putting down the names in the sale-book. He may be taken to have constituted that person his agent for the making of such entries, whom the auctioneer might choose to appoint. If so Pitt [the auctioneer's clerk] was agent for the vendor...".

vendor. The authority of the clerk must, therefore, be derived directly from the vendor; and that he has such authority for certain purposes is, I think, well established....The agency for the vendor...arises from the employment of the auctioneer which by the usages and mode of such sales carries with it the employment of his clerk. The vendor must be presumed to have been aware of and to have adopted these usages, and thus to have given an authority to the clerk, when the occasion should arise, to act as his agent directly in doing those acts which it was necessary for the clerk to do."

The agency of the clerk to sign for the vendor would seem, on this explanation, to be analogous to the auctioneer's agency to sign for a purchaser. In both cases authority is presumed by reason of the nature of the transaction of the sale and it might therefore be expected that the authority of the clerk would be of the same temporary nature as that of the auctioneer. This, indeed, appears to be the law, and it has been stated that the clerk's presumed authority to sign for the vendor ceases upon the conclusion of the sale.

"This implied authority", said Chatterton, V.-C., in another part of his judgment,[1] "must, however, be restricted to the circumstances from which it is implied, and cannot, in my opinion, be fairly extended beyond the auction, including therein the signature, as part of the transaction of the auction, of any agreement so constituted by the terms and conditions of sale....The rule, therefore, applicable to such cases, in my opinion is, that the clerk of an auctioneer has impliedly a direct authority from the vendor to bind him by his signature at, or as part of the actual *res gestae* of the auction, but beyond that he has no such implied authority, and cannot sign for him within the statute without express authority, which may be evidenced of course not only by writing but by parol."

(*b*) *The clerk's authority to sign for a purchaser.* It seems at one time to have been thought that a clerk enjoyed much the same authority as his master to sign a writing on a purchaser's behalf.[2] The case chiefly relied upon as shewing such an authority

[1] (1881) 7 L.R. Ir. 590, 601.

[2] Thus Lord St Leonards, in his work on *Vendors and Purchasers*, 14th ed. 1862, wrote (p. 147) as follows: "And it may now after much controversy be

to be presumed in the clerk was *Bird* v. *Boulter*,[1] the effect of which was stated in the headnote as follows:

"...the clerk is not identified with the auctioneer...and in the business which he performs, of entering the names, &c., he is impliedly authorized by the persons attending the sale, to be their agent".

This case was cited and discussed in *Dyas* v. *Stafford*,[2] and Chatterton, V.-C., considered that it established a presumed authority in the clerk to sign writings on a purchaser's behalf.

"The case of *Bird* v. *Boulter*", said the learned Vice-Chancellor, "decides that the clerk of an auctioneer is an agent for both vendor and purchaser to enter a minute of the sale at the time and as part of the transaction of the auction, and by his signature to such minute to constitute it a note or memorandum of the agreement signed by an agent thereunto lawfully authorized, within the terms of the Statute."

An examination of the judgments in *Bird* v. *Boulter*, however, seems to shew that that case is not to be regarded as resting upon the basis of a presumed authority in the auctioneer's clerk; but that it proceeded upon the ground that the evidence proved authorization:

"It appears to me", said Denman, C.J.,[3] "that the clerk was not acting merely as an automaton, but as a person known to all engaged in the sale, and employed by any who told him to put down his name." "By nodding as their names were called", said Patteson, J.,[4] "they [the purchasers] authorized him [the clerk] to act as he did."

Both Denman, C.J., and Patteson, J., therefore, put the case on the footing of an express authorization. Taunton, J., seemed to think it was a case of authorization to be implied from the proved circumstance of the purchaser's acquiescence. Only in the

laid down generally, that an auctioneer is the agent of both parties upon a sale of land or goods, so as to be enabled to bind them both under the statute. *And an auctioneer's clerk who takes down the biddings openly is considered the agent of both the seller and the purchaser*." (The italics are mine.)

[1] (1833) 4 B. & Ad. 443; 110 E.R. 522.

[2] (1881) 7 L.R. Ir. 590, 600.

[3] (1833) 4 B. & Ad. 443, 447; 110 E.R. 522, 523.

[4] *Ib.* 448; E.R. 524.

judgment of Littledale, J., can any support be found for the view expressed by Chatterton, V.-C., in the passage above quoted.

In *Peirce* v. *Corf*[1] Blackburn, J., clearly regarded *Bird* v. *Boulter* as depending upon proved circumstances and not upon a presumption of law.

"I take it", he said,[2] "as quite clear that the auctioneer's clerk has no authority to sign by the general custom; although, as *Bird* v. *Boulter* decided, there may be special circumstances to shew that an auctioneer's clerk had authority to sign; where the bidder, that is the person to be charged, by word or sign authorizes the auctioneer's clerk to sign on his behalf, he makes him his agent to sign, although by the general custom the auctioneer's clerk would not be the bidder's agent."

Whatever doubts may have remained on this question were finally set at rest by the decision of Stirling, J., in *Bell* v. *Balls*.[3] After quoting Blackburn, J.'s *dictum*, and stating that there was no evidence in *Bell* v. *Balls* of express or other authorization, the learned judge proceeded to consider the argument that "the exigencies of the case require that on sales by auction at the present day the auctioneer's clerk sitting publicly beside him should be held authorized to sign *memoranda* on behalf of purchasers"; that is to say, an argument that such authority should be presumed.

"The ordinary practice at the present time", said Stirling, J., "with reference to sales of real estate was stated by Mr Daw, the plaintiff's own witness, to be that an auctioneer, after he has knocked down a particular lot proceeds with the sale of the following lots and leaves it to the clerk to find out the name of the purchaser and to prepare a record of the contract, which he does by filling up the memoranda appended to two copies of the particulars of sale, one for signature by the purchaser, the other for signature by the auctioneer. Some convenience, no doubt, attends such a practice, and I do not desire to question its validity, but the mere statement of it appears to me to shew that there is no ground for the contention that the exigencies of

[1] (1874) L.R. 9 Q.B. 210.

[2] *Ib.* 215. See also per Archibald, J., p. 219: "I think *the evidence* [italics mine] fails to bring the case within the decision of *Bird* v. *Boulter*...".

[3] [1897] 1 Ch. 663, 670.

the case require that the auctioneer should be held entitled to delegate his authority to his clerk. The practice contemplates that one part of the memorandum should be signed by the auctioneer; and if this be consistent with the requirements of business, why should not the signature of the other by him be also?...I come, therefore, to the conclusion that the memorandum filled in by the clerk does not satisfy the requirements of the Statute of Frauds."[1]

(4) *Authority derived from subsequent ratification.* Subsequent ratification possesses as much efficacy in cases under the Statute as in other cases.

"Now, in all other cases", said Best, C.J., in *Maclean* v. *Dunn*,[2] "a subsequent sanction is considered the same thing in effect as assent at the time. *Omnis ratihabitio retrotrahitur et mandato aequiparatur*: and in my opinion, the subsequent sanction of a contract signed by an agent, takes it out of the operation of the statute more satisfactorily than an authority given beforehand."[3]

III. *Form in which agent must sign.* All that the Statute requires is a *signature*, and the agent may therefore sign either his own name[4] or that of his principal;[5] or he may expressly sign by procuration. But although the form in which the agent signs is immaterial once the fact of agency is established, it may sometimes be a material element in the proof of the agency. For example, if the alleged agent signs the principal's name in the principal's presence and without objection being taken, that circumstance would afford cogent evidence of authorization; whereas the agent's signing his own name would have no such effect.[6]

[1] See also *Sims* v. *Landray*, [1894] 2 Ch. 318.

[2] (1828) 4 Bing. 722, 727; 130 E.R. 947, 949.

[3] See also *Bigg* v. *Strong*, (1857) 3 Sm. & Giff. 592; 65 E.R. 793.

[4] Brokers generally sign their own names on bought and sold notes. See *Sievewright* v. *Archibald*, (1851) 17 Q.B. 103; 117 E.R. 1221. See also *Daniels* v. *Trefusis*, [1914] 1 Ch. 788, where a client was held to be bound by the signature of the firm name of his solicitors.

[5] See *Graham* v. *Musson*, (1839) 5 Bing. (N.C.) 603; 132 E.R. 1232: "...it is clear that a contract may be signed by an agent, on behalf of his principal, and that his signature would satisfy the Statute of Frauds..." (per Tindal, C.J., at p. 607; E.R. 1234).

[6] See per Bramwell, B., in *Mews* v. *Carr*, (1856) 1 H. & N. 484, 488; 156 E.R. 1292, 1293.

(B) *Agency where there is no signature properly so-called*

Where the writing produced bears no regular signature but merely the defendant's name in the text, and that name has been written in the document by some third person, the question arises as to whether the authenticated signature fiction[1] can apply to avert the results of non-compliance with the Statute. The question would seem to cover two classes of cases:

(1) cases where the suggested acts of recognition have been supplied by a third person;

(2) cases where such acts have been supplied by the defendant.

(1) *Acts of recognition supplied by the agent.* It is submitted that the fiction will apply in such cases, provided that the agent is sufficiently authorized. As to the nature of the authority, it is suggested that it would suffice that the agent be authorized either to do the particular acts relied upon as shewing recognition; or else to *sign* on the defendant's behalf, inasmuch as an "authenticated signature" in the eye of the law is no different from a regular signature, which would, of course, be justified by such an authority.

The agent may receive his authority by any of the usual methods; expressly, as in the case of an auctioneer who merely fills the vendor's name into the body of the conditions and particulars of sale, but does not otherwise sign on his behalf; impliedly from the circumstances of the case, as in *Sims* v. *Landray*[2] (referred to below); by presumption of law, as in the case of the auctioneer who writes the purchaser's name into the blanks in a memorandum endorsed on conditions of sale; or by subsequent ratification.

The case of *Sims* v. *Landray*[2] supports the general proposition that the fiction applies in these cases, and it also affords a good example of authority implied from particular circumstances. At an auction sale of land, one of the lots was knocked down to Landray; thereupon the auctioneer's clerk inquired of him his name and address, and wrote these into a memorandum of the

[1] See p. 82 *supra*.

[2] [1894] 2 Ch. 318.

sale endorsed on the particulars and conditions, Landray coming up to the table and standing by while the clerk completed the writing. When asked to sign the memorandum, however, he made some excuse, and subsequently refused to complete the purchase. In these circumstances, Romer, J., held that the clerk was impliedly authorized by the defendant to sign on his behalf; and that the name written into the memorandum was a sufficient signature. "It is clear here", said the learned Judge,[1] "that the auctioneer's clerk had authority from this purchaser to make such a memorandum as was made. The defendant stood by when this memorandum was made by the clerk, and clearly authorized the making of it."

(2) *Acts of recognition supplied by the principal.* Cases in which the acts of recognition are supplied by the principal are not, it is submitted, genuine cases of agency at all, although that term is sometimes used in reference to them, and the acts of recognition are sometimes miscalled "ratification".

The conduct of the defendant may shew that his attention and approval were applied primarily to the acts of the third party and only indirectly and through such acts to the writing. In these circumstances the case would be one of genuine agency, of the class discussed in the last section.[2] *Sims* v. *Landray*,[3] there referred to, affords an excellent illustration.

On the other hand, it may appear that the defendant directed his attention and approval exclusively to the writing, and was quite indifferent as to how his name came to appear therein, or to the person who prepared the writing or wrote his name into it. Such must be the position where a printed name at the top of a bill-head is accepted as a sufficient signature.

"A case was referred to in argument", said Cave, J., in *Evans* v. *Hoare*,[4] "*Schneider* v. *Norris*,[5] in which a printed bill-head was held to amount to a signature within the meaning of the statute....The printed heading there was not put into the document for the purpose of constituting a memorandum of the contract; but it was so used with the assent of the party sought

[1] *Ib.* 320.
[2] P. 118 *supra*.
[3] [1894] 2 Ch. 318.
[4] [1892] 1 Q.B. 593, 598.
[5] 2 M. & S. 286.

to be charged and it therefore was held to have the effect of a signature. This shews that it is unimportant how the name came to be inserted in the document."

Whether the defendant's name appears in the writing by the instrumentality of a printer who is unknown to the defendant, or of a clerk who is present at the time, seems to be quite immaterial if the defendant himself pays no regard to that circumstance, but attends exclusively to the writing. In such a case what is important is that the defendant shall shew that he recognizes the writing as an authentic expression of his contract.

The foregoing contentions are illustrated and supported by the cases of *Durrell* v. *Evans*[1] and *Murphy* v. *Boese*.[2] In *Durrell* v. *Evans* the facts were as follows. The defendant and the plaintiff had been negotiating for the sale by the plaintiff to the defendant of certain hops; after some discussion the defendant went with the plaintiff to the office of the plaintiff's factor, one Noakes, where a contract was ultimately arranged, and in the presence of plaintiff and defendant written out by Noakes. The defendant saw the writing and requested Noakes to alter its date so as to allow further time for payment; and the plaintiff consenting, Noakes altered the writing accordingly. The writing so prepared contained the defendant's name as one of the parties but was not otherwise signed by him. The matter came before the Court of Exchequer Chamber on appeal from a judgment of the Court of Exchequer setting aside a verdict for the plaintiff and directing that a nonsuit should be entered. The Court of Exchequer had held that there was no evidence that Noakes had been authorized by the defendant to sign the writing on the defendant's behalf; but the Exchequer Chamber, after hearing the arguments of both sides, unanimously reversed this decision. The actual grounds upon which the Exchequer Chamber proceeded appear to have been that the defendant, by asking that the writing should be altered, shewed that he recognized the writing thus altered to be a correct exposition of his contract. The matter is somewhat complicated, however, by references in

[1] (1862) 1 H. & C. 174; 158 E.R. 848.
[2] (1875) L.R. 10 Ex. 126.

the judgments to questions of agency and authorization. Thus Crompton, J., after stating the facts, said:[1]

"These facts shew that the defendant J. Evans really intended that a binding record of the contract between the defendants and the plaintiff should be made by Noakes; and if so, Noakes was the agent of both parties for the purpose of making it".

But later on in his judgment, Crompton, J., compared *Durrell* v. *Evans* with *Johnson* v. *Dodgson*,[2] which was clearly a case of "authenticated signature".

"In *Johnson* v. *Dodgson*", he remarked,[3] "Lord Abinger said: 'But when it is ascertained that he meant to be bound by it as a complete contract, the statute is satisfied, there being a note in writing shewing the terms of the contract, and recognized by him'. That expressly applies to the present case. If the parties meant the writing to be a memorandum of their contract, it is binding on them. Here is a document on which the name 'Messrs Evans and Co.' is written by a factor who was appointed to make a binding contract between the parties, and he makes a memorandum containing the names of the buyer and seller, and the terms of the contract. It is true that the words 'Messrs Evans' were not written by the defendant J. Evans, but he saw the document with 'Messrs Evans' on it, and he requested that an alteration might be made, and thereby recognized it as a record of the contract."

Blackburn, J., also likened the case to *Johnson* v. *Dodgson*. After referring to the defendant's request to Noakes to alter the writing, he continued:[4]

"That is evidence for the jury that Noakes was requested to alter this writing, not merely as the seller's account, but as a record of the contract binding on both parties. The document so altered was given to the defendants and kept by them. Therefore, the name of the defendants being written by an authorized agent on a document intended by them to be a memorandum of contract, the case is identical with that of *Johnson* v. *Dodgson*, except that there the buyer wrote the terms of the contract and his name with his own hand; here Noakes wrote the buyer's

[1] (1862) 1 H. & C. 174, 186; 158 E.R. 848, 853.
[2] (1837) 2 M. & W. 653; 150 E.R. 918.
[3] (1862) 1 H. & C. 174, 187; 158 E.R. 853.
[4] *Ib.* 192; E.R. 855.

name....There is the decision of two eminent Judges that, where a document contains the name of the party to be charged, and he intended it to be a binding memorandum of the contract, that is sufficient".

These *dicta* appear to shew that the judges of the Exchequer Chamber felt considerable difficulty in putting the case on the basis of principal and agent; and certainly Crompton, Byles, Blackburn and Willes, JJ., all seem ultimately to rest their judgments on recognition by the defendant of the *writing*.

Durrell v. *Evans* (mentioned in the preceding paragraph) was discussed in the case of *Murphy* v. *Boese*,[1] decided by the Court of Exchequer in 1875. The facts of *Murphy* v. *Boese* were much the same as those in *Durrell* v. *Evans*, except that there was nothing corresponding to the act of the defendant in *Durrell* v. *Evans* in requesting Noakes to alter the writing. On this ground the Court of Exchequer distinguished the earlier case, and held that the action failed for want of a signature to the writing. Pollock, B., referred to *Durrell* v. *Evans* in the following terms:[2]

"I think *Durrell* v. *Evans* can only be supported if it decides that the agency did not commence till after the memorandum was written out, and that will distinguish it from the facts before us. It might be said that the direction given by the defendant to Noakes the factor to alter the instrument, was an adoption of his act in preparing it, or a recognition *ab initio* of the whole document as containing the contract. Or one might go further and say that, from the nature of the transaction, and the meeting of the parties at the office, it might be thought that there was evidence that it was meant that Noakes should act as the scribe of both parties in drawing up a note of the contract. But here there is an entire absence of any act of recognition by the defendant of the traveller as his agent".

If Pollock, B.'s suggestion that *Durrell* v. *Evans* was a case of ratification were to be adopted, however, it would be necessary to shew that at the time Noakes drew up the writing he professed to be acting for the defendant.[3] As Bramwell, B., remarked in

[1] (1875) L.R. 10 Ex. 126. [2] *Ib.* 131.

[3] "The only person who has power effectively to ratify an act is the person in whose name or on whose behalf the act was professedly done...." Bowstead, *Law of Agency*, 8th ed. p. 49.

reference to a similar contention which had been advanced in *Murphy* v. *Boese*,[1] "Did he become agent afterwards by ratification? If so, you would come to this difficulty, that when the agent wrote the paper he did not profess to act for the defendant". And if the suggestion of ratification be rejected, that leaves only two other possible explanations: either Noakes was the common scribe; or the defendant recognized the writing as adequately expounding the contract. Of these two, it is suggested that the latter is more in accordance with the facts of the case and the language of the judges. The decision in *Durrell* v. *Evans*, it is submitted, was merely an example of the application of the authenticated signature fiction in a case where the defendant had himself supplied the acts of recognition.

(C) *The authority of a solicitor to sign writings on his client's behalf*

It is clear that there is no presumption of authority in a solicitor to sign writings binding a client under the Statute. A party seeking to rely on a writing signed by the other party's solicitor must prove that the solicitor was actually authorized to sign the writing.

"It was necessary", said Bankes, L.J., in *Thirkell* v. *Cambi*,[2] "for him [the appellant, plaintiff in the court below] to show that Mr Carr [the respondent's solicitor], in signing the alleged memorandum, was the respondent's agent in that behalf; that he was authorized to make an admission sufficient to bind the respondent to the contract set up by the appellant....In the present case there is no evidence of any actual authority given to Mr Carr."

It is sufficient, however, that it should be proved that the solicitor was authorized to sign a writing correctly expounding

[1] (1875) L.R. 10 Ex. at p. 129.

[2] [1919] 2 K.B. 590, 595. So also Eve, J., at p. 599: "This being an action founded upon a memorandum signed by an agent, the plaintiff cannot succeed unless he has affirmatively proved that the agent was authorized to sign a memorandum of the particular contract on which the plaintiff claims".

the contract: his authority need not go beyond this, nor need it have any reference to the Statute.[1]

Where the solicitor has merely been instructed to prepare a formal document, the execution of which the parties have agreed shall be a condition precedent to the conclusion of a contract, he has no authority to sign a writing binding his client under the Statute, inasmuch as until the formal document has been duly signed, there is no contract in existence of which a writing could be evidence. This would seem to be the effect of the decision and judgments of the Court of Appeal in *Smith* v. *Webster*.[2]

The facts of that case were, briefly, as follows. The plaintiff and the defendant entered into a verbal agreement for the sale and purchase of an inn at the price of £950. Shortly afterwards the defendant called on his solicitors, told them he had entered into a verbal arrangement for the sale of his inn, and instructed them to prepare an agreement. They accordingly prepared a draft agreement and sent it to the plaintiff's solicitor under cover of a letter in the following terms: "Dear Sir,—Mr W. Webster, of the Golden Lion, Worksop, has been with us to-day, and stated that he had arranged with your client, Mr Allen, for the sale to the latter of the Golden Lion for £950. We therefore send herewith draft contract for your perusal and approval". Malins, V.-C., who tried the case in the first instance, took the view that the verbal agreement or arrangement amounted to a concluded contract; and held that the solicitors' letter and its enclosure constituted a sufficient writing under the Statute. The Court of Appeal differed from the Vice-Chancellor on this point and reversed his decision accordingly.

"From the evidence in this case other than that furnished by the letter of the 4th of December 1873", said Baggallay, J.A.,[3] "it appears to me that the arrangement or agreement come to by Mr Webster on the 3rd of December was to sell the Golden Lion for £950, but that that arrangement or agreement was conditional upon a formal contract being signed. It appears to me also clear that the authority which was conferred upon the

[1] *Daniels* v. *Trefusis*, [1914] 1 Ch. 788. See p. 103 *supra*.
[2] (1876) 3 Ch.D. 49.
[3] *Ib*. 57. See also judgment of James, L.J., *ib*.

solicitor by Mr Webster was not to convert that conditional agreement into an absolute agreement, but to prepare, and to procure to be executed, a proper contract which would express the terms of the agreement."

In contrast with *Smith* v. *Webster* is the recent case of *North* v. *Loomes*,[1] the result of which may, it is submitted, be stated as follows. Where a solicitor has been given instructions *to complete* a contract, which has actually been concluded between the parties, such instructions sufficiently authorize him to sign a writing binding his client under the Statute. The facts of *North* v. *Loomes* may be shortly stated. The defendant having verbally agreed to purchase certain premises of the plaintiff, paid the plaintiff a deposit of £50 on account of the price, receiving therefor the following receipt:

"Received of Mr Joseph Goddard Loomes the sum of Fifty pounds deposit on the purchase price Five Hundred and Ninety pounds (£590) for the house and premises and land in the occupation of Mr R. Keene, situate in the High Street, Chinnor, and known as Holmleigh. The balance of the purchase to be paid on or before March 25, 1918.

Purchase price	£590	Frederick J. North
Deposit	50	January 31, 1918".
Balance	£540	

The defendant sent this receipt to his solicitor, with instructions to carry out the agreement; and upon the plaintiff's solicitor submitting a draft contract for perusal and approval, the defendant's solicitor replied by a letter enclosing a copy of the receipt and stating that he considered it a sufficient contract. The question for decision was whether the solicitor's signature to that letter bound the defendant, and Younger, J., held that it did.

"Mr Taylor's instructions from the defendant", he said,[2] "were to complete, not to negotiate, a contract. It was an essential implication that he should, if and when necessary, affirm on behalf of his client the existence and validity, on his side, of the contract he was so instructed to carry out. His authority to write

[1] [1919] 1 Ch. 378. [2] *Ib.* 383.

the letter of February 8 was, therefore, in my opinion, complete and this defence of the Statute fails."

It is apparent from the foregoing authorities that the state of the bargain when the solicitors are instructed is a matter of great importance; and it is sometimes, as *Smith* v. *Webster*[1] shews, a very difficult matter to determine whether the parties have got beyond negotiation, or whether they mean everything to wait upon the preparation and signing of a formal agreement. The considerations affecting this question have been much discussed by the courts, and reference is made to the more important cases in another part of this treatise.[2]

[1] (1876) 3 Ch.D. 49.

[2] P. 43 *supra*.

CHAPTER VII

SEVERAL DOCUMENTS

THERE is no necessity for a writing under the Statute to be on one sheet or connected sheets of paper; it may be, and indeed frequently is, composed of several separate documents. This principle seems first to have been laid down in the case of *Tawney* v. *Crowther*;[1] and since then many cases involving its application have come before the courts. The general tendency exhibited by the more recent decisions has been to relax the restrictions which formerly surrounded the rule, the courts endeavouring here, as in cases involving other aspects of the Statute, to prevent, as far as possible, the defeat of justice by merely technical considerations.

The Statute primarily requires (1) that the whole contract shall be evidenced by writing, and (2) that the writing shall be signed. If the terms of the contract are contained partly in one document and partly in another or others, the question arises as to whether these documents can be connected together to make between them a writing which will satisfy the Statute. To do this parol evidence must be introduced, and it therefore becomes necessary to consider to what extent such evidence may be admitted consistently with the rule that the contract must be wholly proved by writing. Does admitting such evidence amount to allowing the contract to be proved partly by parol?

Again, of the several documents tendered to make up the writing, some may be unsigned. In that case, even if these several documents can be connected together so as *prima facie* to constitute a writing, will it be possible to extend the application of the signature on the signed document or documents to the document or documents which are unsigned?

These are the questions which the courts have had to consider in this matter; the answers have varied somewhat at different times; and even to-day the position is in certain respects obscure.

[1] (1791) 3 Bro. C.C. 318; 29 E.R. 557.

Cases involving several documents fall into two broad classes:

(1) Those where one or more of the documents is signed, the other or others being unsigned.

(2) Those where all the documents are signed.

In cases of the first class, not only is it necessary to connect the several documents together: but in addition, the authenticating influence of the signature in the signed document or documents must in some manner be extended to the unsigned document or documents. In cases of the second class it is only necessary to connect the several documents together. Therefore, while it is clear that any means which would suffice to connect together documents in cases of the first class would be equally efficacious in cases of the second class, it does not follow that the converse proposition would be true. Methods of shewing the connection between documents might be devised which would be useless to discharge the additional task of applying a signature from one document to another. It therefore seems better to consider these two classes of cases separately; and first of all cases where one (or more) of the several documents is unsigned.

I. *Cases where one or more of several documents is signed, the other or others being unsigned.* The principles which determine the conditions upon which several documents, some being unsigned, will constitute a writing sufficient to satisfy the Statute, may ultimately be traced back to the case, already cited, of *Tawney* v. *Crowther*.[1] In that case the defendant had written and signed a letter which referred to an unsigned paper in his possession, and Lord Thurlow, L.C., thus stated the rule which he considered to be applicable in these circumstances:

> "If the letter contains the terms of the agreement, or if it refers to another paper which contains the terms, that is sufficient; for I am of opinion, that if a letter refers so clearly to an agreement, as to shew what was meant by the parties, where the existence of the paper is proved by parol, that will take the case out of the statute".

Where, therefore, the signed document *clearly referred* to the unsigned document, Lord Thurlow considered that parol

[1] (1791) 3 Bro. C.C. 318; 29 E.R. 557.

evidence might be admitted to connect the two by identifying the document to which such reference was made. The principle of a clear reference has become the corner-stone of the law on this matter; and in subsequent cases the attention of the courts has chiefly been directed to working out and elaborating the precise nature and effect of this principle.

The clear reference from the signed document to the unsigned document served two purposes. First, it enabled parol evidence shewing the connection between the documents to be admitted without infringing the rule that the contract should be proved wholly by writing. Such evidence did not prove the contract but merely explained and expounded to the court what was already written.[1] Secondly, it enabled the authenticating influence of the signature in the signed document to be extended to the unsigned document. If a party signs a document which refers, without disapproval or objection, to another document, it seems reasonable to take this signature as evidence that he recognizes the correctness and authenticity of the document so referred to.[2]

[1] Generally as to the admission of parol evidence in reference to writings under the Statute, see p. 59 *supra*, and Part III, chapter i (p. 147), *infra*.

See also Wigram, *Extrinsic Evidence*, 5th ed. p. 8. The learned author's remarks, although made with reference to wills under s. 5 of the Statute of Frauds, would seem to apply *mutatis mutandis* to writings under s. 4. "Courts of law", wrote Wigram, "though precluded from ascribing to a testator any intention not expressed in his will, admit their obligation to give effect to every intention which the will *properly expounded* contains...any evidence is admissible, which, in its nature and effect, simply explains what the testator has written." Certain remarks of the Rt. Hon. T. Pemberton Leigh (afterwards Lord Kingsdown) in delivering the judgment of the Privy Council in *Allen* v. *Maddock*, (1858) 11 Moo. P.C. 427, 441; 14 E.R. 757, 762, may also be quoted. "It may be said", he remarked, "that, on the present occasion, the Court of Probate is, to a certain extent, a Court of construction; for it has to determine what is the meaning of the reference made by the Testatrix in her Codicil, to her last Will and Testament...and whether any, and, if any, what, instrument found at her death is thereby referred to. The question is one of fact which obviously must be explained, and can only be explained by parol evidence."

[2] *Jackson* v. *Lowe*, (1822) 1 Bing. 9; 130 E.R. 4. Here all the terms of the contract were contained in a document not signed by the defendant. The only reason for proving a letter signed by the defendant and referring to this document, therefore, was to extend to such document the authenticating effect of the signature on the letter.

For many years the courts, especially the common law courts, applied this principle of a clear reference in a very strict and narrow manner, holding that nothing less than a direct and express reference from the signed to the unsigned document would suffice.[1] In *Dobell* v. *Hutchinson*,[2] which came before the Court of King's Bench (Lord Denman, C.J., Littledale, Patteson and Williams, JJ.) in 1835, Lord Denman, C.J., summed up the result of the earlier cases in these words:

"The cases on this subject are not at first sight uniform; but, on examination, it will be found that they establish this principle, that, where a contract in writing or note exists which binds one party, any subsequent note in writing, signed by the other, is sufficient to bind him, provided it either contains in itself the terms of the contract, or refers to any writing which contains them. Here the letters of the defendants refer expressly and distinctly to the conditions of sale, and they had in their hands, or in the hands of their auctioneers, at that very time, the conditions of sale signed by the plaintiff, to which reference is made, so that no parol evidence of any kind was requisite to shew a contract binding both parties, except evidence of the handwriting of each, which must be adduced in all cases".

The very narrow attitude adopted by the courts at the time when *Dobell* v. *Hutchinson* was decided, is illustrated by the case of *Smith* v. *Dixon*.[3] In that case there were two letters, each signed by the defendant, so that it might have been expected that the court would have been guided by a somewhat broader rule than that which applied when some of the documents were unsigned; but the court (the Queen's Bench, composed of the same judges as decided *Dobell* v. *Hutchinson*) laid it down that "two distinct written instruments cannot be coupled together

[1] Thus, in *Boydell* v. *Drummond*, (1809) 11 East 142, 151; 103 E.R. 958, 964, Lord Ellenborough, C.J., remarked: "I should add, that I cannot connect the subscription of the plaintiff's name in the book with the prospectus: nor does the defendant's letter refer to the prospectus produced at the trial. It speaks indeed of his engagement with the proprietors of the Boydell Shakespeare; but it cannot be shewn to be the engagement contained in the particular prospectus without parol evidence, which the Statute excludes. If there had been a plain reference to the particular prospectus, that might have helped the plaintiff; but there is nothing of that kind".

[2] (1835) 3 Ad. & E. 355, 371; 111 E.R. 448, 454.

[3] (1839) 3 Jur. 770.

so as to constitute a sufficient memorandum of a contract under the Statute of Frauds, unless, on the face of them, they appear to be necessarily connected with each other".[1]

After *Dobell* v. *Hutchinson* and *Smith* v. *Dixon*, however, the cases disclose a tendency on the part of the courts to relax the severity with which the principle of a clear reference had formerly been applied; and there can be discerned in the reports an ever increasing willingness to connect together documents of which it certainly could not have been said that "on the face of them they appeared to be necessarily connected with each other". Even before *Dobell* v. *Hutchinson*, indications of a possible wider view of the rule were not altogether absent from the reports, and in this connection particular reference may be made to the equity case of *Western* v. *Russell*[2] which came before Grant, M.R., in 1814.

The facts in *Western* v. *Russell* were as follows. The defendant wrote to the plaintiff a note which commenced: "Mr Russell presents his compliments to Mr Western", and then proceeded to set forth an offer to sell certain lands. The plaintiff having written to the defendant accepting this offer, the defendant replied as follows:

"July 11. Dear Sir, I have just received yours; and am glad you have determined to purchase the Watering Farm, as I think it will be an Accommodation to you. I fear you will find but little Timber on the Estate; whatever there may be is at your Service included in the Purchase Money. I have written to Mr Boulton; who will confer with Mr Arnold respecting the Title; and I will write to Mr Harvey to inform him you have agreed to purchase the Estate. I remain, &c. William Russell".

The case was argued on the basis that the defendant's note was unsigned; and the question to be decided, therefore, was whether the defendant's letter sufficiently referred to his note to enable the two to be read together. The Master of the Rolls held that a sufficient reference could be implied.

"I think", he said,[3] "his letter plainly implies, that he had

[1] Quoted from the headnote, which seems accurately to set forth the result of the judgments.

[2] (1814) 3 V. & B. 187; 35 E.R. 450.

[3] 3 V. & B. at p. 191; 35 E.R. at p. 451.

offered to sell upon some Terms, in which he understood the Plaintiff to have acquiesced; for it is evidently not an Assent to any Terms then first proposed to him. It begins, thus: 'I am glad, you have determined to purchase the Watering Farm'; and concludes, 'I will write to Mr Harvey to inform him you have agreed to purchase the Estate'. Determination and Agreement upon the Part of the Plaintiff to purchase do seem necessarily to presuppose some Proposal to sell; for it would be absurd to speak of an original Proposal from the Plaintiff as a Determination and Agreement, bringing the business to such a Close, as that it only remained to the Solicitors to confer upon the Title. This Letter therefore clearly implies an antecedent Proposal, to which it is an Assent. As to the Nature of the Proposal there is no Controversy. It is in Russell's Hand Writing; and, coupling that with the Letter, they amount to an agreement, signed by the Party to be charged within the 4th Section of the Statute of Frauds."

Both the decision in *Western* v. *Russell* and the reasoning by which it is supported seem strangely to anticipate such comparatively modern cases as *Long* v. *Millar*[1] and *Wylson* v. *Dunn*.[2] The similarity between the language of Grant, M.R., and that of Kekewich, J., in the latter case is very marked indeed. But *Western* v. *Russell* was before its time: it was not until after *Dobell* v. *Hutchinson*[3] and *Smith* v. *Dixon*[4] that the cases began consistently to display a tendency towards a less severe application of the rule.

This tendency was clearly displayed in the equity case of *Morgan* v. *Holford*[5] where Stuart, V.-C., decided that two documents could be connected together although the reference from one to the other was not express but had to be inferred. The vendor in *Morgan* v. *Holford* had sent to his solicitors a note setting out the terms of the contract entered into by him with the purchaser (the party to be charged), and instructing them to draw a formal agreement; at the same time he sent a copy of the note to the purchaser. Some days later the purchaser wrote to the solicitors complaining of their delay in sending him "the

[1] (1879) 4 C.P.D. 450.
[2] (1887) 34 Ch.D. 569.
[3] (1835) 3 Ad. & E. 335; 111 E.R. 448.
[4] (1839) 3 Jur. 770.
[5] (1852) 1 Sm. & Giff. 101, 111; 65 E.R. 45, 51.

agreement to be entered into with Mr Crespigny relative to the purchase I have concluded with him for his estate in this county". Referring to this letter the Vice-Chancellor said:

"In the present case, as it is my opinion that the letter of the 29th of November must be considered, on a fair view of the evidence, as referring to the agreement and transaction stated in the letter of the 11th of October [the note sent by the vendor to his solicitors] and therefore to the memorandum [the copy sent to the purchaser] referred to in that letter, and cannot be held as referring to anything else, the difficulty which might otherwise have occurred does not arise...".

Shortly after *Morgan* v. *Holford* came another equity case, which finally went to the House of Lords, viz. *Ridgway* v. *Wharton.*[1] In that case the signed document referred to "instructions", which might have been either written or verbal instructions. The House of Lords decided that parol evidence was admissible to shew that the "instructions" were written and to identify the writing containing them. It was thus finally settled that whatever the nature of the reference necessary to enable an unsigned document to be connected with a signed document, at least it was not required to be an express reference shewing on the face of it that it was to a writing.

Ridgway v. *Wharton* was applied in *Baumann* v. *James.*[2] The only matter calling for mention in this case is Page Wood, L.J.'s statement of the decision in *Ridgway* v. *Wharton.*

"In that case", he said, "'instructions' were referred to. Now, instructions might be either by parol or in writing; but it was held that it might be shewn by parol evidence that instructions had been given in writing, and *that there had been no other instructions than the written document which was produced.*"[3]

It is submitted that *Ridgway* v. *Wharton* contains no warrant for these last (italicized) words. All that it decided was "that parol evidence might be given to identify the instructions referred to with certain instructions in writing".[4]

[1] (1857) 6 H.L.C. 238; 10 E.R. 1287.
[2] (1868) L.R. 3 Ch. 508, 511.
[3] The italics are mine.
[4] Per Field, J., in *Cave* v. *Hastings*, (1881) 7 Q.B.D. 125, 128.

Ridgway v. *Wharton* and *Baumann* v. *James* were relied on by the Court of Appeal in deciding *Long* v. *Millar*,[1] the case which is the foundation of the modern law on the subject. In *Long* v. *Millar* the plaintiff had signed an agreement for the purchase from the defendant of a piece of land. The only document signed by the defendant was a receipt for a deposit on account of the purchase-price, in these words:

"21st September, 1877.
Received of Mr George Long the sum of thirty-one pounds as a deposit on the purchase of three plots of land at Hammersmith.
£31. 0*s*. 0*d*. Chas. W. Millar".

The Court of Appeal held that this receipt sufficiently referred to the agreement signed by the plaintiff to enable parol evidence to be given to connect the two, and thereby constitute a sufficient writing to satisfy the Statute. Bramwell, L.J., put the case on this footing:[2]

"The receipt uses also the word 'purchase', which must mean an agreement to purchase, and it becomes apparent that the agreement alluded to is the agreement signed by the plaintiff, so soon as the two documents are placed side by side. The agreement referred to may be identified by parol evidence". "The true principle", said Baggallay, L.J.,[3] "is that there must exist a writing to which the document signed by the party to be charged can refer, but that this writing may be identified by verbal evidence. I think that in the present case by the words 'purchase of three plots of land' the receipt sufficiently refers to the document signed by the plaintiff."

Thesiger, L.J., based his judgment upon similar grounds:[4]

"...the receipt contains the word 'purchase', which must refer to the purchase of the plots of land mentioned in the document signed by the plaintiff; if we read the two instruments together, we shall not be unduly straining the law by holding that the two, taken together, form a complete contract; our decision will not go beyond the decision in *Allen* v. *Bennet*[5] and in *Baumann* v. *James*[6]".

[1] (1879) 4 C.P.D. 450.
[2] *Ib*. 454.
[3] *Ib*. 455.
[4] *Ib*. 456.
[5] 3 Taunt. 167.
[6] L.R. 3 Ch. 508.

Long v. *Millar* was a Common Pleas case, and it may be regarded as the triumph in the courts of Common Law of the liberal attitude shewn by the Equity Courts in dealing with this question of a reference. The decision of Grant, M.R., in *Western* v. *Russell*[1] has been commented on above;[2] and *Morgan* v. *Holford*,[3] *Ridgway* v. *Wharton*[4] and *Baumann* v. *James*[5] were all equity cases. On the other hand, the Common Law judges, until *Long* v. *Millar*,[6] appeared always to hold to the opinion that nothing short of an express reference to a specific document would suffice.

Perhaps the last case in which the older Common Law view was stated to be the law was *Peirce* v. *Corf*,[7] decided in the Queen's Bench only five years before *Long* v. *Millar* came before the Court of Appeal. In that case there were two documents, an auctioneer's sales ledger, and a printed catalogue of the objects to be sold with conditions of the sale annexed. The actual decision proceeded upon the ground that neither document was signed; but the case contains certain *obiter dicta* on the principles which regulate the use of several documents to form one writing under the Statute.

> "I think", said Quain, J., "they [the catalogue and the sales ledger] do not constitute a contract within the Statute of Frauds, because I cannot see on the face of them anything to connect the one with the other, so as to enable me to read them together. I take the principle to be well laid down in *Dobell* v. *Hutchinson*.[8]...Therefore on the document itself there must be some reference from the one to the other, leaving nothing to be supplied by parol evidence except the identity, as it were, of the document."

Neither *Ridgway* v. *Wharton*[4] nor *Baumann* v. *James*[5] was cited in *Peirce* v. *Corf*. The only case on this point to which Blackburn, J., referred was *Hinde* v. *Whitehouse*,[9] while Quain, J.,

[1] (1814) 3 V. & B. 187; 35 E.R. 450.
[2] P. 131 *supra*.
[3] (1852) 1 Sm. & Giff. 101; 65 E.R. 45.
[4] (1857) 6 H.L.C. 238; 10 E.R. 1287.
[5] (1868) L.R. 3 Ch. 508.
[6] (1879) 4 C.P.D. 450.
[7] (1874) L.R. 9 Q.B. 210, 217.
[8] 3 Ad. & E. at p. 371.
[9] (1806) 7 East 558; 103 E.R. 216.

was content to rely on *Dobell* v. *Hutchinson*.[1] It is submitted that even in 1874 the *dictum* quoted from the judgment of Quain, J., was doubtful law, and that since *Long* v. *Millar*[2] it must certainly be taken as erroneous.

Long v. *Millar*,[2] and the two earlier cases upon which it was based, *Ridgway* v. *Wharton*[3] and *Baumann* v. *James*,[4] shew:

(1) that a reference from the signed to the unsigned document continues to be necessary;

(2) that this reference need not shew on its face that it is to any particular document or even that it is to a document at all; and

(3) that this reference need not be express but may be a matter of inference.

(1) *Reference still necessary*. *Long* v. *Millar*[2] has merely had a broadening effect: although the reference need not be of the direct and precise type which earlier cases shew was once thought essential, nevertheless there must still be some sort of a reference. Otherwise it would be impossible to hold that the authenticating effect of the signature was carried from the signed to the unsigned document. In 1892 the Court of Appeal in *Taylor* v. *Smith*[5] expressly decided that two documents, containing between them all the terms of a contract, were yet insufficient to constitute a writing, inasmuch as the signed document contained no sort of reference to the unsigned document. Kay, L.J., referring to this aspect of the case, said:

"The courts have gone very far in construing referential words so as to connect several documents, and collect the terms of a contract out of them. Here we have an invoice which contains the terms of the contract, but it is not signed by the defendant. There is a carrier's advice note on which is indorsed a memorandum signed by the defendant but neither the advice note nor the indorsement mentions the price, nor refers to the invoice or to any other document. The number of deals mentioned in the advice note corresponds with the number in the invoice, but there are no referential words, nothing on the face of the note to connect it with the invoice".

[1] (1835) 3 Ad. & E. 355; 111 E.R. 448.
[2] (1879) 4 C.P.D. 450.
[3] (1857) 6 H.L.C. 238; 10 E.R. 1287.
[4] (1868) L.R. 3 Ch. 508.
[5] [1893] 2 Q.B. 65, 73.

(2) *The reference need not appear on its face to be to any particular document, or to any document at all.*[1]

(3) *The reference need not be express but may be a matter of inference.* It is the determination of the scope of this rule that presents the chief difficulty in this branch of the law. As *Long* v. *Millar*[2] shews, the courts nowadays allow themselves considerable latitude in deciding whether in the particular case there is any sufficient inference. It is suggested (though with much hesitation) that the principle of the more modern cases may be stated as follows:

If in the signed document there are words, clauses, or provisions which require to be explained before they can be properly comprehended by the court, and such explanation necessarily involves a reference to some unsigned document, then, provided that the signatory knew of the existence and contents of the unsigned document at the time when he signed the signed document, this unsigned document will be considered to be sufficiently connected with the signed document to enable the two to be read together to form one writing.

This statement of the rule receives considerable support from the judgment of Kekewich, J., in *Oliver* v. *Hunting*.[3] After referring to the older rule exemplified by such cases as *Hinde* v. *Whitehouse*[4] and *Boydell* v. *Drummond*[5] Kekewich, J., proceeded to examine the modern cases, and then stated their effect to be as follows:

"...substantially it [parol evidence] never stops short of this, that wherever parol evidence is required to connect two written documents together, then that parol evidence is admissible. You are entitled to rely upon a written document, which requires explanation. Perhaps the real principle upon which that is based is, that you are always entitled in regarding the construction and meaning of a written document to inquire into the circumstances under which it was written, not in order to find an interpretation by the writer of the language, but to ascertain from the

[1] *Ridgway* v. *Wharton*, (1857) 6 H.L.C. 238; 10 E.R. 1287. See p. 133 *supra*.

[2] (1879) 4 C.P.D. 451.

[3] (1890) 44 Ch.D. 205, 209.

[4] (1806) 7 East 558; 103 E.R. 216.

[5] (1809) 11 East 142; 103 E.R. 958.

surrounding facts and circumstances with reference to what, and with what intent, it must have been written. I think myself that must be the principle on which parol evidence of this kind must be admitted. Turning to the case before me, I find a letter of the 12th of September, 1888, written by the Defendant to Mrs Oliver; and in that he says: 'I beg to acknowledge receipt of cheque, value £375, on account of the purchase-money for the Fletton Manor House estate, for which I thank you'. I have two things here perfectly clear, that there is a property called Fletton Manor House estate, which constitutes the subject of a purchase, and, therefore, the subject of a sale. I have also that £375 is part of the purchase-money for that house; but, beyond that, I have no terms of a contract. I am entitled to consider the circumstances under which the letter was written, in order to give any meaning that I properly can to it—not to add terms to it, but to find out what the meaning necessarily must be, having regard to the facts and circumstances—and, having got the evidence which I have in this case, the conclusion is inevitable that it refers to a previous memorandum of terms of agreement under which Mrs Oliver becomes the purchaser of this particular property for the price of £2375, on account of which the cheque for £375 was sent. Having got that evidence in, having got the connection between the two documents, I have then enough to enable me to read the two documents together, and, reading them together, I have a distinct memorandum of contract".

The first sentence quoted from this judgment is, taken by itself, unjustifiably wide; but it must be read in the light of what follows and of the actual decision. The passage as a whole seems to set forth quite accurately the position to which *Long* v. *Millar*[1] has taken the law.

The necessity for the signatory to know of the existence and contents of the document to which it is alleged that the signed document refers, seems to be self-evident; it was emphasized by the judges in *Peirce* v. *Corf*,[2] Quain, J., saying:

"If that letter contained any reference to the sales ledger...that would be sufficient to constitute a good memorandum. But it is manifest, when Maguire [the purchaser] uses the expression 'Lot 49' in the letter, he is referring to the catalogue, and the

[1] (1879) 4 C.P.D. 451. [2] (1874) L.R. 9 Q.B. 210, 217.

catalogue only, which every purchaser or intending purchaser who attends the sale has in his hands, and the only document, as far as we know, in the present case of which the purchaser had any knowledge. The other document, which contained the price, was a document prepared by the auctioneer manifestly for his own use. It contains secret information, such as the reserve price put upon the horses, which was not intended to be communicated to the public".

The rule suggested above[1] may be tested by reference to the cases. In *Long* v. *Millar*[2] the receipt could only be fully comprehended by the court after the agreement for sale and purchase of the land had been given in evidence. In *Taylor* v. *Smith*,[3] on the other hand, there would seem to have been no need to produce the invoice to explain the letter of the defendant refusing to accept delivery of certain deals. The only matter calling for explanation in that letter was the phrase "deals refused by me"; and this could be adequately explained by referring to the carrier's advice note. *Oliver* v. *Hunting*[4] was a case very similar to *Long* v. *Millar*. A complete understanding of the receipt was not possible without a knowledge of the "memorandum of terms of agreement" to which it was held that the receipt referred. In *Wylson* v. *Dunn*[5] the defendant had accepted a written offer by a letter commencing, "I am willing to take". That phrase, Kekewich, J., held, seemed to imply that there was some previous offer: therefore, to properly understand the letter the court had to inquire what had preceded it, and a written offer was accordingly produced.

The latest case bearing on this question is *Stokes* v. *Whicher*,[6] which came before the present Lord Russell of Killowen (Russell, J., as he then was) in 1920. In that case the whole of the contract except the purchaser's name was set out in a writing signed by the vendor's authorized agent, and endorsed on that writing was a receipt for £50 paid on account of the purchase-money. In an action by the purchaser against the vendor, Lord Russell held that he was entitled to inquire into the circumstances

[1] P. 137 *supra*.
[2] (1879) 4 C.P.D. 451.
[3] [1893] 2 Q.B. 65.
[4] (1890) 44 Ch.D. 205.
[5] (1887) 34 Ch.D. 569.
[6] [1920] 1 Ch. 411.

under which the £50 was paid; and on ascertaining that it was part of a cheque for £62 signed by the plaintiff in favour of the defendant's agents, to take the plaintiff's name from that. This case certainly seems to push *Long* v. *Millar*[1] to its extreme limit.[2]

II. *Cases where all of the several documents are signed.* It has already been pointed out[3] that on principle it would seem possible that, where all the documents to be connected together are signed, methods of shewing such connection might be devised which would not suffice where, in addition to bringing the documents together, the authenticating influence of a signature is required to be extended from one document to another or others.

One of the earliest cases involving the connecting together of two signed documents was *Allen* v. *Bennet*,[4] which came before the Court of Common Pleas in 1810. In that case the plaintiff wished to make out a writing from a written order for certain goods and a letter which referred to the same contract as that contained in the order. The court held that this identity of reference was sufficient to allow the two documents to be taken together as one writing, Lord Mansfield, C.J., saying:

> "It [the letter] is in writing, and it is evidently connected with the contract, that no doubt it may be coupled with the order in the order-book; and a valid contract may be established by the evidence of several writings, as we often see at nisi prius".

The same principle was applied by Plumer, M.R., in *Verlander* v. *Codd*,[5] where it was held that two letters, both signed by the defendant and referring to the same lease, were sufficiently connected.

"It has been determined", said the Master of the Rolls, "that

[1] (1879) 4 C.P.D. 451.

[2] See also *Shardlow* v. *Cotterell*, (1881) 18 Ch.D. 280, before Kay, J., reversed on a different ground in the Court of Appeal, 20 Ch.D. 90; *Dewar* v. *Mintoft*, [1912] 2 K.B. 373; and *M'Meekin* v. *Stevenson*, [1917] 1 I.R. 348.
In *Pickles* v. *Sutcliffe*, [1902] W.N. 200, Farwell, J., decided an interesting point, holding that a reference need not be to a particular document but would suffice if it was to a class of documents, such as a standard form of conditions of sale used by members of a law society.

[3] P. 128 *supra*.

[4] (1810) 3 Taunt. 169, 175; 128 E.R. 67, 70.

[5] (1823) Turn. & R. 352, 357; 37 E.R. 1136, 1138.

one written paper, which is signed, may refer to another which is not signed. Here all the essential terms of the contract are contained in the two letters signed by the defendant, explained by the lease to which they refer."

In 1839, however, the Court of King's Bench, in *Smith* v. *Dixon*,[1] delivered a judgment and stated the law in terms very difficult to reconcile with these two earlier cases. The facts in *Smith* v. *Dixon* were almost indistinguishable from those in *Allen* v. *Bennet*,[2] there being a written order, and a subsequent letter referring to the contract set out in the order. Although *Allen* v. *Bennet*[2] was cited, however, the court refused to connect the two documents together.

"In the present case", said Lord Denman, C.J., "the reference to the order, made in the defendant's letter, is not so distinct and clear, that we can say that one document is part of the other, so as to form one entire contract." "These documents", said Patteson, J., "are not necessarily connected together, they may be probably, but they are not necessarily so connected."

In deciding this case, however, it would seem probable that the court (the same, and composed of the same judges, as decided *Dobell* v. *Hutchinson*[3] in 1835) was influenced by the strict rule of an express reference which the common law courts at that time applied in cases where one or more of the several documents was unsigned.

The point next came before the courts in the comparatively recent case of *Studds* v. *Watson*.[4] There neither *Allen* v. *Bennet*,[2] *Verlander* v. *Codd*[5] nor *Smith* v. *Dixon*,[1] was cited, but, on general principles, North, J., decided the point in a manner which accords both with the decisions and the *dicta* in the two former cases.

"But there is a further point", said North, J., "namely, that even assuming the word 'balance' not to be sufficient to connect the two documents, yet there is a parol agreement proved to

1 (1839) 3 Jur. 770, 771.
2 (1810) 3 Taunt. 169; 128 E.R. 67.
3 (1835) 3 Ad. & E. 355; 111 E.R. 448.
4 (1884) 28 Ch.D. 305, 308.
5 (1823) Turn. & R. 352; 37 E.R. 1136.

which both these documents refer. All the terms of this parol agreement are found in one or other of the documents, and are in themselves sufficient to constitute a good memorandum of the agreement within the statute. Moreover, it has been decided that a parol contract may be evidenced by an affidavit made at a different time. And supposing that there were two affidavits evidencing a parol contract, I do not think that it would be necessary for those affidavits to refer to one another. It would, I think, be sufficient that both referred to the same parol contract. That being so, I think it is not necessary in this case that these two documents should refer the one to the other."

Studds v. *Watson*,[1] taken in conjunction with the two earlier cases,[2] would seem to justify the following proposition:

Where two signed documents refer to the same subject-matter they may be connected together to form a writing under the Statute, parol evidence being admissible to identify the subject of reference.

In *Potter* v. *Peters*[3] an argument along these lines was urged before Kekewich, J., and rejected by him; but that learned judge relied solely on *Peirce* v. *Corf*.[4] It has already been submitted that the *dicta* in *Peirce* v. *Corf*, even in 1874, were not an accurate reflection of the law as to several documents; and, moreover, those *dicta* related only to the case of a signed document referring to an unsigned document. In spite of *Potter* v. *Peters*,[3] it is submitted that *Studds* v. *Watson*[1] stands, and that the proposition suggested in the last paragraph correctly sets forth the rule applying to cases where all the documents bear sufficient signatures.

Miscellaneous cases

There is a small group of miscellaneous cases to which reference must be made.

(1) *Letter and envelope*. The Court of Appeal in *Pearce* v. *Gardner*[5] decided that a letter and its envelope may be taken

[1] (1884) 28 Ch.D. 305.
[2] *Allen* v. *Bennet*, (1810) 3 Taunt. 169; 128 E.R. 67; and *Verlander* v. *Codd*, (1823) Turn. & R. 352; 37 E.R. 1136.
[3] (1895) 64 L.J. Ch. 357.
[4] (1874) L.R. 9 Q.B. 210.
[5] [1897] 1 Q.B. 688.

together as one document; and this decision was followed by the same court in *Last* v. *Hucklesby*.[1]

(2) *Two or more documents on the same sheet or sheets of paper* would seem to be regarded as one writing for the purpose of the Statute. For example, it has been held that a reference to particulars of sale is sufficient to incorporate the conditions printed as part of the same document.[2]

(3) Where two documents have been produced at the same time, as, for example, a typed document and its carbon duplicate, it has been suggested that inasmuch as to that extent they originally formed one document, they might subsequently be read together to make one writing under the Statute.[3]

[1] [1914] W.N. 157; 58 S.J. 431.
[2] See per Horridge, J., in *Dewar* v. *Mintoft*, [1912] 2 K.B. 373, 386.
[3] See per Russell, J., in *Stokes* v. *Whicher*, [1920] 1 Ch. 411, 419.

PART III

OPERATION OF THE STATUTE

CHAPTER 1

THE STATUTE AND EXTRINSIC EVIDENCE

THE Statute provides that: "No action shall be brought...unless the agreement upon which such action shall be brought or some memorandum or note thereof shall be in writing...". It follows from these words that the Statute makes the existence of a writing a condition precedent to the bringing of an action. The question therefore arises as to whether and to what extent evidence relating to a contract under the Statute, and extrinsic to the writing, can be received by the courts consistently with the Statutory provision.

In an action where the defendant pleads the Statute, the plaintiff may either fail to produce any sort of writing or produce a writing which on its face shews that it is defective; or produce a writing which completely satisfies the Statutory requirements; or produce a writing which, while *prima facie* sufficient, nevertheless does not in fact comply with such requirements.

Plaintiff producing no writing or writing defective on its face: admissibility of parol evidence on plaintiff's behalf. Where the plaintiff fails to produce any sort of writing to support his contract, the Statute operates to exclude all evidence of such contract; and where a writing, defective on its face, is tendered, the Statute excludes oral evidence to add to, complete, or correct such writing: if documentary evidence should be tendered for any of these purposes its admissibility will depend on the considerations already discussed under the heading of "Several Documents".[1]

"But we think", said Lord Denman, C.J., delivering the judgment of the Court of King's Bench in *Goss* v. *Lord Nugent*,[2] "the object of the Statute of Frauds was to exclude all oral evidence as to contracts for the sale of lands, and that any con-

[1] Part II, chapter VII, p. 127 *supra*.
[2] (1833) 5 B. & Ad. 58, 66; 110 E.R. 713, 716.

tract which is sought to be enforced must be proved by writing only."[1]

Plaintiff produces writing prima facie satisfying Statute: admissibility of parol evidence on plaintiff's behalf. Where the plaintiff produces a writing which *prima facie* satisfies the Statutory requirements, that writing, by virtue of the terms of the Statute, will in general be the only evidence of the contract admissible on the plaintiff's behalf. "The intention of the legislature", said Maule, J., in *Harnor* v. *Groves*,[2] "was, that the writing should be the evidence, and the only evidence, of the contract, and that there should be no occasion to look beyond it." It is not enough that parol evidence should be adduced by the plaintiff to shew that a writing was duly signed by the party to be charged or his agent; the writing itself must be produced, for the Statute makes it the only permissible means of proving the contract. Notwithstanding the Statute, however, secondary evidence of a writing may be given in appropriate circumstances. Thus in *Last* v. *Hucklesby*[3] the Court of Appeal held that secondary evidence was admissible to prove the address on a lost envelope, the envelope and its enclosure being taken together as one document on the principle of *Pearce* v. *Gardner*.[4]

Consistently with the principle stated in the last paragraph, it has been held that parol evidence may not be received on behalf of a plaintiff to add to, vary, subtract from, or contradict a writing *prima facie* satisfying the Statute. Either the writing produced by the plaintiff will be in fact sufficient to satisfy the Statute, in which event evidence of this kind will be unnecessary; or else such writing will not satisfy the Statute, in which event parol evidence to bring the contract apparently disclosed by the writing into line with that pleaded by the plaintiff will be in-

[1] Thus in *Williams* v. *Jordan*, (1877) 6 Ch.D. 517, a writing tendered to prove a contract for a lease was defective by reason of its failure to set forth the name of the lessor; and accordingly the action failed, extrinsic evidence not being receivable to cure the defect.

[2] (1855) 15 C.B. 667, 674; 139 E.R. 587, 590. That case turned on s. 17, but the *dictum* applies with equal force to s. 4. See per Parke, B., in *Marshall* v. *Lynn*, (1840) 6 M. & W. at p. 116; 151 E.R. 345.

[3] [1914] W.N. 157; 58 S.J. 431.

[4] [1897] 1 Q.B. 688.

admissible. Thus in *Giraud* v. *Richmond*,[1] the Court of Common Pleas refused parol evidence tendered by the plaintiff to shew that although the writing produced by him indicated an agreement for yearly payments, nevertheless the true contract was in fact for quarterly payments.

"This appears to me", said Tindal, C.J., "to be a contract within the Statute of Frauds: it was not to be performed within a year....The question, therefore, is whether we can supply an alleged defect in the contract by parol evidence of a contemporaneous or subsequent agreement for the payment of the salary quarterly. I think that would be a direct violation of the statute."

At the time when the Statute was enacted, a rule having an exclusionary effect similar to that of the Statute, had already become established as part of the common law. By this rule (which still exists as part of the law of England), when a contract had been reduced to writing by agreement of the parties, evidence extrinsic to the writing would not be admitted to add to, vary, subtract from or contradict the writing.[2] The question

[1] (1846) 2 C.B. 835, 840; 135 E.R. 1172, 1175. Erle, J., in the same case put the position thus: "I am of the same opinion, on the ground that the contract was one which, by the Statute of Frauds, is required to be in writing. If parol evidence was not admissible to explain, or vary, the terms of the written contract, the salary was payable yearly....The terms of the agreement being free from ambiguity, I think it was not competent to the plaintiff to give such evidence".

See also per Maule, J., in *Harnor* v. *Groves*, (1855) 15 C.B. 667, 674; 139 E.R. 587, 590.

[2] "By the general rules of the common law", said Lord Denman, C.J., in *Goss* v. *Lord Nugent*, (1833) 5 B. & Ad. 58, 64; 110 E.R. 713, 716, "if there be a contract which has been reduced into writing, verbal evidence is not allowed to be given of what passed between the parties, either before the written instrument was made, or during the time that it was in a state of preparation, so as to add to or subtract from, or in any manner to vary or qualify the written contract." In Taylor, *Law of Evidence*, 12th ed. II, p. 723, the rule is expressed thus: "parol testimony cannot be received to contradict, vary, add to, or subtract from, the terms of a valid written instrument".

As to the common law rule being already established as part of the law at the time the Statute was passed, the following references may be given. Wigram, *Extrinsic Evidence*, 5th ed. p. 5: "By the common law (before the Statute) parol evidence was inadmissible to contradict, vary or add to a written instrument". Per Lord Hardwicke, L.C., in *Parteriche* v. *Powlet*, (1742) 2 Atk. 383; 26 E.R. 632: "To add anything to an agreement in writing by admitting parol evidence, which would affect land, is not only contrary to the Statute of Frauds and Perjuries, but to the rule of common law, before the Statute was in being".

therefore suggests itself of whether the exclusion of extrinsic evidence on behalf of a plaintiff in the case of writings under the Statute depends on the effect of the Statute, or whether it is not a particular application of the above-mentioned common law rule.

It is submitted that such exclusion results directly from the terms of the Statute and is independent of the common law rule.[1] This seems to be the view adopted by the courts. "I think that would be a direct violation of the Statute", said Tindal, C.J., in *Giraud* v. *Richmond*,[2] when such evidence was offered by the plaintiff to vary the writing evidencing his contract.[3] It has been judicially said that the intention of the legislature to be discerned in the Statute is that the writing shall be the only evidence of the contract and that there shall be no occasion for the courts to look beyond the writing.[4] Moreover, the Statute requires that the writing shall contain the whole of the contract.[5] Hence it would seem impossible to admit on behalf of a plaintiff parol evidence extrinsic to the writing without directly contravening the Statute. The Statute does not allow a party to prove his contract partly by writing and partly by parol: it demands written evidence of the whole of the contract.[6]

Support for the view that the Statute operates independently

[1] In Wigram's *Extrinsic Evidence*, a similar opinion is expressed with regard to the exclusion of extrinsic evidence in the case of wills made under s. 5 of the Statute of Frauds. In his "Introductory Observations" the learned author stated the purpose of his treatise to be as follows (5th ed. p. 2): "The object of the present work is to answer an important practical question, to which this enactment gives rise, namely—Under what restrictions is the admission of extrinsic evidence, in aid of the exposition of a will, consistent with the provisions of a statute, which makes a writing indispensable to the purpose for which the instrument was made?" Then after noticing the argument that the exclusion of such evidence depended, not on the Statute, but on the common law rule, he continued (p. 4): "The objection points only at the effect or consequences of the statute and does not displace the proposition in the text, that the statute is the source from which those effects or consequences flow".

[2] (1846) 2 C.B. 835, 840; 135 E.R. 1172, 1175.

[3] See also the *dictum* of Lord Hardwicke, L.C., quoted in note 2, p. 149 *supra*.

[4] See *dictum* of Lord Denman, C.J., in *Goss* v. *Lord Nugent*, quoted at p. 147 *supra*; and *dictum* of Maule, J., in *Harnor* v. *Groves*, quoted at p. 148 *supra*.

[5] See p. 55 *supra*.

[6] "But in the present case", said Lord Denman, C.J., in *Goss* v. *Lord Nugent*, (1833) 5 B. & Ad. 58, 66; 110 E.R. 713, 716, "the written contract is not that which is sought to be enforced, it is a new contract which the parties

of the common law rule is to be found in the fact that the Statute applies to evidence and to writings which are outside the scope of the common law rule. That rule will not exclude parol evidence to prove subsequent variations of written contracts[1]; but such evidence is wholly excluded by the Statute.[2] The common law rule does not apply to unilateral writings, or informal writings, but in both of these cases the Statute will operate to exclude extrinsic evidence.[3] It would seem clear, therefore, that the Statute operates quite independently of the common law rule in excluding parol evidence extrinsic to writings *prima facie* complying with its requirements.

Plaintiff produces writing prima facie sufficient, but in fact not satisfying the Statute: admissibility of parol evidence on defendant's behalf. Where the plaintiff produces a writing which, while *prima facie* sufficient, nevertheless does not in fact comply with the Statutory requirements, the question arises as to whether, and to what extent, extrinsic evidence to prove the fact of such non-compliance is admissible on behalf of the defendant. Such evidence may be offered by the defendant

(*a*) to support a plea of the Statute; or

(*b*) where the plaintiff has sued for specific performance, to shew that the plaintiff is acting unconscionably by seeking to impose on the defendant a contract to which the defendant did not agree, and therefore that the plaintiff should not be assisted by a court of equity except on the condition that he admits the actual contract.

Different considerations arise in each of these cases and it is therefore proposed to consider them separately.

(*a*) *Extrinsic evidence to support defendant's plea of the Statute.* There appears to be nothing in the Statute to prevent a de-

have entered into, and that new contract is to be proved, partly by the former written agreement, and partly by the new verbal agreement; the present contract, therefore, is not a contract entirely in writing;...our opinion is not formed upon the stipulation being an essential part of the agreement, but upon the general effect and meaning of the Statute of Frauds, and that the contract now brought forward by the plaintiff is not wholly a contract in writing."

[1] *Phipson on Evidence*, 7th ed. p. 564.

[2] P. 177 *infra*.

[3] Pp. 153–156 *infra*.

fendant from adducing parol evidence for the purpose of defeating the plaintiff's action by shewing that the writing relied upon by the plaintiff does not contain all the terms of the contract, or for some other reason does not express the real contract between the parties.

"It was objected", said Martin, B., delivering the judgment of the Court of Exchequer in *Goodman* v. *Griffiths*,[1] "that this was a contract for the sale of goods above the value of ten pounds, and that as there was nothing to satisfy the 17th section of the Statute of Frauds the plaintiff could not succeed. We are of opinion that this objection must prevail. The bargain was for a price 25 per cent. less than that on the list. The order signed by the defendant did not express the real contract, and it does not preclude the defendant from shewing what the contract was. It is not sufficient under the statute because it does not contain the price agreed on."

As appears from these words, Martin, B., was referring to s. 17 of the Statute; but this section sufficiently resembles s. 4 for the authorities on contracts under the one to be followed, in this respect, with regard to the other.

It is submitted, however, that evidence proffered to shew that the Statute has not been complied with, must be admissible according to the general law of evidence. If the ordinary rules would exclude such evidence, the mere fact that it is being tendered to defeat an action on a contract under the Statute would scarcely seem a sufficient reason to justify its reception. The general exclusionary rule which will most often apply to contracts under the Statute is the common law rule already mentioned;[2] and it is therefore proposed to consider the scope and application of that rule in reference to such contracts.

The underlying basis of the common law rule seems to be that to admit parol evidence extrinsic to those contractual writings to which it applies would be contrary to the intention of the parties in reducing their contract to a written form.

"When the parties have deliberately put their agreement into writing, it is conclusively presumed between themselves and

[1] (1857) 1 H. & N. 574, 577; 156 E.R. 1331, 1332.
[2] P. 149 *supra*.

their privies that they intended the writing to form a full and final statement of their intentions, and one which should be placed beyond the reach of future controversy, bad faith or treacherous memory."[1]

Before the common law rule can apply, however, the circumstances must be such that the court will infer that *both* parties had such an intention with reference to the writing. It is the *common* intention of the parties which is the basis of the rule; as Phipson, in his work on Evidence, expresses it, the contract must have been reduced to writing by "agreement of the parties".[2]

Inasmuch, therefore, as the common law rule is based upon the common intention or agreement of the parties; it does not apply where such common intention or agreement is absent. Accordingly, that rule does not apply, or applies only to a limited extent, in cases of (i) unilateral writings; (ii) writings setting forth part only of the contract; and (iii) informal writings. These cases will be considered in their order.

(i) *Unilateral writings*. A writing not made by agreement of the parties or in fulfilment of any common intention on their

[1] *Phipson on Evidence*, 7th ed. p. 552. In *Taylor on Evidence* a similar view is expressed. The learned author says (12th ed. II, p. 723): "This rule of the common law, which may be traced back to a remote antiquity, is founded on the obvious inconvenience and injustice that would result if matters in writing, made by advice, and on consideration, and intended finally to embody the entire agreement between the parties, were liable to be controlled by what Lord Coke expressively calls, 'the uncertain testimony of slippery memory'. *Lady Rutland's Case*, (1605) Co. 5 Rep. 26*a* 1st Res."

Phipson (*loc. cit.*) notices certain other principles which are sometimes thought to underlie the common law rule, such as that it is an example of the best evidence rule; or that it depends on the doctrine of estoppel. But however this may be, it would seem that the application of the rule depends on whether the courts can, in the particular case, infer an intention common to both the parties that the writing shall be the only and ultimate evidence of their contract. See the next note.

[2] *Phipson on Evidence*, 7th ed. p. 552. In *Allen* v. *Pink*, (1838) 4 M. & W. 140, 144; 150 E.R. 1376, 1378, Lord Abinger, C.B., made particular reference to the need for the writing to be accepted by *both* parties, saying: "The general principle stated by Mr Byles is quite true, that if there has been a parol agreement, which is afterwards reduced by the parties into writing, that writing alone must be looked to to ascertain the terms of the contract; but the principle does not apply here; there was no evidence of any agreement by the plaintiff that the whole contract should be reduced into writing by the defendant".

part will not be affected by the common law rule.[1] If, for example, a party to an action on a contract to which the Statute does not apply, makes an affidavit setting out what he believes to be the contract, there would seem to be no reason why he should not, at a later stage of the proceedings, give evidence contradicting that affidavit, or in some manner amplifying or varying the statements therein contained. His affidavit will perhaps affect the weight which the court will attach to his subsequent evidence, but will not go to raise any question of admissibility.

(ii) *Writings setting forth part only of the contract.* The parties to a contract may reduce certain terms of it to writing, intending that the writing shall be conclusive so far as it goes, but not intending it to be regarded as a complete exposition of the contract. In such a case the common law rule, being based on the intention of the parties, forms no bar to the admission of extrinsic evidence to prove the unwritten terms of the contract, provided that such evidence is not inconsistent with those terms which have been reduced to writing, and that the court is able to infer, either from the writing itself,[2] or from extrinsic cir-

[1] See note 2, p. 153 *supra.*

[2] *Phipson on Evidence*, 7th ed. p. 556: "Where a contract, not required by law to be in writing, purports to be contained in a document which the court infers was not intended to express the *whole agreement* between the parties, proof may be given of any omitted or supplemental oral term, expressly or impliedly agreed between them *before* or at the *time* of executing the document, if it be not inconsistent with the documentary terms".

In this connection the case of *Jeffery* v. *Walton*, (1816) 1 Stark. 267, decided by Lord Ellenborough at *Nisi Prius* may be referred to. There a note of the transaction (a contract for the hire of a horse) was made in the following terms: "Six weeks at two guineas, William Walton Junior". Lord Ellenborough appeared to think that this writing, so far as it went, was intended to be conclusive: he referred to it as the "written agreement", meaning, it is suggested, "that part of the agreement which was in writing"; and while allowing the plaintiff to prove "suppletory matter, as part of the agreement", he refused to admit evidence contradicting the written terms. In *Malpas* v. *London and South Western Railway Co.*, (1866) L.R. 1 C.P. 336, 339, Willes, J., explained Lord Ellenborough's decision in the following way: "The ruling may be sustained, however, on the ground that the memorandum was given by one of the parties to the other at the time as evidence of the agreement between them, and was *acted upon by both parties*, and there was therefore an estoppel in evidence which would sustain the ruling, without any reference to the other doctrine". (The italics are mine.)

A case in which extrinsic evidence was excluded on the ground that the

cumstances,[1] that the writing was not intended to be complete.

(iii) *Informal writings.* A writing may not be intended by the parties to conclude them in any way, and if this appears to the court, then in cases out of the Statute parol evidence will be freely admissible. Such an intention on the part of the contracting parties will generally be inferred from the informal

writing contained all the terms of the bargain, was *Evans* v. *Roe*, (1872) L.R. 7 C.P. 138, 141. There Byles, J., said: "Independently of any reference to the Statute of Frauds, the contract declared upon in this case is a written contract clearly defining all the terms of the bargain. It is in terms a weekly hiring and a weekly service at weekly wages; and it cannot be varied by anything which passed at the time by parol, or, as I should think, by anything which might have passed afterwards". And see the cases collected in *Phipson on Evidence*, 7th ed. pp. 566 *et seq.*

[1] The extent to which the courts may rely on extrinsic circumstances in drawing such an inference does not seem to be very definitely laid down in the authorities. The statement in the text is based on the opinion expressed by Phipson in his *Law of Evidence*, 7th ed. p. 556, relying upon the *Mercantile Bank of Sydney* v. *Taylor*, [1893] A.C. 317. There the appellant had by a contract in writing agreed to release one Griffin from "all debts due by him to the bank [the appellant] at the date of the contract". The question was whether this release extended to a contingent liability on the part of Griffin as a co-surety with the respondent and certain others. To prove that this contingent liability had been intended by the parties to be excepted from the release, the appellant tendered evidence of conversations between its manager, its chairman of directors, and Griffin, which had taken place before the contract had finally been entered into. The Privy Council, affirming the decision of the Supreme Court of New South Wales, held this evidence to be inadmissible. Lord Watson, who delivered the judgment of the Judicial Committee, put the decision on the following ground (at p. 321): "It appears to their Lordships that no foundation was laid at the trial for the admission of any such evidence as the appellants propose to adduce. It had been proved that the whole terms of the agreement under which Griffin became entitled to his release were embodied in the bank's letter of the 5th of April 1889, which he accepted without reservation or qualification. On that assumption, it is plain that the previous verbal communications which had passed between him and the bank were completely superseded, and could not be legitimately referred to, either for the purpose of adding a term to their written agreement, or of altering its ordinary legal construction. But that is what the appellants proposed to do, without attempting to impeach the testimony which established that their letter of the 5th of April, 1889, accepted by Griffin, constituted the sole contract between them". It seems to be fairly inferable from this passage that the Judicial Committee was prepared to look outside the writing in considering whether the parties intended it to be a complete statement of their contract. Before the proffered evidence could be admitted, a *foundation* had to be laid for it: that appears to mean that as the document was *prima facie* complete, evidence of extrinsic circumstances shewing incompleteness had first to be adduced.

nature of the writing.[1] Thus in *Allen* v. *Pink*[2] Allen bought of Pink a horse, Pink orally warranting the horse quiet in harness, and signing the following writing: "Bought of G. Pink, a horse for the sum of £7–2–6". The Court of Exchequer held that evidence of this warranty could be given in spite of the writing which, said Lord Abinger, C.B., appeared "to have been meant merely as a memorandum of the transaction, or an informal receipt for the money, not as containing the terms of the contract itself".

Reverting now to the question of the admissibility of evidence to prove non-compliance with the Statute, it is apparent that writings under the Statute will either be of such a nature as at the same time to fall within the scope of the common law rule, or else they will fall into one or other of the classes of documents outside that rule. If, therefore, evidence extrinsic to the writing is tendered to shew that the Statute has not been complied with, it would seem that such evidence will be admissible only if the writing is one to which the common law rule does not apply.[3] The principles governing the admission of such evidence may, it is submitted, be stated as follows: (1) Where a writing appears to have been intended by the parties to be a complete statement of their contract, the common law rule will prevent the reception of extrinsic evidence to prove that the writing does not contain all the terms of the contract or otherwise does not represent the real contract between the parties and therefore does not comply with the requirements of the Statute. (2) Where, however, the writing, being unilateral or informal, is one to which the common

[1] See *Taylor on Evidence*, 12th ed. II, p. 724; *Phipson on Evidence*, 7th ed. p. 554; *Stephen's Digest*, 11th ed. p. 99, where it is stated that, "oral evidence of a transaction is not excluded by the fact that a documentary memorandum of it was made, if such memorandum was not intended to have legal effect as a contract, or other disposition of property".

[2] (1838) 4 M. & W. 140, 144; 150 E.R. 1376, 1378.

[3] Wigram expresses a similar opinion in regard to the provision of the Statute regarding Wills. "The restrictions under which extrinsic evidence was by the common law (before the statute) admissible, in aid of the exposition of a written instrument, in cases in which the law did not require a writing, will, of course, form a limit beyond which extrinsic evidence cannot be admitted to assist in expounding a writing which a statute makes indispensable." *Extrinsic Evidence*, 5th ed. p. 4.

law rule does not apply, such evidence would appear to be admissible, even though it contradicts the writing. (3) And where, under the common law rule, evidence may be given to *complete* a writing, it would seem that in cases under the Statute, the defendant may adduce such evidence to shew that the writing is incomplete and therefore insufficient to support the action; but such evidence will not be admissible if it contradicts those terms which have been reduced to writing.

The foregoing submissions receive support from the cases of *Goodman* v. *Griffiths*,[1] *Martin* v. *Pycroft*[2] and *North* v. *Loomes*.[3] In the first of these cases, the writing relied upon was in the form of an order for the manufacture of certain goods. At the trial Martin, B., held that the defendant could rely on certain parts of the plaintiff's evidence shewing that the writing failed to set forth the whole of the contract, and he allowed a non-suit accordingly. This ruling was upheld by the Court of Exchequer on the express ground that it was open to a defendant to shew that the contract was other than that alleged by the plaintiff and *prima facie* proved by the writing produced. It is submitted that this decision does not contravene the limitation, suggested in the preceding paragraph, on the reception of extrinsic evidence to prove non-compliance with the Statute, viz. that such evidence must be admissible under the common law rule. The common law rule was not, indeed, expressly referred to in *Goodman* v. *Griffiths*, but the writing relied upon in that case seems to have been in such a form that it might reasonably have been inferred that it was not intended to be complete,[4] and hence extrinsic evidence to add to and complete it would have been allowed by the common law rule; such evidence would therefore be admissible to shew that the Statute had not been satisfied.

In the second case, *Martin* v. *Pycroft*,[2] the writing produced was in legal form and appeared on its face to have been intended by the parties to be the complete and final record of their con-

[1] (1857) 1 H. & N. 574; 156 E.R. 1331.
[2] (1852) 2 De G. M. & G. 785, 794; 42 E.R. 1079, 1083.
[3] [1919] 1 Ch. 378.
[4] See *Jeffery* v. *Walton*, (1816) 1 Stark. 267, referred to in note 2, p. 154 *supra*.

tract. It was alleged by the defendant, however, and admitted by the plaintiff (suing for specific performance of the contract, which was to grant a lease), that the agreement should have contained an additional term, viz. to pay a premium of £200; but nevertheless the court would not receive this evidence to support the defendant's plea of the Statute.

"Now, the first question that here arises", said Knight Bruce, L.J., "seems to be, whether there is a case of latent ambiguity, for patent ambiguity there is none, since the agreement upon the face of it is a contract, intelligible, clear and complete in all its terms. And we think that there is no latent ambiguity, for the evidence before the court does not in our judgment render it impossible to construe the writing satisfactorily. The true interpretation of the writing we conceive to be that premium is excluded, but that the covenant for laying out £200 is included. Then comes, however, the question of the true and real bargain, independently of the point of the mere construction: And we conceive that had the Plaintiff brought an action against the three Pycrofts upon the written agreement, and they had defended themselves at law on the ground merely of the facts now in evidence, with or without the aid of any statute or statutes, the Plaintiff must have recovered, at least if his case ought to be considered as free from fraud. The law prohibits generally, if not universally, the introduction of parol evidence to add to a written agreement, whether respecting or not respecting land, or to vary it. How can a man say that a written contract shall be deemed bad at law for omitting a term verbally agreed upon?... And our opinion is that, where persons sign a written agreement upon a subject, obnoxious or not obnoxious to the statute that has been so particularly referred to, and there has been no circumvention, no fraud nor (in the sense in which the term 'mistake' must be considered as used for this purpose) mistake, the written agreement binds at law and in equity, according to its terms, although verbally a provision was agreed to, which has not been inserted in the document...."[1]

[1] It is to be noticed that in this case it was apparent from the plaintiff's claim that the writing did not in fact satisfy the Statute; yet the common law rule was allowed by the court to debar the defendant from taking advantage of the statutory provisions. And an examination of the cases in which a writing has been held insufficient on the ground that it has omitted a term of the contract, seems to shew that the writings in those cases were either in-

The third case relied on as supporting the above submissions is *North* v. *Loomes*,[1] decided by Younger, J., in 1919. There the plaintiff, in order to comply with the requirements of the Statute, produced a receipt, and the defendant proposed to shew that this receipt was insufficient as omitting a term in the plaintiff's favour. Younger, J., appeared to be of opinion that such evidence would, in general, be receivable; but he refused to allow it in the particular case for three reasons: first, that the defendant had not adequately pleaded the defence; secondly, that the defendant had become estopped from contending that the term was part of the contract inasmuch as "he had previously put forward and obtained the acceptance of his denial" of that term; and thirdly, that the plaintiff could, if he pleased, waive a stipulation exclusively for his own benefit, even though the contract were under the Statute. It is to be noted, however, that Younger, J., did not in any way attempt to deny the general proposition, that in the case of an informal document such as a receipt, evidence might normally be given to shew that it did not satisfy the Statute.

"It was said", remarked the learned judge, "that this receipt... is an insufficient memorandum of the contract in that it contains no reference to the arrangement as to costs to which I have referred. Is this contention open to the defendant *on the defence as it stands?*...Further it must be remembered that the point intended to be raised by the statute must in a pleading be clearly stated: *Pullen* v. *Snelus*.[2] Here this point could not even be conjectured. Therefore, *without amending the defence by asserting this additional term*, the defence of the statute is not, I think, in this respect open."[3]

formal or unilateral, so that the common law rule would not apply to them. For example, in *Blackburn* v. *Walker*, [1920] W.N. 291, which failed on this ground, the writing relied upon was a receipt; in *Nesham* v. *Selby*, (1872) L.R. 13 Eq. 191, it was a letter; and in *Rishton* v. *Whatmore*, (1878) 8 Ch.D. 467, it was an entry in an auctioneer's book. It seems impossible to point to a case in which such evidence has been allowed to defeat an action which has been based on a formal writing appearing on its face to have been intended by the parties to be complete and final, so that it would come within the terms of the common law rule.

[1] [1919] 1 Ch. 378, 383.

[2] 40 L.T. 363.

[3] The italics are mine.

(*b*) *Extrinsic evidence, on behalf of defendant to suit for specific performance, to shew that plaintiff is unconscionably seeking to impose on defendant a contract to which defendant did not agree.* Although extrinsic evidence shewing that the writing does not properly set forth the real contract will not be accepted in support of a plea of the Statute unless it is admissible according to the common law rule, such evidence will nevertheless be admitted where it is tendered merely to shew that a plaintiff suing for specific performance is unconscionably seeking to impose on the defendant a contract to which the defendant did not agree.[1]

"The admission of such evidence", said Lord Redesdale in *Clinan* v. *Cooke*,[2] "as a matter of defence is frequent....It is used to rebut an Equity: the Defendant says, 'The agreement you seek is not the agreement I mean to enter into'; and then he is let in to prove fraud or mistake. It should be recollected what are the words of the Statute....No person shall be charged with the execution of an agreement who has not either by himself or his agent signed a written agreement, but the statute does not say that if a written agreement is signed, the same exception shall not hold to it that did before the statute. Now, before the statute, if a Bill had been brought for specific performance, and it had appeared that the agreement had been prepared contrary to the intent of the Defendant, he might have said, 'that is not the agreement meant to have been signed'. Such a case is left as it was, by the statute; it does not say, that a written agreement shall bind, but that an unwritten agreement shall not bind."[3]

Where a defendant satisfactorily establishes that the writing relied upon by the plaintiff suing for specific performance does

[1] This principle does not apply to enable a defendant to prove a subsequent parol variation of a contract, by way of defence to a suit for specific performance, nor can a plaintiff prove such variations for the purpose of enforcing them upon the defendant. *Price* v. *Dyer*, (1810) 17 Ves. 356; 34 E.R. 137. *Robinson* v. *Page*, (1826) 3 Russ. 114; 38 E.R. 519. *Snelling* v. *Thomas*, (1874) L.R. 17 Eq. 303. See pp. 176 *et seq.*, *infra*.

[2] (1802) 1 Sch. & Lef. 22, 39.

[3] See also per Lord Loughborough, L.C., in *Rich* v. *Jackson*, (1794) 4 Bro. C.C. 514, 518; 29 E.R. 1017, 1019; a fuller note of the judgment is given in 6 Ves. 341 n., 31 E.R. 1081; per Lord Eldon, L.C., in *Townshend* v. *Stangroom*, (1801) 6 Ves. 328, 333; 31 E.R. 1076, 1078; per Grant, M.R., in *Clarke* v. *Grant*, (1807) 14 Ves. 519; 33 E.R. 620.

not properly set forth the contract, the court will offer the plaintiff the choice of accepting a judgment for specific performance of the actual contract, or of having his claim for specific performance dismissed.[1] Thus Grant, M.R., offered a plaintiff such a choice in *Clarke* v. *Grant*.[2] In that case it was one of the

[1] In *Lindsay* v. *Lynch*, (1804) 2 Sch. & Lef. 1, Lord Redesdale refused to allow a plaintiff the alternative of accepting the agreement so proved by the defendant, but dismissed the bill without prejudice to the right of the plaintiff to bring a fresh bill on the agreement as set up by the defendant (*ib.* 10). This judgment, however, was given by Lord Redesdale as Lord Chancellor of Ireland: it appears to be contrary to *Clarke* v. *Grant*, (1807) 14 Ves. 519; 33 E.R. 320, and the cases cited in note 2 *infra*; and Fry, J., in *Smith* v. *Wheatcroft*, (1878) 9 Ch.D. 223, 228, refused to follow it. It is submitted, therefore, that *Lindsay* v. *Lynch* cannot be regarded to-day as an authority against the proposition stated in the text.

[2] (1807) 14 Ves. 519; 33 E.R. 620. See also *Joynes* v. *Statham*, (1746) 3 Atk. 388; 26 E.R. 1023; *Ramsbottom* v. *Gosden*, (1812) 1 V. & B. 165; 35 E.R. 65; *Winch* v. *Winchester*, (1812) 1 V. & B. 375; 35 E.R. 146; and *Martin* v. *Pycroft*, 2 De G. M. & G. 785; 42 E.R. 1079. In *Clowes* v. *Higginson*, (1813) 1 V. & B. 524; 35 E.R. 204, Plumer, V.-C., put the rule allowing evidence on behalf of a defendant upon a narrower basis than the foregoing authorities would appear to warrant. He was willing to admit it to prove circumstances of fraud, mistake, or surprise, if that could be done consistently with the terms of the writing; but he refused to admit evidence, on behalf of a defendant, to shew that the writing did not contain all the terms of the contract. Referring to the evidence offered (which was to prove a declaration made by an auctioneer adding a term to the conditions of sale), the Vice-Chancellor said (527; E.R. 205): "In Sales by Auction the real object of introducing Declarations by the Auctioneer or other Persons is to explain, alter, or contradict, the written Contract; in Effect to Substitute another Contract; and, independent of Authority, I should be much disposed to reject such Declarations, as open to all the Mischief, against which the Statute was directed, and also violating the Rule of Law, which prevailed previously; whether offered by a Plaintiff, seeking a Performance, or by a Defendant, to get rid of the Contract: a Distinction, which it is difficult to adopt, where the Evidence is introduced to shew, that the Writing, purporting to be the Contract, is not the Contract; that there is no Contract between them, if, that, which is proved by parol, does not make a Part of it. That does not depend upon the Principle, on which a Defendant is permitted to shew Fraud, Mistake, or Surprise, collateral to, and independent of, the written Contract: the Object in the other Case being to get rid of the Contract by explaining it away".

Although, however, the Vice-Chancellor excluded the evidence in question, he dismissed the plaintiff's suit on other grounds; and his remarks as to the admissibility of evidence on behalf of a defendant did not pass without criticism. "This judgment", wrote Lord St Leonards in his *Law of Vendors and Purchasers of Estates*, 14th ed. p. 161, "does not seem to be warranted by the principles of the Court. It is manifest that the learned Judge was disposed to overrule the settled distinction. It is not necessary, in order to render the evidence admissible, that its object should be to shew fraud, mistake, or

terms of contract for a lease that the defendant might subsequently select some other part of a certain close than that mentioned in the writing, and he did in fact select, and entered upon the occupation of, another part of the close. The plaintiff afterwards brought an action for specific performance of the agreement as set out in the writing, and the defendant tendered evidence, by way of defence, to prove the true contract.

"If the evidence be admissible," said the Master of the Rolls,[1] "it appears, that this written agreement was only signed in consequence of the promise of the four trustees to consent to such alterations with regard to the spot, as would be for the convenience of the Defendant; so that but for this promise there would probably never have been any agreement at all. It would then be against equity, and a fraud on the Defendant, to insist upon his performance of an agreement, which he only signed on the faith of an alteration being made in one of its terms. It has been ruled, that it is not open to a Plaintiff to supply or correct a term of a written agreement by parol; but it has never been determined, that a Defendant cannot set up a parol engagement in opposition to a party, who, having entered into it, seeks to have a written agreement specifically performed independently of it. The Statute of Frauds has not altered the situation of a Defendant, against whom a specific performance is prayed. A Defendant in such a case may give the same evidence now, which he might have given before...there can, I think, be no doubt, that a Defendant is at liberty to urge such a parol promise as a bar to a specific performance of a written agreement....I there-

surprise, collateral to or independent of the written contract, although that usually is its tendency; but the evidence is admissible where, by way of defence, the object is to get rid of the contract by shewing that it is not the contract really entered into by the parties, although where, even as a defence, the evidence is used to shew that the terms of the contract are not the real ones, the evidence, when admitted, must be very powerful to induce the Court to believe that the terms expressed are not the real ones." Then after referring to *Winch* v. *Winchester*, (1812) 1 V. & B. 375; 35 E.R. 146, and pointing out that there Grant, M.R., had admitted evidence on a defendant's behalf which *contradicted* the writing, Lord St Leonards continued (*ib.* 162): "The evidence, it is submitted, in the latter case, was admissible in equity as a defence, simply on the ground that the plaintiff, who ought to come into equity with clean hands, sought to commit a fraud in evading to pay for the timber, although the auctioneer declared that it was to be paid for". Lord St Leonards' criticism of *Clowes* v. *Higginson* appears to have been approved by Stuart, V.-C., in *Dear* v. *Verity*, (1869) 38 L.J. Ch. 297, 302.

[1] 14 Ves. 524; 33 E.R. 622.

fore think, the Bill must be dismissed; unless the Plaintiffs will agree to execute such a lease, as the Defendant has submitted he is ready to accept."[1]

It would seem, however, that the principle of *Clarke* v. *Grant* is subject to the qualification that where the parties intentionally adopt a particular legal shape for their transaction (as, for example, having arranged for a reciprocal transfer of estates, they accept for their contract a writing expressing the transaction as two separate sales), they will not be heard subsequently to say that the transaction was other than it appears from the writing to be. In such a case, assuming that there are no omitted or inaccurate terms, it cannot be regarded as fraudulent or unconscionable in either party to demand specific performance on the construction of the transaction which both parties intentionally adopted by accepting the writing as their contract. This would appear to be the result of the case of *Croome* v. *Lediard*.[2] There, the plaintiff and the defendant were negotiating for the mutual sale or exchange of two estates, and an agreement was ultimately arrived at. The written contract, accepted by both parties, put the agreement as two independent sales. On a suit for specific performance, the defendant, relying upon *Clarke* v. *Grant*,[3] desired to introduce extrinsic evidence shewing that in fact the transaction had been intended to be an exchange; but this evidence was refused, Lord Brougham, L.C., distinguishing *Clarke* v. *Grant* as follows:[4]

[1] In *Dear* v. *Verity*, (1869) 38 L.J. Ch. 297, it was said by Stuart, V.-C., that *Clarke* v. *Grant*, (1807) 14 Ves. 519; 33 E.R. 620, was a case of part performance. Nevertheless, Vesey Junior's report, the accuracy of which Stuart, V.-C., did not question, seems to make it clear that while the facts of *Clarke* v. *Grant* would have justified an application of the doctrine of part performance, yet Grant, M.R., actually based his judgment on the principle that a defendant to a suit for specific performance may shew that the writing fails to set forth the true contract. This principle, indeed, is implicit in Stuart, V.-C.'s own judgment in *Dear* v. *Verity*, for he decided that case on the ground that the evidence adduced by the defendant was inadequate for the purpose of shewing that the contract apparently disclosed by the writing was not the contract actually agreed upon by the parties. The principle in question would seem to have been accepted by the Lords Justices when *Dear* v. *Verity* came before them on appeal: see per Selwyn, L.J., 38 L.J. Ch. 487.

[2] (1833) 2 My. & K. 251; 39 E.R. 940.

[3] (1807) 14 Ves. 519; 33 E.R. 620.

[4] 2 My. & K. 261; 39 E.R. 943.

"In *Clarke* v. *Grant* the parol evidence admitted was of a stipulation entered into by the Defendant prior to, and as a condition precedent to, the execution of the agreement. There was an express promise, on the part of the Plaintiff, antecedent to the execution of the agreement; and 'but for that promise', observes Sir William Grant, 'the agreement would probably never have been made'. It was observable, moreover, that the stipulation of which parol evidence was admitted in that case did not seek to vary the substance of the agreement; on the contrary, it was a stipulation that 'such alteration should be made in the memorandum of agreement as should be consistent with, and agreeable to the substance thereof'. In the present case, the purpose for which the parol evidence was tendered on the part of the Defendant was, not to enforce a collateral stipulation, but to shew that the transaction was conducted on the basis of an exchange...".

It would appear from the foregoing passage from Lord Brougham's judgment that he regarded the parol stipulation in *Clarke* v. *Grant*[1] as "collateral" in the sense in which that term is used in a subsequent chapter of this treatise,[2] as implying a stipulation, in the nature of an independent contract, forming the consideration for the making of some other contract. Nevertheless, it does not seem to have been an essential feature of *Clarke* v. *Grant*[1] that the parol stipulation in that case was collateral to the contract sought to be enforced: indeed, it would rather appear that that stipulation was part of the contract. In *Joynes* v. *Statham*,[3] decided by Lord Hardwicke on the same principle as (it is submitted) was adopted by Grant, M.R., for his judgment in *Clarke* v. *Grant*, there was certainly no question of the parol term being collateral: it was most plainly a portion of the contract. Lord Brougham's further suggestion that *Clarke* v. *Grant* could be distinguished on the ground that the evidence in that case did not have the effect of varying the substance of the agreement, can hardly be sustained: nothing seems to be clearer than that to substitute for the parcel of land mentioned in an agreement for a lease, another parcel of land subsequently selected by the lessee in accordance with a parol

[1] (1807) 14 Ves. 519; 33 E.R. 620.

[2] See p. 188 *infra*.

[3] (1746) 3 Atk. 388; 26 E.R. 1023.

stipulation reserving that liberty to him, is to vary the substance of and to contradict the written agreement. In *Winch* v. *Winchester*[1] the principle of *Clarke* v. *Grant* was applied by Grant, M.R., although the parol evidence plainly contradicted the writing.

It is submitted, however, that *Croome* v. *Lediard*[2] can be distinguished from *Clarke* v. *Grant* and supported upon the following grounds. It would have been contrary to the intention of the parties and therefore fraudulent and unconscionable, for the plaintiff in *Clarke* v. *Grant* to have enforced the agreement in that case, without allowing the defendant the benefit of the parol term. In *Croome* v. *Lediard*, however, the plaintiff's conduct was in no way fraudulent or unconscionable, for he was merely seeking specific performance of a contract intentionally entered into by himself and the defendant. He was asking nothing more than that the court should take that view of the transaction which he and the defendant, with their eyes open, and uninfluenced by fraud or anything of a fraudulent nature, had deliberately adopted. This seems to be quite different from the position which arose in *Joynes* v. *Statham*,[3] *Clarke* v. *Grant*,[4] *Winch* v. *Winchester*,[1] and similar cases.[5]

Where the writing does not properly set forth the contract

[1] (1812) 1 V. & B. 375; 35 E.R. 146.
[2] (1833) 2 My. & K. 251; 39 E.R. 940.
[3] (1746) 3 Atk. 388; 26 E.R. 1023.
[4] (1807) 14 Ves. 519; 33 E.R. 620.
[5] The criticism of *Croome* v. *Lediard*, (1833) 2 My. & K. 251; 39 E.R. 940, offered in the text is supported by the opinion regarding that case expressed by Lord St Leonards in his *Law of Vendors and Purchasers of Estates*, 14th ed. p. 163: "The decision in the above case [*Croome* v. *Lediard*] was probably well founded. The evidence, it is submitted, was inadmissible, not because it was not to enforce a collateral stipulation, but because it did not prove that by fraud, mistake, or surprise, the agreement did not state the alleged real contract, viz., for an exchange between the parties. The defendant was an attorney, and fraud was not alleged, nor indeed was mistake or surprise, for he had himself prepared the agreement, and he preferred making it a mutual contract for sale and purchase, instead of an exchange, and of course he could not be permitted to alter its character by parol evidence of the mode in which the negotiation was conducted, and of the views of the parties, in order to avoid the consequences which attached to the nature of the contract which the parties with their eyes open, having regard to other objects, had thought it proper to adopt".

between the parties, a defendant may well be in a position to defeat the plaintiff's suit by pleading the Statute; but, as has already been submitted,[1] evidence in support of such a plea must be admissible under the common law rule which regulates the reception of parol evidence to add to, vary or contradict documents. It may perhaps be asked why a party defending a suit for specific performance should be fettered by this common law rule when he produces extrinsic evidence to support a plea of the Statute, while he is in no way affected by it when he produces the same evidence to shew that the plaintiff in seeking to enforce the contract as set forth in the writing is acting unconscionably and therefore should not be assisted by a court of equity. The distinction in question appears to be a result of the maxim that "Equity follows the law".

"The Court of Chancery never claimed to override the Courts of Common Law. 'Where a rule, either of the common or statute law, is direct, and governs the case with all its circumstances, or the particular point, a Court of Equity is as much bound by it as a Court of Law, and can as little justify a departure from it.'[2] It is only when there is some important circumstance disregarded by the common law rules that equity interferes."[3]

Hence, in the absence of any special ground of equitable relief such as fraud or part performance, a contract unenforceable at law will be equally unenforceable in equity.

"The real question", said Lord Loughborough, L.C., in *Rich* v. *Jackson*,[4] "is, whether in this court any more than at law, where the judges have said, I ought not to have admitted the evidence, and I approve their determination, it ought to be admitted; whether there is any distinction in a Court of Equity, where a party comes to enforce a written agreement by obtaining a more formal instrument, and to add in doing that a term not expressed in the written agreement, and of such a nature, as to bear against the written agreement. I have looked into all the cases; and I cannot find, that this court has ever taken upon

[1] See p. 156 *supra*.
[2] Story, *Equity Jurisprudence*, 3rd English ed. p. 34.
[3] Snell, *Principles of Equity*, 20th ed. p. 14.
[4] (1794) 6 Ves. 341 n.; 31 E.R. 1081.

itself in executing a written agreement by a specific performance to add to it by any circumstance, that parol evidence could introduce: but it has often with great propriety, where an attempt has been made to obtain by a decree of this court a farther security or more ample interest, than the party was in possession of by the paper itself, refused, if it appeared, the demand was fraudulent or unfair."

A defence of the Statute of Frauds is merely a defence that the contract is unenforceable at law, and therefore should not be enforced by courts of equity. Accordingly, where that defence is pleaded, it must be made out on evidence which would be available at law, and the above-mentioned common law rule applies. Where, however, the question is whether some purely equitable relief shall be granted, Courts of Equity take into account matters of conscience which are not relevant at common law and hence the common law rule in question is to this extent excluded.

"It cannot be said", remarked Lord Eldon, L.C., in *Townshend* v. *Stangroom*,[1] "that because the legal import of a written agreement cannot be varied by parol evidence, intended to give it another sense, therefore in Equity, when once the court is in possession of the legal sense, there is nothing more to enquire into. Fraud is a distinct case, and perhaps more examinable at law; but all the doctrine of the court as to cases of unconscionable agreements, hard agreements, agreements entered into by mistake or surprise, which therefore the court will not execute, must be struck out, if it is true, that, because parol evidence should not be admitted at law, therefore it shall not be admitted in Equity, upon the questions whether, admitting the agreement to be such as at law it is said to be, the party shall have a specific execution, or be left to that court, in which, it is admitted, parol evidence cannot be admitted. A very small research into the cases will shew general indications by judges in Equity, that that has not been supposed to be the law of this court."

[1] (1801) 6 Ves. 328, 333; 31 E.R. 1076, 1078.

CHAPTER II

EXTRINSIC EVIDENCE PROVING SUBSEQUENT VARIATION OR RESCISSION OF CONTRACTS UNDER THE STATUTE

THE discussion in the preceding chapter has been confined to the admissibility of extrinsic evidence to shew that, even when the writing was first drawn up, it failed adequately to set forth the contract between the parties. Where, however, the writing in its inception accurately states the contract, it may yet happen that the contract will subsequently be rescinded or varied by the parties, so that the writing ceases to represent the true arrangement between them. In such a case it becomes necessary to consider whether, and if so, to what extent, extrinsic evidence can be admitted to prove the subsequent rescission or variation.

Goman v. *Salisbury*,[1] decided only seven years after the passing of the Statute, would seem to be the first case in which the question was raised as to the admissibility of parol evidence to prove the total rescission of a contract under the Statute. Vernon's report is short, and may be quoted in full:

"The single point of this case was, whether an agreement in writing made since the Statute of *Frauds* and *Perjuries* might be discharged by *parol*? And *Lord Keeper* [Sir Francis North, afterwards Earl of Guilford] held it might. And therefore dismissed the bill, which was brought to have the agreement executed *in specie*."

Goman v. *Salisbury* was cited in *Buckhouse* v. *Crossby*,[2] which came before Lord Hardwicke, L.C., in 1737; but the Lord Chancellor seemed to doubt whether the principle of the earlier case would apply to a parol agreement rescinding a contract relating to land.

"...his Lordship said", runs the report (an 'abridgment'),[3]

[1] (1684) 1 Vern. 240; 23 E.R. 440.
[2] (1737) 2 Eq. Ca. Abr. 32, pl. 44; 22 E.R. 28.
[3] *Ib.* p. 33; E.R. 29.

"that though he would not say that a Contract in Writing could not be waived by Parol, yet he should expect in such a case a very clear proof; and the proof in the present case he thought very insufficient to discharge a Contract in Writing; and observed, that the Statute of Frauds and Perjuries requires that 'all Contracts and Agreements concerning Land should be in Writing'. Now an Agreement to Waive a Purchase Contract is as much an Agreement concerning Lands, as the original Contract. However, his Lordship said, there was no Occasion now to determine this Point."

The solution of the difficulty suggested by Lord Hardwicke would, however, seem plain. The Statute affects only the enforcement of contracts, and not their rescission.

"It is to be observed", said Lord Denman, C.J., in *Goss* v. *Lord Nugent*,[1] "that the statute does not say in distinct terms that all contracts or agreements concerning the sale of lands shall be in writing; all that it enacts is, that no action shall be brought unless they are in writing. And as there is no clause in the Act which requires the dissolution of such contracts to be in writing, it should rather seem that a written contract concerning the sale of lands may still be waived and abandoned by a new agreement not in writing, and so as to prevent either party from recovering on the contract which was in writing."[2]

Lord Hardwicke's doubts on this question do not appear to have been shared by any subsequent judge, and since his time it seems never seriously to have been doubted that a contract under the Statute could be wholly rescinded by a parol agreement. In 1826 Lord Lyndhurst (then Sir J. S. Copley, M.R.), was able to say:[3]

"Unquestionably, waiver, even by parole, would be a sufficient answer to the Plaintiff's claim. But it has been laid down in all the cases, that such a defence must be established with the greatest clearness and precision; and the circumstances of waiver and abandonment must amount to a total dissolution of the contract, placing the parties in the same situation in which they

[1] (1833) 5 B. & Ad. 58, 65; 110 E.R. 713, 716.
[2] See also Fry, *Specific Performance of Contracts*, 6th ed. p. 479.
[3] *Robinson* v. *Page*, (1826) 3 Russ. 114, 120; 38 E.R. 519, 521.

stood before the agreement was entered into. In *Price* v. *Dyer*,[1] Sir William Grant, speaking of the waiver of a certain agreement, says, 'The waiver spoken of in this case is an entire abandonment and dissolution of the contract, restoring the parties to their former situation'. The question, therefore, in this cause, is, whether, under the circumstances which are here brought before me, I am satisfied that there was an absolute dissolution and abandonment of the contract of the 5th of March".

In *Noble* v. *Ward*[2] it was treated as settled law by Willes, J., and the Court of Exchequer Chamber that a contract under the Statute could be validly rescinded by parol.

"Mr Holker has contended", said Willes, J., in delivering the judgment of the court in that case, "that...*since the parties might have entered into a mere verbal contract to rescind simpliciter*,[3] we are to say what would have resulted if the contract had been valid, will take place though it is void...." "What was really decided [by *Noble* v. *Ward*]", said Viscount Haldane, addressing the House of Lords in *Morris* v. *Baron*,[4] "was that while the parties might have entered into a parol contract to rescind *simpliciter* the second, just as they had so rescinded the first, they had not done so."

If, however, a contract under the Statute can validly be rescinded by an express parol agreement to that effect, it would seem that a like result should follow where the agreement is not express but has to be implied from the circumstances of the case; and this, indeed, is now clearly established as the law. An argument on these lines was advanced in *Price* v. *Dyer*,[5] but Grant, M.R., held that the circumstances of that case were not sufficient to justify an inference that the parties had agreed to rescind their contract.

"It is then said", remarked the Master of the Rolls, "that the agreement was waived; and that a written agreement may be so far waived by parol, that the court will refuse the interposition of its equitable jurisdiction to enforce it....I incline to

[1] (1810) 17 Ves. 356; 34 E.R. 137; not quite accurately quoted by the Master of the Rolls.
[2] (1867) L.R. 2 Ex. 135, 137.
[3] The italics are mine.
[4] [1918] A.C. 1, 17.
[5] (1810) 17 Ves. 356, 363; 34 E.R. 137, 140.

think, that upon the doctrine of this court such would be the effect of a parol waiver, clearly and satisfactorily proved: but here there was no such waiver."

A similar argument was urged in *Robinson* v. *Page*,[1] but there also it was held that the facts did not warrant the inference of a complete rescission being drawn. In dealing with this question, Lord Lyndhurst, in the passage from his judgment quoted above,[2] followed Grant, M.R., in stating that the evidence, in order to justify the inference of rescission, should be clear and precise. *Stead* v. *Dawber*,[3] which came before the King's Bench in 1839, was perhaps the first case in which it was decided that a defence of this nature had been sufficiently made out. It was followed a year later by the Court of Exchequer in *Marshall* v. *Lynn*;[4] and thus the principle was finally settled, that rescission of a contract under the Statute might properly be established by inference from the circumstances of the case, as well as by evidence of an express agreement for rescission. *Morris* v. *Baron*,[5] decided by the House of Lords in 1917, affords a recent illustration of this principle.[6]

A detailed examination into the nature of the circumstances which will justify the court in implying a rescission would be outside the scope of this treatise; but it may be stated generally that these circumstances must be such as to prove, "with the greatest clearness and precision", that the parties intended to rescind.[7] Particular reference must, however, be made to the class of case in which the circumstance, or one of the circumstances, relied upon to afford such proof is a subsequent contract inconsistent in its terms with the earlier contract.

Rescission by subsequent contract not complying with Statute. The general principle may be stated quite shortly: "Where the parties to a contract come to a fresh agreement of such a kind that the two cannot stand together, the effect of the second agree-

[1] (1826) 3 Russ. 114; 38 E.R. 519.
[2] P. 169 *supra*.
[3] (1839) 10 A. & E. 57; 113 E.R. 22.
[4] (1840) 6 M. & W. 109; 151 E.R. 342.
[5] [1918] A.C. 1.
[6] See also *Cutts* v. *Taltal Railway Co.*, (1918) 62 S.J. 423.
[7] Per Copley, M.R. (Lord Lyndhurst), in *Robinson* v. *Page*, (1826) 3 Russ. 114; 38 E.R. 519.

ment is to rescind the first".[1] But the application of this principle to cases under the Statute presents certain difficulties. If the second agreement comes within the Statute, and does not comply with the Statutory requirements, it may be asked whether it is consistent with the provisions of the Statute to allow such second agreement to operate even to the limited extent of rescinding the first. And if it be allowed that the Statute will offer no bar to such rescission, it may yet be urged that the injustice which may ensue through the rescission of an enforceable contract by a contract which is itself unenforceable, must be taken into account in deciding whether the circumstances actually afford proof "of the greatest clearness and precision" of an intention in the parties to rescind.

It is now definitely established by the decision of the House of Lords in *Morris* v. *Baron*,[2] that the Statute does not bar the admissibility of evidence to prove a subsequent parol agreement not complying with the Statute, if such evidence is tendered merely for the purpose of establishing the rescission of a prior contract.[3] Even in such early cases as *Price* v. *Dyer*[4] and *Robinson* v. *Page*[5] this seems to have been assumed to be the law; and the Court of Exchequer Chamber in *Noble* v. *Ward*[6] would clearly appear to have recognized the principle. In *Noble* v. *Ward*, the plaintiff had been non-suited on the ground that the contract on which he was suing had been impliedly rescinded by a subsequent unenforceable contract. But on a motion to set aside the non-suit and for a new trial, it was laid down by the Court of Exchequer Chamber that whether this result followed was not a question of law for the judge, but of fact for the jury.

[1] Fry, *Specific Performance of Contracts*, 6th ed. p. 481.

[2] [1918] A.C. 1.

[3] In *Morris* v. *Baron*, [1918] A.C. 1, the prior contract was also required (by s. 4 of the Sale of Goods Act, 1893) to be, and was in fact, in writing. It would seem clear, however, that the principle that a contract under the Statute, but not complying with the Statutory requirements, may be given in evidence to prove the rescission of an earlier contract, applies equally whether the earlier contract is one affected by the Statute or not. See per Lord Dunedin, *Morris* v. *Baron*, [1918] A.C. at p. 28, quoting from Fry's *Specific Performance of Contracts*.

[4] (1810) 17 Ves. 356; 34 E.R. 137.

[5] (1826) 3 Russ. 114; 38 E.R. 519.

[6] (1867) L.R. 2 Ex. 135, 137.

"Mr Holker has contended", said Willes, J., in delivering the judgment of the Exchequer Chamber, "that though the contract of the 27th of September cannot be looked on as a valid contract in the way intended by the parties, yet since, if valid, it would have had the effect of rescinding the contract of the 18th, and since the parties might have entered into a mere verbal contract to rescind simpliciter, we are to say that what would have resulted if the contract had been valid, will take place though the contract is void; or, in other words, that the transaction will have the effect which, had it been valid, the parties would have intended, though without expressing it, although it cannot operate as they intended and expressed. But it would be at least a question for the jury, whether the parties did intend to rescind —whether the transaction was one which could not otherwise operate according to their intention; and a material fact on that point is, that, while they expressly rescinded the contract of the 12th of August, they simply made a contract as to the carrying into effect that of the 18th, though in a mode different from what was at first contemplated."

In *Morris* v. *Baron*,[1] however, it was contended in argument that *Noble* v. *Ward*[2] established that a contract, unenforceable under the Statute, could not be proved to shew that it rescinded a prior contract, but this argument was rejected by all the law Lords.

"It was not decided by *Noble* v. *Ward*,"[2] said Viscount Haldane,[3] "that the Statute of Frauds prevents a parol agreement, if it plainly purports to do so, from rescinding in its entirety a previous written contract. Even although itself incapable of being sued on, a parol contract may have that effect. The question is whether there is an intention in any event to rescind, independent of any further intention which may exist to substitute a second contract. I think that *Noble* v. *Ward*[2] affirms what seems to result from principle, that in such a case the agreement to rescind must receive effect."

Subsequent contract containing express rescission of earlier contract. It follows that if the second contract should contain a

[1] [1918] A.C. 1.
[2] (1867) L.R. 2 Ex. 135.
[3] [1918] A.C. at p. 18.

term expressly rescinding the first, effect will be given to this term by the courts.

"For it would be an extraordinary result", said Lord Dunedin in *Morris* v. *Baron*,[1] "that although a parol contract to rescind a written contract is good, as to which there can be no doubt, yet the same thing cannot happen if after rescinding the first contract the parties go on to make another contract which may or may not be enforceable. Accordingly, if express words to that effect are used there can be no doubt."[2]

Subsequent contract not containing express rescission of earlier contract. Where, however, there is no term in the second contract expressly rescinding the first, it would seem that rescission will be implied only where the second contract, taken in conjunction with other relevant circumstances (if any),[3] affords evidence of an unconditional intention to rescind, independent of any further intention to substitute a new contract for the first.[4] If "the parties have entered into a new contract entirely or to an extent going to the very root of the first inconsistent with it", this fact will afford sufficient evidence of such an actual and independent intention. That was the ground of the decision in *Morris* v. *Baron*,[5] and the following passages from the speeches of Lords Dunedin and Atkinson shew how the House applied this principle to the facts of that case.

"I now turn", said Lord Dunedin,[6] "to the facts of this case. There has been alleged breach of contract *A* on both sides, and action raised with counterclaim. Now the first term of the new contract *B* is to put each party to withdraw legal proceedings; then to give three months' credit to the defendants in the payment of a sum admittedly due for goods already delivered; then to allow them £30 in satisfaction of the expenses they had incurred by reason of non-delivery under contract *A*; and lastly

[1] [1918] A.C. at p. 27. [2] But see note 1, p. 176 *infra*.

[3] Although the subsequent agreement will usually be the most important circumstance to be considered by the court, other relevant circumstances must, of course, be regarded. See per Lord Parmoor in *Morris* v. *Baron*, [1918] A.C. at p. 37, quoted in the text at p. 180 *infra*.

[4] Per Viscount Haldane in *Morris* v. *Baron*, [1918] A.C. at p. 18, quoted in the text at p. 173 *supra*. See also per Lord Atkinson in *British and Beningtons Ltd.* v. *N.W. Cachar Tea Co.*, [1923] A.C. at p. 62.

[5] [1918] A.C. 1. [6] *Ib.* at p. 27.

to substitute for the right of the plaintiff to supply and the duty of the defendants to take 277 pieces of cloth, an option on the defendants' part to take them if they pleased. My Lords, it seems to me impossible to come to any conclusion on this but that the parties agreed that the old contract should be abrogated."

Lord Atkinson expressed the result in these words:[1]

"It is quite impossible, in my opinion, to reconcile the agreement of April 22, 1915, with that of September 24 previous. With the exception already pointed out as to price, they are in conflict in all those material and fundamental provisions which go to the root of each of them. It is, I think, impossible to arrive at any rational conclusion as to the meaning, aim, and effect of this new arrangement other than this, that it was the clear intention of both the appellant and the respondents to put aside, in their future dealings, the original agreement, and to treat it thenceforth as abandoned or non-existent".

Where, however, the second agreement is not "entirely or to an extent going to the very root of the first inconsistent with it" and there are no other circumstances sufficient to establish an unconditional intention to rescind, it would seem that the courts will regard the rescission which would normally be implied under the general rule,[2] as being conditional on the enforceability of the second contract.

"If the implication be no more than this", said Lord Dunedin in *Morris* v. *Baron*,[3] "that the second contract if valid would displace the first, that by itself is not enough, for, as Willes, J., says in *Noble* v. *Ward*,[4] 'It is quite in accordance with the cases of *Doe d. Egremont* v. *Courtenay*[5] and *Doe d. Biddulph* v. *Poole*,[6] overruling the previous decision of *Doe d. Egremont* v. *Forwood*,[7] to hold that, where parties enter into a contract which would have the effect of rescinding a previous one, but which cannot operate according to their intention, the new contract shall not operate to affect the previously existing rights. This is good sense and sound reasoning, on which a jury might at least hold that there was no such intention.' The cases there cited are all cases of surrenders of leases upon new leases granted in which

[1] [1918] A.C. p. 33.
[2] See p. 171 *supra*.
[3] [1918] A.C. at p. 27.
[4] L.R. 2 Ex. at p. 138.
[5] (1848) 11 Q.B. 702.
[6] (1848) 11 Q.B. 713.
[7] (1842) 3 Q.B. 627.

it was held that the surrender, whether express or implied, was conditional upon the new lease being good."[1]

An example may be suggested to illustrate this point. Two parties enter into a contract for the sale and purchase of a house. This contract is reduced to writing and signed; and it contains terms *A* (setting out the agreement for sale and purchase), *B*, *C*, *D* and *E*. The parties subsequently decide to substitute for term *E* a new term *Ea*; and accordingly draw up, but fail to sign, a writing repeating terms *A*, *B*, *C*, and *D* and containing also *Ea*. It is submitted that in these circumstances the second contract would not effect an unconditional rescission of the first.

Subsequent contract producing variation merely. A distinction has, however, been drawn between the admission of evidence of a subsequent agreement, not complying with the Statute, for the purpose of proving or assisting to prove an *independent and unconditional rescission* of a previous contract, and the admission of such evidence for the purpose of proving a *variation* of a prior

[1] It is to be noted with regard to this principle, however, that the authorities cited from the Queen's Bench Reports were both cases where the second lease, being voidable, was subsequently avoided, and it may be open to argument whether Willes, J., did not consider that the second contract in *Noble* v. *Ward*, (1867) L.R. 2 Ex. 135, was also void. See per Lord Finlay, L.C., in *Morris* v. *Baron*, [1918] A.C. at p. 11; *contra*, Lord Haldane, at p. 16; and Lord Dunedin at p. 31. Even if this were so, however, it would still seem possible to support his statement. These leasehold cases proceeded on the implication of a condition, viz. that the surrender should operate only if the second lease were valid. "The surrender", said Erle, J., in *Doe* v. *Poole*, (1848) 11 Q.B. 713, 717; 116 E.R. 641, 642, "is in consideration of the grant; and, if the grant fails, contrary to the intention of the parties, it seems unreasonable that an absolute surrender should be presumed to have been intended." In the same way it might well be said, with regard to cases under the Statute, that where the second contract proves to be unenforceable, contrary to the intention of the parties, it would be unreasonable that an absolute rescission should be presumed to have been intended; unless, of course, there be other sufficient evidence of such intention. See also per Coleridge, J., delivering the judgment of the Queen's Bench in *Doe* v. *Courtenay*, (1848) 11 Q.B. 702, 712; 116 E.R. 636, 640.

It may be remarked that in *Doe* v. *Poole* the court applied this principle to a case where the second lease contained an express surrender of the first. It may be, therefore, that an analogous rule would apply to contracts under the Statute where the second contains an express rescission of the first; and that the principle stated in the text (pp. 173, 174 *supra*) on the authority of a passage quoted (*ib.*) from the speech of Lord Dunedin in *Morris* v. *Baron* should be expressed to be subject to the non-implication of a condition of the sort now under discussion.

contract *coming within the Statute and complying with its requirements*. In the latter case, evidence of the subsequent agreement is rigorously excluded.

"Now we cannot get over the difficulty", said Tindal, C.J., in *Stowell* v. *Robinson*,[1] "which has been pressed upon us, that to allow the substitution of a new stipulation as to the time of completing the contract by reason of a subsequent parol agreement between the parties to that effect, in lieu of a stipulation as to time contained in the written agreement signed by the parties, is virtually and substantially to allow an action to be brought on an agreement relative to the sale of land partly in writing signed by the parties, and partly not in writing, but by parol only, and amounts to a contravention of the Statute of Frauds."

Evidence, therefore, being inadmissible to prove the variation, the parties must stand or fall by their original contract.

This principle was recognized by Lord Hardwicke, L.C., in the case of *Parteriche* v. *Powlet*.[2] It was stated as the law by Grant, M.R., in *Price* v. *Dyer*,[3] and again by Lord Lyndhurst in *Robinson* v. *Page*.[4] A good illustration of the principle is afforded by the case of *Goss* v. *Lord Nugent*.[5] There the plaintiff had agreed to sell the defendant certain land. It subsequently appeared that the plaintiff could not make a proper title to a portion of the land, and accordingly the plaintiff and the defendant agreed verbally for the waiver of the defendant's right to require such title. Later, the defendant refused to go on with the contract, and the plaintiff commenced an action for damages, offering parol evidence to prove the agreement to waive title. This evidence, however, was rejected by the Court of King's Bench, the rights of the parties being left to be determined by the original agreement; and accordingly the plaintiff failed in his action.[6]

[1] (1837) 3 Bing. (N.C.) 928, 937; 132 E.R. 668, 672.
[2] (1742) 3 Atk. 383, 384; 26 E.R. 632.
[3] (1810) 17 Ves. 356; 34 E.R. 137.
[4] (1826) 3 Russ. 114; 38 E.R. 519.
[5] (1833) 5 B. & Ad. 58; 110 E.R. 713.
[6] See also *Stowell* v. *Robinson*, (1837) 3 Bing. (N.C.) 928; 132 E.R. 668; *Vezey* v. *Rashleigh*, [1904] 1 Ch. 634; and *Morris* v. *Baron*, [1918] A.C. 1. The principle stated in the text was applied by the House of Lords in *British and Beningtons Ltd.* v. *N.W. Cachar Tea Co.*, [1923] A.C. 48.

What is a variation? The principle, therefore, being that verbal evidence may not be given to prove the subsequent variation of a contract under the Statute, it becomes necessary to inquire what constitutes a variation. A variation, it is submitted, is a contract to vary by addition,[1] subtraction,[2] or substitution,[3] some portion of a prior contract between the same parties. Every variation, it would seem, is in the nature of a substituted contract, which, if it is to operate, must first rescind the prior or varied contract. This substituted contract would appear to be composed partly of the new terms (if any) introduced by the variation, and partly (or wholly, as the case may be) of such terms of the old contract as are not affected by the variation. It is therefore implied, either partly or wholly, from the circumstance that the parties have allowed the unaltered terms to remain, thereby evincing an intention to continue bound by them; for although these terms were formulated as part of the old contract, the continuance of their contractual force would seem to be solely attributable to a new contract that they should still operate.

That every variation constitutes a substituted contract seems to be the view of the matter which has consistently been adopted by the courts.

"By the general rules of the common law", said Denman, C.J., in *Goss* v. *Lord Nugent*,[4] "...after the agreement has been reduced into writing it is competent to the parties, at any time before breach of it, by a new contract not in writing...in any manner to add to, or subtract from, or vary or qualify the terms of it, and thus to make a new contract; which is to be proved, partly by the written agreement, and partly by the subsequent verbal terms engrafted upon what will thus be left of the written agreement....But, in the present case, the written agreement is not that which is sought to be enforced, it is a new contract which the parties have entered into, and that new contract is to be proved, partly by the former written agreement, and partly by the new verbal agreement; the present contract, therefore,

[1] *Price* v. *Dyer*, (1810) 17 Ves. 356; 34 E.R. 137.
[2] *Stowell* v. *Robinson*, (1837) 3 Bing. (N.C.) 928; 132 E.R. 668.
[3] *Goss* v. *Lord Nugent*, (1833) 5 B. & Ad. 58; 110 E.R. 713.
[4] (1833) 5 B. & Ad. 58, 65; 110 E.R. 713, 716.

is not a contract entirely in writing....''[1] "The foundation, I think", said Lord Atkinson in *Morris* v. *Baron*,[2] "on which that rule rests is that after the agreed variation the contract of the parties is not the original contract which had been reduced into writing, but that contract as varied, that of this latter in its entirety there is no written evidence, and it therefore in its entirety cannot be enforced."

Distinction between substituted contract producing rescission and substituted contract producing variation. Although, however, every variation is in the nature of a substituted contract, every such contract will not prove an unconditional intention to rescind.[3] "If the implication be no more than this", said Lord Dunedin[4], "that the second contract if valid would displace the first, that by itself is not enough...." This principle has already[5] been discussed in relation to substituted contracts in general, and it would seem that variations are merely substituted contracts of the type which does not prove an intention to rescind independently of the enforceability of the variation. In other words, the rescission produced by a variation is conditional on the enforceability of the variation.

"But", said Viscount Haldane,[6] "if the construction placed by the Courts on such words is not accepted injustice will result. For it would then be in the power of a defendant to insist that

[1] "The decision in *Goss* v. *Lord Nugent*", said Parke, B., in *Marshall* v. *Lynn*, (1840) 6 M. & W. 109, 117; 151 E.R. 342, 345, "the principle of which I have no doubt is perfectly correct, has clearly established, with respect to the case of a contract relating to the sale of an interest in lands, that if the original written contract be varied, *and a new contract, as to any of its terms, substituted in the place of it* [the italics are mine], that new contract cannot be enforced in law, unless it also be in writing."

"The plaintiffs say", remarked Bramwell, B., in *Sanderson* v. *Graves*, (1875) L.R. 10 Ex. 234, 236, "that there is no new agreement, but a substituted performance. As this performance, however, could only be substituted for the other by agreement of the two parties, the plaintiffs and defendant, it seems to me manifest there was a new agreement, and not a new agreement as to part, but a new agreement as to the whole. The old agreement was entirely gone, and a new agreement arose incorporating such parts of the old agreement as the parties did not choose to alter."

See also per Shearman, J., in *Williams* v. *Moss Empires, Ltd.*, [1915] 3 K.B. 242, 246, 247. As to this case generally see note 1, p. 183 *infra*.

[2] [1918] A.C. 1, 31. [3] See p. 174 *supra*. [4] [1918] A.C. at p. 27.

[5] P. 175 *supra*. [6] [1918] A.C. at p. 18.

the contract to be sued on by the plaintiff must be the entire new contract comprising the old one with the parol variations, and then to defeat the plaintiff by setting up the statute. The Courts, in order to avoid this result, have read the language as implying that the original formal contract is not, in any question of evidence in proceedings, to be treated as varied by a subsequent contract which is informal, and therefore of imperfect obligation."

How, then, does a contract of which evidence may be given to prove a rescission, differ from a variation? Solely, it would seem, in its evidentiary effect. In the one case an independent and unconditional intention to rescind is proved; in the other the evidence is insufficient to produce this result. The second contract is merely a circumstance tending to prove rescission, and it will be considered by the courts along with other relevant circumstances (if any) to ascertain whether the evidence, *as a whole*, establishes that the parties intended unconditionally to dispose of the earlier contract.

"The next point that arises for consideration", said Lord Parmoor in *Morris* v. *Baron*,[1] "is whether, taking into consideration the parol arrangement of April as part of the acts and conduct of the parties, there was an intention to rescind the earlier contract of September, 1914."

On the totality of the evidence, there must

"have been made manifest the intention in any event of a complete extinction of the first and formal contract and not merely the desire of an alteration, however sweeping, in terms which still leave it [the first contract] subsisting".[2]

If the evidence fails to prove an independent and unconditional intention to rescind, the second contract will be accounted a mere *variation*, and neither party will be able to rely on it for any purpose.[3]

[1] [1918] A.C. at p. 37; and see at p. 38.
[2] Per Viscount Haldane in *Morris* v. *Baron*, [1918] A.C. at p. 19.
[3] Per Lindley, J., in *Hickman* v. *Haynes*, (1875) L.R. 10 C.P. 598, 605: "The result of these cases appears to be that neither a plaintiff nor a defendant can at law avail himself of a parol agreement to vary or enlarge the time for performing a contract previously entered into in writing, and required so to be by the Statute of Frauds".

In accordance with the foregoing principles, it is submitted that where the new arrangement proceeds by subtracting terms from or adding them to the old contract, such new arrangement will, in general, fail to afford proof of an unconditional and independent intention to rescind the earlier contract, and will constitute a variation merely.

"The waiver spoken of in these cases", said Grant, M.R., in *Price* v. *Dyer*,[1] "is an entire abandonment and dissolution of the contract, restoring the parties to their former situation. From the history of the transaction, in the answer and evidence of the solicitor, *all they at any time meant was to add to or modify the terms of the original agreement*".[2]

The materiality of the terms added or subtracted appears to be irrelevant.[3] Where, however, the effect of the new agreement is to substitute for the transaction contemplated by the first agreement a new and different transaction, then it would seem that an intention completely and unconditionally to rescind the first agreement will be inferred;[4] and the mere fact that the second

[1] (1810) 17 Ves. 356, 364; 34 E.R. 137, 140. The italics are mine.

[2] See also *Goss* v. *Lord Nugent*, (1833) 5 B. & Ad. 58; 110 E.R. 713.

[3] "I must also observe", said Parke, B., in *Marshall* v. *Lynn*, (1840) 6 M. & W. 109 at p. 117; 151 E.R. 342 at p. 345, "that it seems to me to be unnecessary to inquire what are the essential parts of the contract, and what not, and that every part of the contract, in regard to which the parties are stipulating, must be taken to be material...."

[4] *Marshall* v. *Lynn*, (1840) 6 M. & W. 109 seems to have been a case of this sort. There the defendant agreed to buy from the plaintiff a shipload of potatoes to be shipped in the plaintiff's ship on her next arrival. When the ship arrived, the defendant asked the plaintiff to send her to load a cargo of some other potatoes which the defendant had bought, and at the same time offered to accept the plaintiff's potatoes when the ship should return; to these proposals the plaintiff agreed. The defendant subsequently refusing to take the plaintiff's potatoes, the plaintiff sued for breach of contract; but was nonsuited on the ground that the second arrangement was not a variation, but the substitution of one contract for another, that other being unconditionally rescinded.

The following illustration may also be suggested. *A* enters into a contract with *B* for the sale and purchase of lot 1 on a building estate; subsequently, however, *A* changes his mind and the parties verbally agree that for lot 1 shall be substituted lot 2. It is submitted that although only one term is altered in the old contract, yet the new and the old relate to entirely different ventures or undertakings; and accordingly the second will afford adequate evidence of an independent intention to rescind the first.

contract incorporates certain of the terms of the first will not reduce it to the position of a variation of the first.

If the view is correct that every variation is in the nature of a substituted contract, it follows that in deciding whether the variation is enforceable, what has to be considered is not the original contract, nor yet the alterations introduced by the variation; but the new contract as a whole. It is submitted that if the result of the variation is to produce a substituted contract which does not come within the Statute, then it is irrelevant to consider the fact of the original contract being one to which the Statute applied. This is the principle of the decision in *Williams* v. *Moss Empires Ltd.*;[1] and in spite of the criticism of this case which fell from Viscount Haldane in *Morris* v. *Baron*,[2] it would seem that the decision and Shearman, J.'s statement of the law are in accordance both with principle and authority. The plaintiff in *Williams* v. *Moss Empires Ltd.* contracted with the defendants to perform at their theatres for a period of about three and a half years, at an agreed salary. When less than a year of the engagement had still to run, the parties verbally agreed for a new rate of salary; and it was decided by Shearman and Sankey, JJ., that inasmuch as the new contract composed of the variation as to salary and the unaltered terms of the original contract, was not within the Statute, it might be proved to the court by parol evidence.

"Those cases[3]", said Shearman, J.,[4] "shew that whenever the parties vary a material term of an existing contract they are in effect entering into a new contract, the terms of which must be looked at in their entirety, and if the new contract is one which is required to be in writing, then it must be wholly disregarded and the parties are relegated to their rights under the original contract. But if on the other hand there is nothing in the terms of the new contract which necessitates a written contract, then, although the original contract was one which was bound to be

[1] [1915] 3 K.B. 242.

[2] [1918] A.C. at pp. 19, 20. See note 1, p. 183 *infra*.

[3] *Goss* v. *Lord Nugent*, 5 B. & Ad. 58; *Stead* v. *Dawber*, 10 Ad. & E. 57; *Giraud* v. *Richmond*, 2 C.B. 835; *Marshall* v. *Lynn*, 6 M. & W. 109; and *Stowell* v. *Robinson*, 3 Bing. (N.C.) 928.

[4] [1915] 3 K.B. at p. 247.

in writing, the new parol contract can be enforced because although it is not in writing it is nevertheless an effective contract."[1]

Subsequent arrangements not constituting variations. A subsequent verbal arrangement or agreement amounting to no more than (1) the acceptance of a substituted performance of the original contract or (2) a voluntary forbearance at the request of the party to be charged, will not constitute a variation of the original contract; and accordingly parol evidence to prove such arrangement or agreement will not be excluded by the Statute.

(1) *Substituted performance.* If one party to a contract tenders a performance different from that specified in the contract, and the other party accepts such performance in satisfaction of his rights, such acceptance, it would seem, will not constitute a variation, nor yet afford evidence of a rescission. The reason for this appears to be that such an acceptance cannot be construed as amounting to a contract, as it imposes no sort of obligation on either party; and if it is not a contract it cannot amount to a variation. This, it is submitted, is the result of the decision of the Court of Queen's Bench (Cockburn, C.J., Blackburn, Mellor, and Archibald, JJ.) in *Leather Cloth Co.* v. *Hieronimus*.[2] There the defendant ordered some goods from the plaintiffs to be sent by the Ostend route. Actually the goods were sent by the Rotterdam route; and the defendant, by his conduct, assented to this substituted performance. The goods being subsequently damaged through the stranding of the ship by which they were sent, the defendant refused to pay for them, and the plaintiffs sued on their contract. It was held that the plaintiffs

[1] Viscount Haldane, in *Morris* v. *Baron*, [1918] A.C. at pp. 19, 20, criticizes unfavourably both the decision of *Williams* v. *Moss Empires, Ltd.* and the judgments of Shearman and Sankey, JJ., in that case. Nevertheless it is submitted that that decision was strictly in accordance with principle; and that the judgment of Shearman, J., correctly states the law. The judgment of Sankey, J., however, is on a different footing; as Lord Dunedin pointed out ([1918] A.C. at p. 25) "it ignores the distinction between variation and rescission", and both Lord Dunedin and Lord Parmoor disapproved of it. Neither Lord Dunedin nor Lord Parmoor, however, suggested that the actual decision was wrong; and Lord Parmoor, in his speech ([1918] A.C. at p. 39), quoted with approval Shearman, J.'s statement of the law.

[2] (1875) L.R. 10 Q.B. 140, 146.

might prove that the defendant had assented to the substituted performance which had been tendered.

"The plaintiffs", said Blackburn, J., "do not rely on a substituted contract but on the original contract; and they say, You, the defendant, on being told of the substituted delivery, did not object, but, by your conduct, assented to it. I cannot see why the assent to a substituted mode of performing one of the terms of a contract need be in writing and may not be by parol, though the original contract must have been in writing. They are quite different things, the proof of a substituted contract and the proof of a ratification or approval, after performance, of the substituted mode of performance."

Where, however, the effect of the new arrangement is to impose obligations on the parties—that is, where it is executory and not executed—the ordinary rules apply: the new arrangement may afford evidence of an independent intention to rescind; or it may amount to a variation only, and evidence of it will then be disregarded.[1] If, for example, the parties in the *Leather Cloth Case* had verbally agreed, *before* despatch of the goods, that they should be sent by the Rotterdam route, it would perhaps have been a question whether this new contract did not prove an intention unconditionally to rescind the earlier contract; but otherwise evidence of the arrangement would not have been admissible, and the parties would have had to stand or fall by the original contract.

(2) *Request by defendant for time, followed by voluntary forbearance on part of plaintiff.* Where the new arrangement consists of a request by the defendant for time, followed by a voluntary forbearance on the part of the plaintiff, who nevertheless does not bind himself to forbear, this will not amount to a variation of the original contract, and parol evidence will accordingly be admissible to prove the request and consequent forbearance. The reason for this rule would seem to be much the same as that for the substituted performance rule: an arrangement of this sort is not a contract, and therefore is not a variation.

[1] See, e.g. *Sanderson* v. *Graves*, (1875) L.R. 10 Ex. 234, where Bramwell, B., in a judgment which had the sanction of Pigott, B., held that the new agreement, although unenforceable itself, proved an unconditional intention to rescind the earlier agreement.

Ogle v. *Earl Vane*[1] is generally considered to be the first case[2] in which this rule was judicially recognized and applied. In that case the plaintiff sued the defendant for not delivering iron in pursuance of a written contract, and sought to recover as damages the difference between the contract price of the iron, and the market price, not at the time of the defendant's breach, but at a later time, the plaintiff having been requested by the defendant to wait, and having waited accordingly. At the trial, judgment was given for the plaintiff for the full amount of his claim, and this judgment was upheld by the Court of Queen's Bench and the Court of Exchequer Chamber.

"There is no evidence", said Blackburn, J.,[3] "that the plaintiff ever bound himself to wait for a later delivery, or that he ever made a fresh contract. And I do not think that the evidence establishes either of Mr Jones's propositions, that what the plaintiff did was either inoperative altogether, or amounted to a contract which was void under the Statute of Frauds. I agree that the plaintiff did not make a binding contract at law, because he never contracted at all; but I think that what he did operated so far that it amounted to a postponement of the day at which he might go into the market, and at which the jury might calculate the measure of damages."

Lush, J., put his judgment on the same ground.

"In *Stead* v. *Dawber*[4]", he said,[5] "and the other cases cited, the parties, before the time of the performance of the contract had come, intended to alter the contract, and agreed to extend the time for performance; and the question was, whether the substituted contract could be enforced, and it was held that it could

[1] (1867) L.R. 2 Q.B. 275; 3 Q.B. 272.

[2] It would seem, indeed, that this rule, or a principle closely analogous to it, was relied upon by Lord Ellenborough, C.J., in delivering the judgment of the Court of King's Bench in *Cuff* v. *Penn*, (1813) 1 M. & S. 21; 105 E.R. 8. That case, however, was for some time after its decision very much doubted (see per Parke, B., in *Marshall* v. *Lynn*, (1840) 6 M. & W. 109, 116; 151 E.R. 342, 345) and the rule is nowadays regarded as resting on the cases of *Ogle* v. *Earl Vane*, (1867) L.R. 2 Q.B. 275; 3 Q.B. 272, and *Hickman* v. *Haynes*, (1875) L.R. 10 C.P. 598. McCardie, J., in *Levey and Co.* v. *Goldberg*, [1922] 1 K.B. 688, 691, actually called the rule by the names of these cases, describing it as "the *Ogle* v. *Earl Vane* and *Hickman* v. *Haynes* principle".

[3] L.R. 2 Q.B. at p. 281.

[4] 10 Ad. & E. 57.

[5] L.R. 2 Q.B. at p. 284.

not, because it was partly in writing and partly by parol, and, being for the sale of goods, was within the Statute of Frauds. But here there is no agreement shewn to alter the contracts. After the expiration of the time limited for the performance of the contracts, the plaintiff being entitled at once to sue for damages for the breach, the defendant, the seller, requested the plaintiff, the buyer, to wait and postpone his remedy, in order to enable the seller, if he could, to deliver the iron; the plaintiff accordingly waited. At no time was there any binding contract on the plaintiff to wait, and the defendant remained all along in default."

As these passages shew, it is essential that the plaintiff's forbearance shall be *voluntary*. If he *binds* himself to forbear, the position is entirely different. The arrangement, in that event, will be at least a variation; and in certain cases may even afford evidence that the original contract has been unconditionally rescinded.[1]

The necessity for the forbearance to be at the request of the defendant was emphasized in *Plevins* v. *Downing*.[2] In *Plevins* v. *Downing* there was no such request, and on this ground the Court of Common Pleas distinguished that case from *Hickman* v. *Haynes*.[3] Although, however, it must appear that the forbearance was requested by the defendant, it is sufficient that this request shall appear by implication from the circumstances of the case; it need not be express.[4]

It has been decided that an agreement to extend the time for the acceptance of an offer, which, if accepted, will produce a contract within the Statute, need not be in writing. The Statute relates to contracts only, and anything done prior to the making of the contract is outside its application. Thus, in *Morrell* v. *Studd and Millington*,[5] the defendants offered to purchase from the plaintiff a lease, the offer to remain open for a month and to

[1] *Ogle* v. *Earl Vane* was followed by the Court of Common Pleas in *Hickman* v. *Haynes*, (1875) L.R. 10 C.P. 598 (see per Lindley, J., at p. 606), and the principle of these cases was expressly recognized by Lord Atkinson in *Morris* v. *Baron*, [1918] A.C. 1, 31.

[2] (1876) 1 C.P.D. 220.

[3] (1875) L.R. 10 C.P. 598.

[4] See judgment of Kelly, C.B., in *Ogle* v. *Earl Vane*, L.R. 3 Q.B. 272, 279.

[5] [1913] 2 Ch. 648, 659.

be withdrawn if not accepted within that time. An acceptance of this offer was sent out of time, but the defendant's conduct and other circumstances of the case shewed "either an agreement to enlarge the time or to treat the actual acceptance as a proper acceptance"; and Astbury, J., held that the Statute did not operate to prevent this agreement from being proved.

"Now s. 4 of the Statute of Frauds", said the learned judge, "only requires a note or memorandum of the agreement referred to in the section, which agreement does not come into existence until the offer and acceptance are complete, and therefore an agreement to extend the time for acceptance, or an agreement that an acceptance, which by reason of its date need not be treated as an acceptance, shall be so treated so as to create a contract, is not an agreement which the statute requires to be evidenced in writing, if the note or memorandum contained in the signed offer is otherwise sufficient."

CHAPTER III

ADMISSION OF EXTRINSIC EVIDENCE TO PROVE COLLATERAL CONTRACTS

NEITHER the Statute nor the common law rule[1] will prevent the proof and enforcement of a contract outside the provisions of the Statute but *collateral to*, and not inconsistent with, another coming within such provisions. A contract is collateral to another when the consideration for the first is the making of that other.

"It is evident", said Lord Moulton, in *Heilbut, Symons and Co.* v. *Buckleton*,[2] "both on principle and on authority that there may be a contract the consideration for which is the making of some other contract. 'If you will make such and such a contract I will give you one hundred pounds', is in every sense of the word a complete legal contract. It is collateral to the main contract, but each has an independent existence, and they do not differ in respect of their possessing to the full the character and status of a contract."

The principle that parol evidence may be given of a contract not in writing and not within the Statute but collateral to another contract to which the Statute applies, seems first to have been laid down in the comparatively late case of *Lindley* v. *Lacey*.[3] In that case the plaintiff and defendant were negotiating for the sale of a business; the terms agreed upon were ultimately reduced to writing, but when the plaintiff was asked by the defendant to sign the writing he demurred until the defendant verbally undertook to settle an action then pending against the plaintiff at the suit of one Chase. On these facts it was held that the defendant's undertaking was a separate and collateral contract, which, not being inconsistent with the contract in writing, could be duly proved and enforced. The ground of this decision was thus expressed by Erle, C.J.:

1 P. 149 *supra*.

2 [1913] A.C. 30, 47.

3 (1864) 17 C.B. (N.S.) 578, 586; 144 E.R. 232, 235.

"I think, therefore, the intention of the parties was that this settlement of Chase's bill should form the subject of a distinct collateral promise—a preliminary matter to be done at once. I take it to be substantially the same as if, the agreement for the sale of the goods being before them, Lacey had said to Lindley, 'In consideration of your signing that agreement, I will settle Chase's action'....I think it is clear from the evidence here that there was a distinct collateral agreement that Chase's action should be settled by the defendant, and that evidence of that agreement, which was perfectly consistent with the written agreement, was admissible".

Lindley v. *Lacey* was cited in *Morgan* v. *Griffith*,[1] where the Court of Exchequer gave a similar decision. There the plaintiff had agreed to take from the defendant a lease of certain lands; but finding the lands overrun with rabbits, he refused to sign the lease unless the defendant would undertake that the rabbits should be destroyed. The defendant refused to insert such an undertaking in the lease, but verbally agreed that he would destroy the rabbits; and thereupon the plaintiff signed the lease. The defendant having failed to destroy the rabbits, the plaintiff sued for the breach of the verbal agreement. The trial judge admitted evidence of this agreement and left it to the jury to say whether the lease had been signed upon the faith of it. The jury found for the plaintiff and the defendant appealed on the ground of misreception of evidence. The Court of Exchequer dismissed the appeal, holding that the verbal agreement was collateral to the lease, and therefore could be proved by oral evidence.

"The verbal agreement in this case", said Pigott, B.,[2] "although it does affect the mode of enjoyment of the land demised, is, I think, purely collateral to the lease. It was on the basis of its being performed that the lease was signed by plaintiff, and it does not appear to me to contain any terms which conflict with the written document."

Morgan v. *Griffith* was followed by the Lords Justices in *Erskine* v. *Adeane*;[3] and by the Court of Queen's Bench in

[1] (1871) L.R. 6 Ex. 70.
[2] *Ib.* at p. 73.
[3] (1873) L.R. 8 Ch. 756.

Angell v. *Duke*;[1] and these cases were applied by the Court of Appeal in deciding *De Lassalle* v. *Guildford*.[2] There the plaintiff and defendant had agreed for a lease from the defendant to the plaintiff, but the plaintiff refused to hand over the counterpart that he had signed unless he received an assurance that the drains were in good order. The defendant accordingly gave a verbal assurance to this effect, thereupon receiving the counterpart from the plaintiff. The drains were not in good order and the plaintiff commenced an action for damages. It was decided by the Court of Appeal that the defendant's assurance was a "warranty" collateral to the lease, and parol evidence was accordingly admitted.

In order that the principle of the foregoing cases should apply, it must clearly be proved that the parties intended the undertaking to constitute a contract.[3]

[1] (1875) L.R. 10 Q.B. 174. Here the court expressly said that their judgment appeared to run counter to the judgment of the King's Bench in *Mechelen* v. *Wallace*, (1837) 7 A. & E. 49; 112 E.R. 389; and this case, it is submitted, must now be considered as overruled.

[2] [1901] 2 K.B. 215. Approved and followed by a Divisional Court consisting of Swift and Macnaghten, JJ., in *Miller* v. *Cannon Hill Estates, Ltd.* [1931] 2 K.B. 113.

[3] The collateral undertakings in *Lindley* v. *Lacey*, (1864) 17 C.B. (N.S.) 578; 144 E.R. 232, *Morgan* v. *Griffith*, (1871) L.R. 6 Ex. 70, *Erskine* v. *Adeane*, (1873) L.R. 8 Ch. 756, and *Angell* v. *Duke*, (1875) L.R. 10 Q.B. 174, were all executory and therefore clearly capable of standing alone as distinct contracts. At first sight, however, *De Lassalle* v. *Guildford*, [1901] 2 K.B. 215, presents a difficulty; there the undertaking was that a certain state of affairs existed; and not in terms that something was to be done. Can such an undertaking, then, constitute a contract? "It is to be observed", wrote Salmond in Salmond and Winfield's *Law of Contracts*, p. 13, "that an essential distinction between contracts and all other kinds of agreements is that contracts are necessarily, in the technical language of the law, executory, whereas all non-contractual agreements are necessarily executed. An executory agreement means one in which after the making of it there remains something to be done by one or both of the parties in performance thereof. It is this executory element which constitutes the obligation of the contract." See also the definition of a contract in Anson's *Law of Contract*, 17th ed. p. 8. It would seem, however, that an undertaking in the form that a certain state of things exists, really amounts to a promise to pay damages if it does not exist, and hence can rightly be regarded as a contract. To quote again from Salmond and Winfield's *Law of Contracts* (at p. 32): "He who warrants a horse to be sound does in truth and in fact promise that, if it is not sound, he will pay to the purchaser by way of damages any deficiency in value caused by its unsoundness. It is in this promissory obligation to pay damages that the contractual obligation of a warranty consists". See also per Lord Moulton in *Heilbut, Symons and Co.* v. *Buckleton*, [1913] A.C. at p. 47.

"Not only the terms of such contracts", said Lord Moulton in *Heilbut, Symons and Co.* v. *Buckleton*,[1] "but the existence of an animus contrahendi on the part of all parties to them must be clearly shewn....There is in the present case an entire absence of any evidence to support the existence of such a collateral contract....Neither the plaintiff nor the defendant were asked any question or gave any evidence tending to shew the existence of an animus contrahendi other than as regards the main contracts. The whole case for the existence of a collateral contract therefore rests on the mere fact that the statement was made as to the character of the company, and if this is to be treated as evidence sufficient to establish the existence of a collateral contract of the kind alleged the same result must follow with regard to any other statement relating to the subject-matter of a contract made by a contracting party prior to its execution. This would negative entirely the firmly established rule that an innocent representation gives no right to damages. It would amount to saying that the making of any representation prior to a contract relating to its subject-matter is sufficient to establish the existence of a collateral contract that the statement is true and therefore to give a right to damages if such should not be the case."

It is in virtue of the operation of such an undertaking as a separate contract that parol evidence may be given of it although the contract to which it is collateral is within the Statute. Such evidence does not affect the contract under the Statute: it merely goes to prove a separate and independent contract. For the same reason, the collateral contract does not seem to constitute an addition to or variation of the contract under the Statute, so as to conflict with the common law rule.[2] Nevertheless the

[1] [1913] A.C. at p. 47.

[2] P. 149 *supra*. Certain *dicta* in the cases would suggest that the principle under discussion in the text consists merely in that exception to the common law rule, whereby extrinsic evidence may be given (notwithstanding the common law rule) to complete a writing appearing on the face of it or by inference from the surrounding circumstances not to be intended to be complete. See p. 154 *supra*. Thus in *Lindley* v. *Lacey*, (1864) 17 C.B. (N.S.) 578, 586; 144 E.R. 232, 235, Erle, C.J., remarked: "If the instrument shews that it was meant to contain the whole bargain between the parties, no extrinsic evidence can be admitted to introduce a term which does not appear there. But, if it be clear that the written instrument does not contain the whole, and the jury find that there was a distinct collateral verbal agreement between the parties, not inconsistent with the written contract, the law does not prohibit such distinct collateral agreement from being enforced". And in *De Lassalle* v. *Guildford*, [1901] 2 K.B. 215, 222, A. L. Smith, M.R. (who delivered the

collateral contract must not be inconsistent with the contract under the Statute.[1]

If the injured party is unable to establish that *animus contrahendi* referred to by Lord Moulton, the undertaking relied upon by him may perhaps amount to a misrepresentation entitling him to rescind the contract and affording a defence to a claim for specific performance; and if made fraudulently it will support an action for damages *ex delicto*.[2] But unless this *animus*

judgment of the Court of Appeal), also made reference to the incompleteness of the writing (a lease) evidencing the main contract. "It appears to me in this case clear", he said, "that the lease did not cover the whole ground, and that it did not contain the whole of the contract between the parties." Notwithstanding these *dicta*, however, it is submitted that the collateral contract principle is entirely independent of the common law rule. Perhaps, indeed, the writing in *Lindley* v. *Lacey* was in such a form as to justify the inference that it was not intended to be a complete statement of the contract between the parties. In none of the other cases (*Morgan* v. *Griffith*, (1871) L.R. 6 Ex. 70, *Erskine* v. *Adeane*, (1873) L.R. 8 Ch. 756, *Angell* v. *Duke*, (1875) L.R. 10 Q.B. 174, and *De Lassalle* v. *Guildford*, [1901] 2 K.B. 215), however, would evidence not amounting to proof of an independent contract have been admitted to add to the terms contained in the writing, for in none of those cases could it have been said that the form of the writing (in each case a lease) suggested anything but finality and completeness; and it does not appear that any circumstance (apart from the collateral undertaking itself) was proved, tending to indicate incompleteness. Indeed, it may be doubted whether evidence of surrounding circumstances would be available for this purpose in the case of a document so plainly final and complete as a lease. The only fact upon which A. L. Smith, M.R., could have based his *dictum* was the very collateral undertaking of which it was sought to admit oral evidence. Neither in *Morgan* v. *Griffith*, (1871) L.R. 6 Ex. 70, *Erskine* v. *Adeane*, (1873) L.R. 8 Ch. 756, nor *Angell* v. *Duke*, (1875) L.R. 10 Q.B. 174, did the court refer to the common law rule; and it is submitted that the real basis of the principle exemplified by those cases, is the operation and existence of the collateral undertaking as a separate contract.

[1] See per Pigott, B., in *Morgan* v. *Griffith*, (1871) L.R. 6 Ex. at p. 73; per Mellish, L.J., in *Erskine* v. *Adeane*, (1873) L.R. 8 Ch. at p. 766; and per A. L. Smith, M.R., in *De Lassalle* v. *Guildford*, [1901] 2 K.B. at p. 222.

[2] On the law as to innocent misrepresentation inducing a contract, see Anson, *Law of Contract*, 17th ed. pp. 178–186; as to fraudulent misrepresentation, *ib.* pp. 196–208. *Heilbut, Symons and Co.* v. *Buckleton*, [1913] A.C. 30, affords an example of a case where the undertaking relied upon by the plaintiff amounted neither to a collateral contract nor to a fraudulent misrepresentation. In *De Lassalle* v. *Guildford*, [1901] 2 K.B. 215, A. L. Smith, M.R., considered at some length whether the undertaking in that case was anything more than an innocent misrepresentation (*ib.* pp. 220–221).

Angell v. *Duke*, (1875) 32 L.T. 320, is interesting in this respect. The proceedings in the case reported in L.R. 10 Q.B. 174 (referred to *supra*) were upon demurrer; but at the trial Blackburn, J., held that the plaintiff failed to

contrahendi is clearly proved, the undertaking will not operate as a contract.[1]

establish, as to one of the terms of the alleged collateral contract, anything more than a mere representation made during the course of negotiation. Accordingly he rejected evidence of this term; and his ruling was upheld by the Court of Queen's Bench. "Here", he said (32 L.T. 321), "the lease expresses the whole of the terms; the defendant agrees to let, and the plaintiff to take, the house and furniture at a certain rent; there is said to have been an arrangement made beforehand during the negotiation, that the defendant should let the plaintiff have more furniture for the same rent; how is this collateral? I cannot perceive that it is." See, with reference to this case, *De Lassalle* v. *Guildford*, [1901] 2 K.B. at p. 223.

[1] Long before the doctrine of collateral contracts was established in the courts of common law, it had been held by Lord Thurlow, L.C., in *Pember* v. *Mathers*, (1779) 1 Bro. C.C. 52; 28 E.R. 979, that where a contract is entered into by a plaintiff on the faith of a parol undertaking by the defendant, evidence to prove that undertaking is admissible, inasmuch as it would be a fraud on the plaintiff if it were excluded. The importance of this decision has, however, been greatly diminished by the growth and development of the above-mentioned common law doctrine. It would seem, nevertheless, that the principle of *Pember* v. *Mathers* and the common law rule as to collateral contracts are not entirely coincident. The equitable principle could apply even if the collateral agreement were a contract within the Statute, whereas in such a case, the common law rule, which depends on the collateral agreement being itself a valid and enforceable contract, would not help the plaintiff.

CHAPTER IV

EFFECT OF STATUTE ON CONTRACTS NOT COMPLYING WITH ITS REQUIREMENTS

Statute merely renders contracts unenforceable. It is now well settled that the Statute affects merely the enforceability, and not the existence, of contracts. For many years after the enactment of the Statute, however, the result of non-compliance with its provisions remained uncertain; and it was not until 1852 that it was finally and expressly determined (in *Leroux* v. *Brown*[1]) that such non-compliance did not render the alleged contract void. In *Case* v. *Barber*[2] indeed, decided by the Court of King's Bench in 1681, the court appeared clearly to appreciate the position of contracts not complying with the statutory requirements. "Admit the agreement would bind", runs Sir Thomas Raymond's report, "yet now by the Statute of Frauds and Perjuries, 29 Car. 2, this agreement ought to be in writing, or else the plaintiff could have no remedy thereon." But in later cases, the judges more commonly spoke of the Statute as *avoiding* contracts which, being within its terms, were not evidenced by writing. Thus in *Chater* v. *Beckett*,[3] which came before the King's Bench in 1797, Lord Kenyon, C.J., said:

"When the cause came on to be tried, I referred to the case of *Read* v. *Nash*,[4] to shew that this was a case within the Statute of Frauds; and though the court ruled that that case itself was not within the Statute, what was said by Lord Chief Justice Lee is decisive to shew that this promise is void by the Statute".[5]

[1] (1852) 12 C.B. 801; 138 E.R. 1119.

[2] Raym. Sir T. 450; 83 E.R. 235, 236.

[3] (1797) 7 T.R. 201, 204; 101 E.R. 931, 933.

[4] 1 Wils. 305.

[5] Many such *dicta* are to be found in the earlier reports. "The question", said Lord Mansfield, C.J., in *Simon* v. *Metivier*, (1766) 1 Black. W. 599, 600; 96 E.R. 347, "is singly upon the Statute of Frauds, whether the contract is void by the provisions of that positive law." "The agreement being void as to the land must be void also as to the personal property which was to be sold with it...", said Macdonald, C.B., in *Cooke* v. *Tombs*, (1794) 2 Anst. 420, 425; 145 E.R. 922, 924. In the course of his judgment in *Matson* v. *Wharam*,

It may, however, be suggested, that by "void" the judges in this case, and in others where the word has been similarly used, meant nothing more than "unenforceable". In favour of this suggestion is the fact that where an action is brought to enforce an alleged contract, it is immaterial, for the immediate purpose of determining the result of the action, whether such contract be void or merely unenforceable: in either event the action fails.[1] In such cases, therefore, the judges quite probably described the contracts sued on as "void", without adverting to the distinction in question.

In *Carrington* v. *Roots*,[2] however, the point was expressly taken in argument; and the Court of Exchequer (Lord Abinger, C.B., Parke, Bolland and Gurney, BB.) unanimously declared that the Statute wholly avoided contracts within its terms and not in writing. "I think, therefore", said the learned Chief Baron, "that the meaning of the Statute is, not that the contract shall stand for all purposes except that of being enforced by action, but it means that the contract shall be altogether void." This case was followed by the same court (composed, on this occasion, of Pollock, C.B., Parke and Alderson, BB.), in *Reade* v. *Lamb*.[3]

These two decisions of the Court of Exchequer did not dispose of the question, however. In the first place, the Statute itself merely said that "no action should be brought" on contracts not complying with its provisions; and that, *prima facie*, would seem to be different from saying that such contracts should be void. Moreover, a void contract is a nullity; but long before the decision in *Carrington* v. *Roots* it had been established that the writing required by the Statute need not come into existence contemporaneously with the contract but might be

(1787) 2 T.R. 80, 81; 100 E.R. 44, 45, Buller, J., remarked that "the general line now taken is, that if the person to whose use the goods are furnished be liable at all, any other promise to pay that debt must be in writing, otherwise it is void by the Statute of Frauds".

[1] The distinction between the terms "void" and "unenforceable" has not always been drawn as carefully as definition would demand: see per Lord Dunedin in *Morris* v. *Baron*, [1918] A.C. 1, 24.

[2] (1837) 2 M. & W. 248, 255; 150 E.R. 748, 751.

[3] (1851) 6 Ex. 130; 155 E.R. 483.

written or adopted by the party to be charged, at some later time.[1] Yet if the contract had in its inception been a nullity, it would have been impossible for any subsequent writing, not being itself a contract, to have brought it into existence.

Not only, however, did the decision of *Carrington* v. *Roots* present these and other difficulties of principle, but it was also contrary to the opinion expressed by the Court of King's Bench in *Crosby* v. *Wadsworth*.[2]

> "This brings us to the question", said Lord Ellenborough, C.J., in the latter case, "whether the plaintiff had under the agreement and circumstances stated any legal title to this growing crop at the time when the injury [by way of trespass *quare clausum fregit*] complained of was done; or whether his supposed title thereto was not wholly void, as being created by parol, under any, and which of the provisions in the Statute of Frauds, or on any other and what account?...But the statute does not expressly or immediately vacate such contracts, if made by parol; it only precludes the bringing of actions to enforce them by charging the contracting party or his representatives, on the ground of such contract and of some supposed breach thereof; which description of action does not properly apply to the one now brought, viz. a mere general action of trespass, complaining of an injury to the possession of the plaintiff, however acquired, by contract or otherwise."

In this state of the authorities *Leroux* v. *Brown*[3] came before the Court of Common Pleas in 1852. In that case the plaintiff based his action upon an oral contract not to be performed within a year, made in France, and fully valid there. By the rules of private international law, questions relating to procedure and evidence are determined by the *lex fori*, and questions as to

[1] "It is not necessary", said Lord Ellenborough in *Shippey* v. *Derrison*, (1805) 5 Esp. 190, 193; 170 E.R. 782, 783, "that the note in writing, to be binding under the statute, should be cotemporary with the agreement. It is sufficient if it has been made at any time and adopted by the party afterwards, and then anything under the hand of the party, expressing that he had entered into the agreement, will satisfy the statute which was only intended to protect persons from having parol agreements imposed on them." See also *Tawney* v. *Crowther*, (1791) 3 Bro. C.C. 318; 29 E.R. 557.

[2] (1805) 6 East 602, 610; 102 E.R. 1419, 1423.

[3] (1852) 12 C.B. 801, 824; 138 E.R. 1119, 1129.

the "rights and solemnities of the contract" by the *lex loci contractus*. It was therefore contended for the plaintiff, that the Statute affected the existence of the contract and not merely the evidence by which it was to be proved; but the Court of Common Pleas held that this contention could not be sustained.

"The statute, in this part of it", said Jervis, C.J., "does not say, that, unless those requisites are complied with, the contract shall be void, but merely that no action shall be brought upon it: and, as was put with great force by Mr Honyman, the alternative, 'unless the agreement, or some memorandum or note thereof, shall be in writing',—words which are satisfied if there be any written evidence of a previous agreement—shews that that statute contemplated that the agreement may be good, though not capable of being enforced if not evidenced by writing. This therefore may be a very good agreement, though, for want of a compliance with the requisites of the statute, not enforceable in an English court of justice. This view seems to be supported by the authorities; because, unless we are to infer that the courts thought the agreement itself good, though not made in strict compliance with the statute, they could not consistently have held, as was held in the cases referred to by Sir Edward Sugden, that a writing subsequent to the contract, and addressed to a third person, was sufficient evidence of an agreement within the statute."

Leroux v. *Brown* definitely established that the Statute went merely to the enforceability of the contract. In *Williams* v. *Wheeler*,[1] indeed, Willes, J., expressed a doubt as to the soundness of the decision in *Leroux* v. *Brown*; but in subsequent cases its validity and correctness have been fully recognized.

"It has been determined at law", said Lord Selborne, L.C., in his speech to the House of Lords in *Maddison* v. *Alderson*,[2] "(and, in this respect, there can be no difference between law and equity), that the 4th section of the Statute of Frauds does not avoid parol contracts, but only bars the legal remedies by which they might otherwise have been enforced: *Crosby* v. *Wadsworth*;[3] *Leroux* v. *Brown*;[4] *Britain* v. *Rossiter*.[5]" "I think

[1] (1860) 8 C.B. (N.S.) 299; 141 E.R. 1181.
[2] (1883) 8 App. Cas. 467, 475. [3] (1805) 6 East 602; 102 E.R. 1419.
[4] (1852) 12 C.B. 801; 138 E.R. 1119. [5] 11 Q.B.D. 130.

it is now finally settled", said Lord Blackburn in the same case,[1] "that the true construction of the Statute of Frauds, both the 4th and the 17th sections, is not to render the contracts within them void, still less illegal, but it is to render the kind of evidence required indispensable, when it is sought to enforce the contract." "The real truth", said Kay, J., in *Bristol, Cardiff and Swansea Aerated Bread Co.* v. *Maggs*,[2] "is that the statute was not meant to affect contracts in any way, but only the evidence of them."[3]

The Statute and the doctrine of consideration.[4] At one time during the eighteenth century, it seemed likely that a writing under the Statute might be accepted as an alternative to consideration in constituting a contract. In 1765, Lord Mansfield had laid it down that consideration was required merely as evidence of the existence of the contract.

"I take it", he said in *Pillans* v. *Van Mierop*,[5] "that the ancient notion about the want of consideration was for the sake of evidence only: for when it is reduced into writing, as in covenants, specialties, bonds, etc., there was no objection to the want of consideration. And the Statute of Frauds proceeded upon the same principle."

From this it was argued that where the contract was in writing, and especially where the writing had been adopted in pursuance of the requirements of the Statute, consideration was unnecessary. This doctrine, however, was but short-lived: it was emphatically rejected by the judges when consulted by the House of Lords in *Rann* v. *Hughes*;[6] and it received its final death-blow at the hands of the Court of Queen's Bench in *Eastwood* v. *Kenyon*.[7]

Effect of a contract rendered unenforceable by the Statute. A contract, therefore, which should have been evidenced by writing to comply with the Statute, may not be enforced by an

[1] 8 App. Cas. at p. 488.
[2] (1890) 44 Ch.D. 616, 622.
[3] See also *In re Hoyle*, [1893] 1 Ch. 84, 97, per Lindley, L.J.; *Morris* v. *Baron*, [1918] A.C. 1.
[4] See Holdsworth, *History of English Law*, VIII, p. 35.
[5] (1765) 3 Burr. 1663, 1669; 97 E.R. 1035, 1038.
[6] (1778) 7 T.R. 350n. (*a*); 101 E.R. 1014.
[7] (1840) 11 A. & E. 438; 113 E.R. 482.

action brought directly for this purpose, nor will damages be recoverable for its breach;[1] moreover, it would seem that it will not support proceedings, criminal or otherwise, the indirect effect of which would be to enforce it for the benefit of the prosecutor or plaintiff. Thus in *Banks* v. *Crossland*[2] the prosecutor preferred an information under the Master and Servant Act, 1867, against the defendant for failing to enter into the prosecutor's service in accordance with a contract made between them. This contract was, in fact, within the Statute of Frauds, and not evidenced by writing. Accordingly the justices dismissed the information, and their decision was upheld by the Court of Queen's Bench.

"I also think the first ground good", said Blackburn, J., "which the magistrates took under s. 4 of the Statute of Frauds, which says that no action shall be brought, inter alia, upon any agreement that is not to be performed within one year from the making, unless the agreement shall be in writing. That, I think, is equivalent to saying that such an agreement shall not be enforced generally, and to proceed under the new statute would be to enforce the agreement."

If, then, such a contract may not be enforced by action, the question arises as to whether and to what extent it will be available for other purposes. In the language of jurisprudence, an unenforceable contract creates "imperfect" rights; that is to say, the right lacks the character of enforceability which is the mark of a perfect right.[3] An imperfect right may produce any or all of the following effects:

(1) It may be good as a ground of defence.

(2) It may be sufficient to support any security that has been given for it.

(3) Its discharge may afford sufficient consideration to support a subsequent contract.

[1] It would seem, however, that the loss of a contract unenforceable under the Statute may be taken into account in estimating the *quantum* of damages for which a defendant will be liable in an action for the breach of another contract. *Waters* v. *Towers*, (1852) 8 Ex. 401; 155 E.R. 1404.

[2] (1874) L.R. 10 Q.B. 97, 100.

[3] Salmond, *Jurisprudence*, 8th ed. p. 253.

(4) It may possess the capacity of becoming perfect.[1]

It is proposed, therefore, to consider whether rights arising from contracts rendered unenforceable by the Statute produce any or all of these results.

(1) *Availability as a defence.* If rights have been created,[2] money paid,[3] property transferred or possession given and taken,[4] by or in pursuance of a contract which the Statute renders unenforceable, it would seem that the owner of the right, payee, transferee or person in possession may prove and rely upon such contract to justify and protect his position as against a plaintiff seeking to establish some countervailing claim.[5] In such circumstances a defendant does not seek to charge the plaintiff upon the unenforceable contract; he merely endeavours to defeat the plaintiff's action. Thus in *Miles* v. *New Zealand Alford Estate Co.*,[6] the plaintiff was an equitable mortgagee of certain shares belonging to a bankrupt shareholder of the defendant company. The company, however, claimed to be entitled to a prior charge on these shares in pursuance of a contract which, it was suggested, should have been in writing under the Statute. The company having refused to allow any transfer of the shares unless its lien should first be satisfied, the plaintiff commenced an action, claiming, *inter alia*, a declaration that his charge took priority over the company's lien. By way of defence to this claim the company set up its unenforceable contract, and North, J., held that it might do so.

"It is not an action", said North, J., "brought whereby to charge the Plaintiff with the agreement in favour of the De-

[1] As to (1), (2) and (4), and generally see Salmond, *Jurisprudence*, 8th ed. pp. 254, 255. As to (3), see Salmond and Winfield, *Law of Contracts*, p. 26. The distinction between perfect and imperfect rights was well known in Roman Law; an imperfect right being there called *naturalis obligatio*. As to this, see Moyle's *Imperatoris Justiniani Institutiones*, 5th ed. pp. 480–481.

[2] *Miles* v. *New Zealand Alford Estate Co.*, (1886) 32 Ch.D. 280.

[3] *Simmons* v. *Simmons*, (1847) 6 Hare 352; 67 E.R. 1202; *Thomas* v. *Brown*, (1876) 1 Q.B.D. 714; *Jones* v. *Jones*, (1840) 6 M. & W. 84; 151 E.R. 331.

[4] *Crosby* v. *Wadsworth*, (1805) 6 East 602; 102 E.R. 1419.

[5] Cf. however, the decision of the High Court of Australia in *Perpetual Executors and Trustees Association of Australia, Ltd.* v. *Russell*, (1931) 45 C.L.R. 146; see especially the judgment of Evatt, J. (pp. 153 *et seq.*).

[6] (1886) 32 Ch.D. 266, 279.

fendants, and I cannot extend it and say the section can be read as if it were 'any action in which the plaintiff seeks to charge the defendant, or the defendant seeks to set up against the plaintiff any counter-claim of his own'. If this were a case in which the defendant had by a counter-claim set up a charge of his, and sought to enforce that, I should have considered that was equivalent to a separate action, and the plaintiff might in answer to the counter-claim, beyond all question, set up the *Statute of Frauds*: but there is nothing like a counter-claim, and it seems to me I should be enlarging that section of the *Statute of Frauds* if I said the Plaintiff was entitled to set up the *Statute of Frauds* in answer to the case made by the Defendants."

The case went to the Court of Appeal, but there the point became immaterial; Bowen, L.J., however, expressed a similar opinion to that of North, J.

"The only effect of the *Statute of Frauds*", he remarked,[1] "is to prevent the active prosecution of claims in the Law Courts which are not supported by written evidence at the trial."

In *Thomas* v. *Brown*[2] the purchaser of land paid to the vendor a deposit on account of the purchase-money; but subsequently she decided not to go on with the purchase and brought an action to recover the deposit. On her behalf it was contended that the contract did not comply with the Statute and hence could not be relied upon by the defendant to justify his retention of the money. It was held, however (by Mellor and Quain, JJ.), that the plaintiff could not support her case merely by shewing non-compliance with the Statute.

"Now where, upon a verbal contract for the sale of land", said Quain, J., "the purchaser pays the deposit and the vendor is always ready and willing to complete, I know of no authority to support the purchaser in bringing an action to recover back the money."[3]

[1] *Ib.* 296.

[2] (1876) 1 Q.B.D. 714, 723.

[3] A contract rendered unenforceable by the Statute may also serve as a defence by preventing the implication of any different contract respecting the same subject-matter. Where the plaintiff bases his action upon a contract which he alleges can be implied from the acts of the parties, it is open to the defendant to prove that those acts were in fact done in pursuance of a contract rendered unenforceable by the Statute. "It seems to me impossible", said Brett, L.J., in *Britain* v. *Rossiter*, (1879) 11 Q.B.D. 123, 127, "that a new con-

(2) *Availability to support securities.* Although a contract may be unenforceable by reason of the Statute, it would seem that it will yet suffice to support any security which may be given for it. Thus in *Jones* v. *Jones*,[1] the defendant gave the plaintiff a promissory note to secure the payment of the purchase price of a house and land which the plaintiff had verbally agreed to sell to the defendant. The defendant having refused to pay the note, the plaintiff commenced an action. The defendant contended that there was no consideration for the note, inasmuch as the contract of sale was unenforceable, but the Court of Exchequer overruled this objection.

"It is clear", said Lord Abinger, C.B., "that this is a case where the parties have paid their money down—or, what is equivalent, given a promissory note payable on demand—for a future conveyance. Can anybody say that they are not bound to pay it, unless they shew that the plaintiffs have refused to execute that conveyance?"

The position of a contract rendered unenforceable by the Statute is closely analogous to that of a simple contract rendered unenforceable by the Statute of Limitations.[2] Even though a simple contract debt becomes unenforceable by lapse of time, a mortgage or pledge securing it will remain perfectly valid.[3]

The decision of the Court of Appeal in *Ex parte Hall*[4] is not, it is submitted, contrary to the view advanced in the preceding paragraphs. In that case, a customer borrowed from his bankers,

tract can be implied from the doing of acts which were clearly done in performance of the first contract only, and to infer from them a fresh contract would be to draw an inference contrary to the fact." See also per Lyndhurst, C.B., in *Snelling* v. *Lord Huntingfield*, (1834) 1 C.M. & R. 20, 25; 149 E.R. 976, 978.

[1] (1840) 6 M. & W. 84, 88; 151 E.R. 331, 333.

[2] 21 Jac. I, c. 16, s. 3. See *In re Rownson*, (1885) 29 Ch.D. 358. While, however, the Court of Appeal, in that case, recognized the analogy of a contract rendered unenforceable by the 21 Jac. I, c. 16, s. 3, it declined to accept this analogy as a sufficient reason for extending the doctrine of the executor's right to retain statute-barred debts to the case of his debts made unenforceable by the Statute of Frauds. It was said (p. 362) that the executor's right to retain statute-barred debts was a special case, and not an instance of a general principle.

[3] *London and Midland Bank* v. *Mitchell*, [1899] 2 Ch. 161. See also per Jessel, M.R., in *Ex p. Sheil*, (1877) 44 Ch.D. 789, 792.

[4] (1879) 10 Ch.D. 615, 621.

Messrs Hall and Co., £200, and verbally agreed to charge in the bankers' favour certain rent not then due. Accordingly, he wrote out and handed to his bankers a letter addressed to his tenants, as follows:

> "Dear Sirs—When your Michaelmas rent becomes due to me, I hereby authorize and request you to pay to Messrs Hall & Co., of Brighton, £200 to my credit, for which I will accept their receipt as so much of your rent discharged".

This letter was duly sent by the bankers to the tenants. Shortly afterwards and before the rent had become due, the customer was adjudicated bankrupt. It was argued for the bankers that the letter created an equitable assignment; but the Court of Appeal took the view that the letter merely constituted a revocable authority, and was accordingly revoked by the bankruptcy.

> "The Chief Judge", said James, L.J., "held that the letter was a revocable authority to receive the rent, like the authority which a customer frequently gives to his banker to receive his dividends for him. To prevent the possibility of revocation it is necessary to prove the prior agreement, which is the only thing which gives the bankers any equity."

Inasmuch, therefore, as the letter failed to constitute an equitable assignment of the rent, the bankers were forced to rely upon the verbal contract; but this contract related to land and hence the Statute excluded all evidence of it. In *Ex parte Hall*, therefore, the court merely decided that the bankers had failed to prove an equitable assignment;[1] it is submitted that the decision is no authority against the proposition that a contract rendered unenforceable by the Statute will nevertheless support a security.

(3) *Is the discharge of an unenforceable contract sufficient consideration to support a subsequent contract?* It is submitted that, on principle, the discharge of the imperfect obligation or right resulting from an unenforceable contract under the Statute should be sufficient consideration to support a subsequent contract, or to prevent a deed from being regarded by the courts as

[1] See *Greenaway* v. *Atkinson*, (1881) 29 W.R. 560, 561.

voluntary. The Statute merely forbids the bringing of actions to charge persons upon certain specified contracts not evidenced by writing. And it is submitted that to adduce evidence of such a contract merely as incidental to proving its discharge is the exact contrary of proving the contract to charge the defendant upon it: the defendant is charged upon the subsequent contract, not upon the discharged verbal contract.

Certain of the decisions, however, seem to go in the opposite direction. One of the earliest was *Walker* v. *Constable*,[1] which came before the Court of Common Pleas in 1798, as an appeal from a non-suit ruling by Eyre, C.J., at *Nisi Prius*.[2] In that case the plaintiff, having contracted to buy an estate from the defendant, paid a sum of money by way of deposit, and incurred certain expenses in investigating the title. Subsequently the parties agreed that the deal should be off and that the defendant should repay to the plaintiff the deposit together with interest thereon, and re-imburse the plaintiff for the expenses to which he had been put in examining the title. At *Nisi Prius*, Eyre, C.J., had non-suited the plaintiff, and the Court of Common Pleas upheld this ruling. Both Eyre, C.J., and the Court of Common Pleas appeared to consider that the Statute applied to the proof of contracts for any purpose, and ignored the express words of the Statute whereby it is made to apply only where an action is brought to charge a person upon a contract not evidenced by writing. Moreover, the plaintiff's case was not argued upon the basis of the discharge of the earlier contract being a consideration to support the subsequent agreement; but was put upon two grounds, first, that sales by auction were not within the Statute; and secondly, that the discharge of a contract could be proved without giving that contract in evidence. In addition, it was by no means universally accepted in 1798 that the Statute merely rendered contracts unenforceable: Eyre, C.J., described the contract as "void". "This", said he,[3] "is a question on the sale of lands...and I am of opinion that such contract is void, if there is no note in writing of it produced." It is submitted that

[1] (1798) 1 B. & P. 306; 126 E.R. 919.
[2] 2 Esp. 659; 170 E.R. 488.
[3] 2 Esp. 661; 170 E.R. 489.

these reasons would amply justify a court at the present time in refusing to follow, or overruling, *Walker* v. *Constable*, so far as it relates to the question under discussion.

The other cases on the point, of which *Warden* v. *Jones*[1] is the most important, turn chiefly on the question of whether post-nuptial marriage settlements, entered into in pursuance of verbal ante-nuptial contracts made in consideration of marriage, are void against creditors under the 13 Eliz. c. 5, or the 27 Eliz. c. 4, as being voluntary. In *Warden* v. *Jones* it was argued both before Romilly, M.R., who heard the case in the first instance, and Lord Cranworth, L.C., who heard it on appeal, that the verbal ante-nuptial contract was void, *Randall* v. *Morgan*[2] being relied upon. There Grant, M.R., had said:

"Supposing, however, that this letter refers to some parol promise before the marriage, I doubt extremely, whether that would be sufficient to entitle the court to construe this into an acknowledgment of debt: for, the promise being itself a nullity, producing no obligation, a written recognition, after the marriage, would give it no validity".

The defendant in *Warden* v. *Jones* did, indeed, take the point that the Statute did not avoid the contract; but *Leroux* v. *Brown*[3] was not cited, the defendant relying upon Vesey Junior's report of *Dundas* v. *Dutens*.[4] That report, however, merely goes to shew that Lord Thurlow, L.C., considered a settlement reciting an ante-nuptial agreement could constitute a sufficient writing evidencing that agreement; and it was in regard to this proposition that Romilly, M.R., in the course of his judgment in *Warden* v. *Jones*, referred to *Dundas* v. *Dutens*. "I am at loss", said Romilly, M.R.,[5] "to understand how that decision is to stand with the case of *Randall* v. *Morgan*, which is express on this point...." In *Randall* v. *Morgan*, in which Grant, M.R., disapproved of *Dundas* v. *Dutens* (as reported by Vesey Junior),[6]

[1] (1857) 23 Beav. 487; 53 E.R. 191; on appeal 2 De G. & J. 76; 44 E.R. 916.
[2] (1805) 12 Ves. 67, 73; 33 E.R. 26, 29.
[3] (1852) 12 C.B. 801; 138 E.R. 1119.
[4] (1790) 1 Ves. Jun. 196; 30 E.R. 298.
[5] 23 Beav. 495; 53 E.R. 195.
[6] See May, *Fraudulent and Voluntary Dispositions of Property*, 3rd ed. pp. 296–297; especially note (*r*) on p. 297.

the point was whether a letter written after the marriage and setting forth the terms of an ante-nuptial contract, could be a sufficient writing under the Statute; and the decision of Grant, M.R., was "express" that it would not suffice.

Counsel for the wife, in *Warden* v. *Jones*, supported their argument that the ante-nuptial contract, although unenforceable, would yet prevent the post-nuptial settlement from being voluntary, by submitting that if the wife had sued for specific performance of the ante-nuptial agreement, and the husband had omitted to plead the Statute, a valid decree might have been made. Romilly, M.R., declined to consider the implications of this argument, saying that the case before him did not raise the question. "No doubt", he said,[1] "it would not have been obligatory on the husband to have pleaded the statute, but it is unnecessary for me to consider what would be the effect of that upon his creditors, for no such case arises before me."

When *Warden* v. *Jones* came before Lord Cranworth, L.C., he treated the ante-nuptial agreement as productive merely of a moral obligation, so that a post-nuptial settlement in pursuance of that agreement would be grounded upon a "moral" consideration only. "The argument here was", he said,[2] "first that the parol agreement being proved, the parties were under a moral, though not legal, obligation to perform, so that the settlement could not be fraudulent." In deciding the point, Lord Cranworth relied upon an *obiter dictum* of Lord Northington, L.K., in *Spurgeon* v. *Collier*,[3] decided in 1758.

> "It is admitted", remarked Lord Northington, "that, since the statute, though such promise was made, Dr Alston [the beneficiary] could have no remedy. Then the settlement was voluntary, for it could not be compelled. It was made to a person having no right to demand it; for where there is no remedy there is no right."

It would seem, therefore, that Lord Northington also considered that the effect of the Statute was to avoid the contract; "the

[1] 23 Beav. 497; 53 E.R. 195.
[2] 2 De G. & J. 84; 44 E.R. 919.
[3] (1758) 1 Eden 56, 61; 28 E.R. 605, 607.

remedy being taken away, the right also disappeared", said he. But although the general rule is *ubi jus ibi remedium*, it is clearly recognized, to-day, that the fact that the special form of remedy by way of action is not available, does not of itself reduce the right to the position of a merely moral right.[1] As *Leroux* v. *Brown*[2] and *Maddison* v. *Alderson*[3] shew, this is certainly not the effect of the absence of a right of action in cases under the Statute.

Of *Warden* v. *Jones*, then, it may be said, that it was decided at a time when so eminent an authority as Willes, J., still thought the principle of *Leroux* v. *Brown*[2] open to doubt.[4] Moreover *Leroux* v. *Brown* was not cited, either before the Master of the Rolls or the Lord Chancellor. The Master of the Rolls seemed not to appreciate the argument that the settlor was not being charged upon the ante-nuptial agreement, and the Lord Chancellor regarded it as an endeavour to support the post-nuptial deed by reference to an agreement productive of merely moral rights. For these reasons, it is submitted that *Warden* v. *Jones* can scarcely be regarded at the present day as a satisfactory authority.

Three years after the decision of *Warden* v. *Jones*, Romilly, M.R., followed that case in *Goldicutt* v. *Townsend*.[5] *Goldicutt* v. *Townsend* is open to precisely the same objections as *Warden* v. *Jones*, and takes the matter no further.

The next case is *Trowell* v. *Shenton*,[6] decided in the Court of Appeal in 1878, and therefore, like the preceding cases, before the doctrine of *Leroux* v. *Brown*[2] had been finally recognized by the House of Lords in *Maddison* v. *Alderson*.[3] In *Trowell* v. *Shenton* it was alleged that an infant had entered into an ante-nuptial agreement to settle certain property on his intended wife. Eleven years after the marriage, a settlement was in fact entered into; but the ante-nuptial agreement was never ratified in writing in accordance with the requirements of Lord Tenter-

[1] See Salmond, *Jurisprudence*, 8th ed. p. 254.
[2] (1852) 12 C.B. 801; 138 E.R. 1119. [3] (1883) 8 App. Cas. 467.
[4] *Williams* v. *Wheeler*, (1860) 8 C.B. (N.S.) 299; 141 E.R. 1181.
[5] (1860) 28 Beav. 445; 54 E.R. 437.
[6] (1878) 8 Ch.D. 318.

den's Act,[1] which rendered such ratification essential before an action could be maintained on such an agreement. It was held by the Court of Appeal (Jessel, M.R., Collins and Thesiger, L.JJ.), that the settlement was voluntary, the court, as would appear from the judgment of Collins, L.J., following *Warden* v. *Jones*.[2] It is suggested, however, that even apart from that case, the settlement in *Trowell* v. *Shenton* could not have been supported as having been made in consideration of the discharge of the ante-nuptial agreement: it would rather appear to have been an entirely different transaction from that contemplated by such agreement. "The deed does not refer to the agreement", said Thesiger, L.J.[3]; "fourteen years had elapsed since it was entered into. The property is not the same, and the limitations of the deed are different from those provided for by the agreement."

Since 1883, when *Maddison* v. *Alderson*[4] was decided by the House of Lords, there has been no case in which it has been held that the discharge of an agreement, unenforceable under the Statute for want of a writing, would yet not provide a sufficient consideration to support a subsequent contract or prevent a subsequent deed from being voluntary. In *In re Holland*,[5] which came before the Court of Appeal in 1902, *Warden* v. *Jones*[2] was, indeed, discussed; but the court's decision proceeded on the ground that the post-nuptial settlement, which contained a recital of the ante-nuptial agreement, was a sufficient writing to satisfy the Statute.

On the other hand, the case of *In re Davies*,[6] decided by Horridge, J., in 1921, affords considerable support to the view that the discharge of a contract rendered unenforceable by the Statute, will constitute an adequate consideration to support a subsequent contract. In that case, one Davies assigned to the respondent his interest in certain lands, and was immediately afterwards adjudicated bankrupt. The question was whether the assignment was not void as being a "fraudulent convey-

[1] 9 Geo. IV, c. 14.
[2] (1857) 23 Beav. 487; 53 E.R. 191; on appeal 2 De G. & J. 76; 44 E.R. 916.
[3] 8 Ch.D. 326.
[4] (1883) 8 App. Cas. 467.
[5] [1902] 2 Ch. 360.
[6] [1921] 3 K.B. 628.

ance".[1] An assignment made in pursuance of a valid prior agreement would not, in the circumstances of *In re Davies*, have been a fraudulent conveyance, but in *In re Davies* the assignment had been made in pursuance of a prior verbal agreement which was unenforceable for want of a writing under the Statute. Horridge, J., therefore had to consider whether the Statute would prevent the court from taking cognizance of the prior agreement. He came to the conclusion that the Statute did not have this effect, his judgment being chiefly based upon the view of the Statute adopted by the House of Lords in *Maddison* v. *Alderson*[2] and re-stated by Vaughan Williams, L.J., in *In re Holland*.[3]

"The effect of s. 4", said Horridge, J.,[4] "is dealt with in the judgment of Vaughan Williams, L.J., in *In re Holland*.[3] 'The Statute of Frauds does not deal with the validity of the agreement...it deals only with the evidence to prove the agreement, the statute requiring that the agreement shall be evidenced by a writing signed by the party thereto against whom the action is sought to be enforced.' Now what was the position when this document of December 10 [the assignment] was entered into? There was a valid agreement under which this assignment was required to be made, but the bankrupt, when proceedings were taken against him, was entitled to set up the Statute of Frauds in answer to that agreement. Does his failure to avail himself of the provisions of that statute constitute an act of bankruptcy? I cannot think it does. If a suit had been brought against him and he had not availed himself of the statute and a decree for specific performance had been made against him could it be said that the non-pleading of the statute in that action was an act of bankruptcy in the sense that it was an assignment of his property in such a way as to hinder or delay his creditors? I do not think so. I think the absence of the memorandum under the Statute of Frauds did not prevent the principles laid down in the case to which I have just referred[5] from applying here and

[1] Bankruptcy Act, 1914, s. 1, sub-s. 1 (*b*).

[2] (1883) 8 App. Cas. 467.

[3] [1902] 2 Ch. 360.

[4] [1921] 3 K.B. 631.

[5] *Ex parte Hauxwell*, (1883) 23 Ch.D. 626, the principle referred to by Horridge, J., being contained in a *dictum* quoted by Baggallay, L.J. (at p. 642), from the judgment of James, L.J., in *Ex parte Kilner*, (1879) 13 Ch.D. 245, 253: "Where a document is set up which upon the face of it is an act of

therefore I think that this assignment was not an act of bankruptcy."

It is submitted that the principles which guided Horridge, J., in deciding *In re Davies* are correct and in accordance with modern opinion as to the effect of the Statute. It follows that *Warden* v. *Jones*[1] and similar cases should be regarded as being based on the erroneous assumption that the Statute avoids contracts not complying with its requirements. It would seem, therefore, that in spite of *Warden* v. *Jones*[1] and other cases decided prior to *Maddison* v. *Alderson*, the discharge of a contract unenforceable under the Statute for want of a signed writing can yet constitute a sufficient consideration to support a subsequent contract or prevent a deed made in pursuance thereof from being voluntary.[2]

(4) *Capacity to become perfect.* Imperfect rights arising from contracts which the Statute renders unenforceable for want of a signed writing, can be perfected at some subsequent time by the provision of a writing satisfying the requirements of the Statute. The writing must, however, be in existence prior to the

bankruptcy, that is, an assignment of all a man's goods for a past consideration, if it is said that it is not an act of bankruptcy because it is warranted by a prior agreement, the onus probandi is always upon the person who sets up the prior agreement to prove, not only that the agreement did exist in fact, but that it was in all respects a bona fide agreement".

[1] (1857) 23 Beav. 487; 53 E.R. 191; on appeal 2 De G. & J. 76; 44 E.R. 916.

[2] It is interesting to note that the principle suggested in the text appears to have been acted upon by Lord Thurlow, L.C., in *Dundas* v. *Dutens*, (1790) 2 Cox 235; 30 E.R. 109. According to Cox's report of that case, Lord Thurlow decided it on the ground that a verbal ante-nuptial agreement would be sufficient to prevent a post-nuptial settlement from being voluntary. "The *Lord Chancellor*", runs Cox's report (p. 240.; E.R. 111), "said he could not conceive that a settlement made after marriage in pursuance of an agreement before marriage, though only parol, could ever be reckoned a fraudulent settlement; that the cases, though they had gone a great way, in treating settlements after marriage as fraudulent, had never gone to such a length as that; and he was therefore clearly of opinion that the settlement was in itself valid." The report of Vesey Junior, however (1 Ves. Jun. 196; 30 E.R. 298), varies considerably from Cox's, and puts the judgment on other grounds. But as is pointed out in May, *Fraudulent and Voluntary Dispositions of Property*, 3rd ed. p. 296, n. (*n*), Cox was one of the counsel engaged in the case, and that would seem to justify his report being preferred to Vesey's. Cox's report does not seem to have been referred to in *Warden* v. *Jones*, (1857) 23 Beav. 487; 53 E.R. 191; on appeal 2 De G. & J. 76; 44 E.R. 916.

commencement of the action wherein it is proposed to rely upon it; or where the party proposing to rely upon it is joined after the commencement of the action, then prior to such joinder.[1]

[1] See p. 78 *supra*.

CHAPTER V

THE STATUTE AND QUASI-CONTRACTS

THE Statute does not affect the common law principles relative to quasi-contracts. Where one of the parties to a contract which fails to comply with the requirements of the Statute, has rendered services to the other party under circumstances which would normally afford the former a quasi-contractual action against the latter, this action will not be barred merely because such services were rendered in pursuance of the unenforceable contract.[1] The term quasi-contract is perhaps not a very happy one when applied to English law,[2] but it possesses the advantage of comprehensiveness. It is used here to include obligations of the following kinds:

(1) Obligations enforceable in an action for money paid at the request of another;

(2) Obligations enforceable in an action for money had and received;

(3) Obligations arising upon a *quantum meruit*; and

(4) Obligations arising upon an account stated.

These quasi-contracts are independent of any contractual intention in the parties; they are "imposed by implication of law, quite apart from and without regard to the probable intention of the parties, and sometimes even in opposition to their expressed or presumed intention".[3] They are sometimes called "contracts implied by the law",[4] or implied contracts, simply; and they must be distinguished from genuine contracts established by inference from the circumstances of the case, such contracts being also called "implied contracts".[5] The implica-

[1] See *Snelling* v. *Lord Huntingfield*, (1834) 1 C.M. & R. 20, 25; 145 E.R. 976, 978, per Lyndhurst, C.B.; and *Britain* v. *Rossiter*, (1879) 11 Q.B.D. 123, 133, per Thesiger, L.J.

[2] As to the use of the term "quasi-contract" in reference to English law, see Winfield, *The Law of Tort*, pp. 116–117.

[3] *The Laws of England*, ed. Halsbury, VII, p. 463, para. 944.

[4] Winfield, *op. cit.* pp. 124–125.

[5] *The Laws of England*, ed. Halsbury, VII, p. 463, para. 944. See also per Lindley, L.J., in *In re Rhodes*, (1890) 44 Ch.D. 94, 107.

tion of a contract of the latter kind will be impossible where there is already in existence an express contract dealing with the same subject-matter, even though that express contract should be unenforceable for want of a writing under the Statute.

"It is a proposition which cannot be disputed", said Brett, L.J., in *Britain* v. *Rossiter*,[1] "that no new contract can be implied from acts done under an express contract, which is still subsisting; all that can be said is that no one can be charged upon the original contract because it is not in writing."

As has been stated, however, the Statute does not affect the common law principle relating to quasi-contracts.

"Then", said Lord Lyndhurst, C.B., in *Snelling* v. *Lord Huntingfield*,[2] "if there was a contract in fact...although, by the Statute of Frauds, no action can be brought upon it, how can another contract be implied? *It is not like the case of a demand for services rendered;* it is a claim for damages against the defendant for not continuing the plaintiff for the year, and a contract of hiring for a year must be proved."

If the plaintiff's claim had been for services rendered (i.e. quasi-contract), it could have been maintained in spite of the previous verbal contract.

It is now proposed briefly to consider, in relation to contracts rendered unenforceable by the Statute, the several kinds of quasi-contracts mentioned above.

(1) *Money paid at the request of another.* "Where a payment is made at the request of another, a promise to repay the amount will be implied, even though the person at whose request the payment was made has not thereby been relieved from any legal claim."[3] In *Knowlmann* v. *Bluett*,[4] the defendant, who was the father of certain illegitimate children of the plaintiff, verbally agreed with the plaintiff to pay her an annual sum for so long as she should maintain and educate the children. After a time he discontinued the payments, but the plaintiff still maintained

[1] (1879) 11 Q.B.D. 123, 127.
[2] (1834) 1 C.M. & R. 20, 25; 149 E.R. 976, 978. The italics in the quotation are mine.
[3] *The Laws of England*, ed. Halsbury, VII, p. 465, para. 946.
[4] (1874) L.R. 9 Ex. 307, 308.

the children, and later brought an action for the arrears. The Court of Exchequer Chamber held that even if the agreement were within the Statute, the plaintiff could maintain an action for "money paid at the defendant's request".

"It is said", remarked Blackburn, J., "that the action is not maintainable because there is no memorandum in writing of the bargain. But the plaintiff has performed her part of it, and it would be unjust if she could not obtain payment of the sums she has expended. She could have maintained an action for 'money paid at the defendant's request', and it would have been no answer to have said that the term in respect of which she was suing was longer than a year, and that the agreement which fixed the rate of remuneration was one not to be performed within a year. We think that in substance her present claim is for money paid, although the declaration is in form upon a special contract."

(2) *Money had and received.* Where a person has received another's money under such circumstances that the court considers it unjust that he should retain it, an action for money had and received will lie against him for its recovery.[1] This action covers a multifarious class of cases, and it would probably be impossible to devise a formula which would comprehend them all.[2] Special reference need be made here to one only of these cases, viz. where money has been paid on a consideration which has entirely failed. Under these circumstances the payor will usually be entitled to recover back such money from the payee.[3] Where, however, money has been paid in accordance with the terms of a contract rendered unenforceable by the Statute, the mere fact of the unenforceability of the contract is not a sufficient failure of consideration to support this action. Provided the defendant is ready and willing to perform the contract, he can rely upon it as a defence to an action for the recovery of moneys paid to him in pursuance of it.[4]

[1] *The Laws of England*, ed. Halsbury, VII, p. 473, para. 965.

[2] Winfield, *The Law of Tort*, p. 155, citing per Scrutton, L.J., in *Holt* v. *Markham*, [1923] 1 K.B. 504, 514.

[3] *Strickland* v. *Turner*, (1852) 7 Ex. 208; 155 E.R. 919.

[4] See *Thomas* v. *Brown*, (1876) 1 Q.B.D. 714, per Mellor, J., 722, 723; per Quain, J., 723. And see *supra*, pp. 200, 201.

(3) *Quantum meruit.*

"Where one party has disabled himself from performing the contract or has repudiated it, the other party is entitled to treat the contract as at an end. In that case he is not only entitled to damages for breach of contract, but if he has performed his part of the contract wholly or in part, he has a right to sue on a *quantum meruit* for what he has done. This right does not arise out of the original contract, but is based on an implied promise by the other party arising from the acceptance of an executed consideration."[1]

In the case of contracts rendered unenforceable by the Statute, the injured party will have no action for damages, but if the other party has refused to pay for services rendered to and accepted by him, an action will lie for the reasonable value of such services.

"If a party to a contract", said Salter, J., in *Scott* v. *Pattison*,[2] "which is unenforceable under the Statute of Frauds, has rendered services under that contract to the other party, and the other party has accepted and benefited by those services, then I think that the party who has rendered the services can sue the other party in debt on an implied contract to pay him according to his deserts."[3]

The price which was to have been paid for the services under the verbal contract will doubtless be a circumstance which the court will consider in determining the "reasonable value" of such services.

The action on a *quantum meruit* in cases where services have been rendered in pursuance of contracts which are unenforceable for non-compliance with the Statute, is not in the nature of a common law counterpart of the equitable doctrine of part-performance. The common law action is limited in its operation to recouping a party for services which have already been rendered; the amount recoverable is independent of the terms of the actual contract; and relief cannot be obtained in this

[1] *The Laws of England*, ed. Halsbury, VII, p. 440, para. 901.

[2] [1923] 2 K.B. 723, 727.

[3] See, for example, *Pulbrook* v. *Lawes*, (1876) 1 Q.B.D. 284; and *Mavor* v. *Pyne*, (1825) 3 Bing. 285; 130 E.R. 522.

action for the non-performance by the other party of his obligations under that contract. The equitable doctrine produces different results: the contract is performed specifically, so that the plaintiff gets for the services precisely what has been agreed upon.

At one time, indeed, there was a tendency to confuse the common law remedy with the doctrine of equity, and it was supposed that where a contract had been executed on one side, the Statute ceased to apply to it. Certain *dicta* in the judgment of Tindal, C.J., in *Souch* v. *Strawbridge*[1] were usually relied upon for this proposition. In that case an action had been brought for services rendered by the plaintiff in boarding and lodging a child at the request of the defendant. Tindal, C.J., in the course of his judgment said:

> "In the first place, it appears to me that this is not an action which is within the prohibition of the statute. It is brought for a by-gone or executed consideration, viz. the support and maintenance of a child at the request of the defendant. There was evidence enough to shew that the child was placed under the care of the plaintiff at the charge of the defendant, with his assent, and that he had made payments on account of its maintenance. That is equivalent to the proof that is ordinarily given in an action for goods sold and delivered, whence the law implies a promise on the defendant's part to pay for them....It [the Statute] has no application to an action in the present form, founded upon an executed consideration".

Souch v. *Strawbridge* was cited in *Kelly* v. *Webster*[2] as supporting the argument that the Statute did not apply to contracts executed on one side, but the Court of Common Pleas rejected this contention. The same argument was advanced in *Sanderson* v. *Graves*,[3] and again it was unsuccessful.

> "The plaintiff", said Amphlett, B., in that case, "also contended that the Statute of Frauds did not apply to executed contracts, although executed on one side only, and there are some old dicta, and even some decisions, that appear to bear out that view, and had it been sustained, Courts of Law would have

[1] (1846) 2 C.B. 808, 813; 135 E.R. 1161, 1164.
[2] (1852) 12 C.B. 283; 138 E.R. 912.
[3] (1875) L.R. 10 Ex. 234, 241.

certainly made a long stride towards the adoption of the equitable doctrine of part performance."

The question was once again raised in the recent case of *Scott* v. *Pattison*,[1] and on this occasion the judges (Darling and Salter, JJ.) pointed out that the remarks of Tindal, C.J., in *Souch* v. *Strawbridge* had no general application but were made in reference to the particular case then before the court, which was an action in the nature of a claim on a *quantum meruit*.

"We must therefore look", said Darling, J., "in order to see what was the form of the action in that case [*Souch* v. *Strawbridge*]. The first words of the report are: 'Assumpsit for board, lodging, etc., supplied by the plaintiff to a child at the request of the defendant. Plea, non assumpsit'. That explains that it was an action upon an implied promise by the defendant—that was the assumpsit—to pay for the board and lodging which had already been supplied by the plaintiff at the request of the defendant. It is therefore perfectly plain that it was not an action upon a contract which was within the Statute of Frauds, but was an action upon a contract for a consideration which had been already executed, and was therefore one which Tindal, C.J., held was capable of being sued upon because it had been executed."

Scott v. *Pattison* may be regarded as having completely rebutted the suggestion that the Statute does not apply to executed contracts: all that Tindal, C.J., meant in *Souch* v. *Strawbridge* was that the Statute had no application to contracts implied in law (quasi-contracts) from the acceptance of an executed consideration.

(4) *Account stated.*

"Where parties mutually agree that a certain sum is due from one to the other an 'account stated' is said to arise, and the law implies a promise on the part of the one from whom such sum has been agreed to be due to pay the same, on which the other party may sue without being put to proof of the correctness of the account."[2]

[1] [1923] 2 K.B. 723, 725.

[2] *The Laws of England*, ed. Halsbury, VII, p. 489, para. 991. See also *Camillo Tank S.S. Co. Ltd.* v. *Alexandria Engineering Works*, (1921) 38 T.L.R. 134, per Viscount Finlay, p. 141, quoting from Bullen and Leake's *Pleadings*, 2nd ed. (1863).

Dr Winfield, in his analysis of the term "account stated",[1] points out, following Viscount Cave in *Camillo Tank S.S. Co. Ltd.* v. *Alexandria Engineering Works*,[2] that it has three meanings:

(i) It is applied to the case where a claim for payment by one party is admitted by the other to be correct; an action can then be brought on the admission.

(ii) It denotes the liability which arises when, after mutual dealings between the parties, several items of claim are brought into account, on either side, and a balance is struck; by virtue of this process the party against whom the balance stands becomes liable to pay the amount of it to the other party.

(iii) It is also applied to cases where one party has made a claim against the other, and that other has, for valuable consideration, agreed to accept it as correct.

In case (i) it would seem that the admission merely has the effect of changing the burden of proof. Proof of the admission is presumptive proof of an obligation to pay the sum admitted to be due, but it does not discharge the original contract.[3] When, therefore, a party claiming under a contract not complying with the Statute is in a position to rely upon an account stated of this kind, he is absolved from the necessity of proving anything more than the admission, and hence will not be embarrassed by the absence of a signed writing. Thus, in *Cocking* v. *Ward*,[4] the defendant promised the plaintiff, who was the tenant of a farm, that he would pay her £100 if she would surrender her tenancy and induce the landlord to accept him in her place. This the plaintiff did, but when the defendant was asked to pay the £100, he admitted his liability and asked for time. The Court of Common Pleas considered that the original contract was unenforceable by reason of the Statute, but held that the plaintiff could recover upon an account stated.

"There was distinct evidence in this case", said Tindal, C.J., "that after the plaintiff had given up possession, and after the

[1] Winfield, *The Law of Tort*, p. 167. [2] (1921) 38 T.L.R. 134, 143.

[3] See per Viscount Cave in *Camillo Tank S.S. Co. Ltd.* v. *Alexandria Engineering Works*, (1921) 38 T.L.R. 134, 143.

[4] (1845) 1 C.B. 858, 868; 135 E.R. 781, 785.

defendant had succeeded to it through the plaintiff's application to the landlord, the defendant admitted that he owed the £100 to the plaintiff. And this appears to us to be sufficient evidence to enable the plaintiff to recover on the account stated."[1]

In case (ii) the original contract is discharged, and a new liability arising from quasi-contract takes its place.[2] It is immaterial that some or all of the debts which form items of the account should have been unenforceable by reason of the Statute, for the plaintiff does not sue upon the original debts but upon the new quasi-contractual liability which replaces them. Thus in *Re Laycock* v. *Pickles*,[3] the plaintiff owed the defendants £111, while they owed him £67 and held an equitable mortgage over certain of his lands. It was agreed that the defendants should take the lands at £70; and on this basis an account was stated shewing a balance of £22 due to the plaintiff. It was objected by counsel for the defendants, that the action was really for the purchase-price of land, and the plaintiff had

[1] It would seem that the admission of a debt will not operate as an account stated, unless at the time when the admission is made, the consideration for the debt has been executed. This appears to be the effect of the decision of the Court of Exchequer in *Earl of Falmouth* v. *Thomas*, (1832) 1 C. & M. 89; 149 E.R. 326. There the plaintiff agreed to let to the defendant a farm, and in consideration of such lease the defendant agreed to pay the plaintiff for the existing crops at valuation. The crops were duly valued but the defendant refused to pay the amount at which they were assessed, and accordingly the plaintiff commenced an action. There was no writing to support the contract, and the plaintiff relied upon (*inter alia*) an account stated. It was held by the Court of Exchequer, however, that this claim could not be sustained, as the consideration for the original debt had not been executed at the time the account was alleged to have been stated. "The plaintiff's object, therefore", said Lord Lyndhurst, C.B. (rep. 110; E.R. 335), "upon the account stated, is to take the case out of the operation of the Statute of Frauds, and to charge the defendant upon a new contract, a contract which the law would imply from the defendant's taking the crops and receiving the benefit of the work, labour and materials; but this object the defendant has defeated, by shewing that the account was stated when the case stood wholly upon the original contract, and before the mowing of the crops, which was to raise a new contract, had occurred." See also per Scrutton, L.J., in *Joseph Evans and Co.* v. *Heathcote*, [1918] 1 K.B. 418, 437.

[2] Dr Winfield points out (*The Law of Tort*, p. 168) that scientifically this liability could well be classified as "contractual", for all the points requisite to a valid contract seem to be met with in such cases.

[3] (1863) 4 B. & S. 497, 507; 122 E.R. 546, 549.

failed to produce a signed writing; but this argument was overruled by the Court of King's Bench.

"The defendants object", said Blackburn, J., "that, inasmuch as this transaction was by word of mouth, they could not enforce the agreement for the transfer of the equity of redemption, but, if the £70 had been actually paid down, the defendants could not have recovered it back without shewing that the plaintiff had made default in transferring the equity of redemption, or had refused to transfer it; in which case they might have opened the account. But there is no attempt to shew that the plaintiff ever refused to perform the agreement, or that he set up the Statute of Frauds in order to be off his bargain. I therefore think that here was sufficient evidence of an account stated, and that the plaintiff was entitled to succeed."

In case (iii) it would seem that the liability to pay the agreed sum is purely contractual. As Dr Winfield remarks,[1] "there seems to be no need to resort to quasi-contract in order to explain what is, on the face of it, an ordinary contract". With regard to the account being partly or wholly made up of debts which would have been unenforceable by reason of the Statute, the position appears to be the same as in case (ii) *supra*. The plaintiff would sue upon the new contract, and therefore he would not be prejudiced by the fact that the contracts giving rise to the original debts could not have been enforced.

[1] Winfield, *The Law of Tort*, p. 168.

CHAPTER VI

THE EQUITABLE DOCTRINE OF FRAUD IN ITS RELATION TO CONTRACTS UNDER THE STATUTE

VERY soon after the passing of the Statute it began to be laid down by courts of equity that the Statute, as its preamble shewed, was intended to prevent fraud and therefore would not be allowed by equity to become an instrument of fraud. Thus, in 1720, Lord Parker, L.C. (afterwards the Earl of Macclesfield), in delivering judgment in *Montacute* v. *Maxwell*,[1] remarked: "In cases of fraud, equity should relieve, even against the words of the Statute...". Some years later Lord Hardwicke, L.C., in *Attorney-General* v. *Day*,[2] enunciated the same principle, saying that,

> "on all questions on that statute in this court the end and purport of making it has been considered, viz. to prevent frauds and perjuries....Then there are other cases, well known, taken out of the statute, not so much on the principle of no danger of perjury, as that the statute was not intended to create or protect fraud".

The principle was lately affirmed in the House of Lords by Viscount Sumner, who in his speech in *Blackwell* v. *Blackwell*,[3] quoted with approval the following passage from the judgment of Lord Westbury in *McCormick* v. *Grogan*:[4]

> "The Court of Equity has, from a very early period, decided that even an Act of Parliament shall not be used as an instrument of fraud; and if in the machinery of perpetrating a fraud an Act of Parliament intervenes, the Court of Equity, it is true, does not set aside the Act of Parliament, but it fastens on the individual who gets a title under that Act, and imposes upon him a personal obligation, because he applies the Act as an instru-

[1] (1720) 1 P. Wms. 618, 620; 24 E.R. 541, 542.
[2] (1748–1749) 1 Ves. Sen. 218, 221; 27 E.R. 992, 994.
[3] [1929] A.C. 318, 336.
[4] (1869) L.R. 4 H.L. 82, 97.

ment for accomplishing a fraud. In this way the Court of Equity has dealt with the *Statute of Frauds*, and in this manner, also, it deals with the *Statute of Wills*."

Fraud,[1] as understood in Courts of Equity, is a very broad term, and it would seem to include any conduct of an unfair or unconscionable nature on the part of either party to the contract. "But fraud is infinite in variety", said Lord Macnaghten in *Reddaway* v. *Banham*;[2] "sometimes it is audacious and unblushing; sometimes it pays a sort of homage to virtue, and then it is modest and retiring; it would be honesty itself if it could only afford it. But fraud is fraud all the same; and it is the fraud, not the manner of it, which calls for the interposition of the court." "Fraud", wrote Fry,[3] "of course includes not only misrepresentation when fraudulent...but also all other unconscionable and deceptive dealing of either party to any contract." "We must also remember", wrote Anson,[4] "that judges in the Court of Chancery never had occasion to define fraud with precision as an actionable wrong. They therefore, not unnaturally, used the term 'fraudulent' as applicable to all cases in which they refused specific performance or set aside an instrument on the ground that one of the parties had not acted in good faith; and somewhat unfortunately they applied the same term to representations which were made in good faith though they afterwards turned out to be untrue."[5]

When, then, may it properly be said that a party is making the Statute an engine of fraud? In other words, when will it be a fraudulent and unconscionable thing for him to plead the Statute? In its broadest sense the principle under discussion might well amount to a complete negation of the Statute, inas-

[1] The term fraud, when used with reference to doctrines of equity, must be carefully distinguished from that term when used with reference to the tort of deceit for which the common law allows an action for damages. Equitable fraud includes common law fraud; but it includes as well innocent misrepresentation which was not actionable at common law, and indeed much else besides. See text. In this chapter the term "fraud" is employed to denote equitable fraud.

[2] [1896] A.C. 199, 221.

[3] *Specific Performance of Contracts*, 6th ed. p. 330.

[4] *Law of Contract*, 17th ed. p. 180.

[5] See also per Viscount Haldane, L.C., in *Nocton* v. *Ashburton*, [1914] A.C. 932, 951–954.

much as in general the mere making of a contract imposes a moral obligation to perform it. The Courts of Equity have, however, restricted the operation of this principle to two classes of cases, viz.:

(i) Cases where one party has partly or wholly performed his side of the contract, and the other thereupon, designing to secure the benefit of such performance without performing in return the obligations which the contract imposes on him, sets up a plea of non-compliance with the Statute; and

(ii) Cases where such a plea is set up by one who has by fraud prevented the execution of a sufficient writing.

In cases of the first class, the general principle has gradually become so modified and developed as to constitute a separate body of rules, to which the name 'doctrine of part performance" has been applied. This topic will be discussed in the next chapter. In the present chapter it is proposed to consider the general principle as it applies to cases of the second class.

Fraud in preventing the execution of a sufficient writing. Where the drawing up of a sufficient writing evidencing the contract has been prevented by the fraudulent conduct of one of the parties, the absence of the writing will afford no defence to the party guilty of the fraud.

"First, it is said", remarked Turner, L.J., in the course of his judgment in *Wood* v. *Midgley*,[1] "that the defendant has so acted as to avoid signing the agreement, holding the other party bound by the agreement, and *Maxwell* v. *Mountacute*[2] is referred to on this head. But the principle of that and similar cases is fraud. If a party has been guilty of fraud, beyond all doubt the court will not let him take advantage of the Statute of Frauds." "So, if an agreement is, by fraud, prevented from being reduced into writing, the court will relieve, notwithstanding the statute", said Lord Thurlow, L.C., in *Shelburne* v. *Inchiquin*.[3]

What will constitute fraud of the kind referred to by Turner, L.J., and Lord Thurlow is difficult to define in express language.

[1] (1854) 5 De G. M. & G. 41, 45; 43 E.R. 784, 786.

[2] Prec. Ch. 526.

[3] (1784) 1 Bro. C.C. 338, 344; 28 E.R. 1166, 1169. See also per Thurlow, L.C., in *Whitchurch* v. *Bevis*, (1789) 2 Bro. C.C. 559, 565; 29 E.R. 306, 309.

It was at one time thought that where the parties, after entering into a parol contract, had agreed that a writing evidencing it should be prepared and signed, a subsequent refusal of either of them to sign the writing would amount to fraud. Thus in *Leake* v. *Morris*,[1] a bill brought for the specific performance of a contract relating to lands contained an allegation that the parties had agreed that the contract should be put into writing. The defendant pleaded the Statute, but Lord North, L.K., ordered that he should answer so much of the bill as charged that the contract was to be put into writing.[2] In *Montacute* v. *Maxwell*,[3] however, it was laid down by Lord Parker, L.C., that to constitute fraud in these cases something more was necessary than the mere refusal subsequently to sign the writing. Lord Parker's judgment, as reported in *Precedents in Chancery*, contains the following passage:[4]

> "if there were any agreement for reducing the same [the contract] into writing and that is prevented by *the fraud* and *practice* of the other party...this court will in such case give relief; as where instructions are given, and preparation made for the drawing of a marriage settlement, and before the compleating of it the woman is drawn, by the assurances and promises of the man, to perform it and after to marry him."

Lord Thurlow, L.C., in *Whitchurch* v. *Bevis*,[5] expressed a similar opinion.

The effect of *Montacute* v. *Maxwell* was stated in the following terms by Stuart, V.-C., in the course of his judgment in *Wood* v. *Midgley*:[6] "if, the terms of the agreement having been settled and reduced into writing, the signature by the Defendant was only postponed for his convenience or by his contrivance, the Defendant cannot successfully insist on the Statute of Frauds". In *Wood* v. *Midgley* the defendant had approved of a draft agreement, but had asked that, in order to save him the

[1] (1682) 1 Dick. 14; 21 E.R. 171.

[2] See also *Hollis* v. *Whiteing*, (1682) 1 Vern. 151; 23 E.R. 380.

[3] (1720) 1 P. Wms. 620; 24 E.R. 542; *sub nom. Maxwell* v. *Mountacute*, Prec. Ch. 526; 24 E.R. 235.

[4] Prec. Ch. 526; 24 E.R. 236.

[5] (1789) 2 Bro. C.C. 559, 565; 29 E.R. 306, 309.

[6] (1854) 2 Sm. & Giff. 115, 122; 65 E.R. 327, 330.

trouble of waiting till it was fairly copied, he might be allowed to call and sign the fair copy in the morning. Subsequently he refused to sign, and Stuart, V.-C., decided that his conduct was such as to preclude him from relying upon the Statute as a defence. When *Wood* v. *Midgley* came before the Lords Justices,[1] however, they reversed the Vice-Chancellor's decision and laid it down that the presence of fraud beyond the mere refusal to sign was essential before the defendant could be deprived of his right to rely on the Statute.

"Is there then", said Turner, L.J., in the course of a judgment in which Knight Bruce, L.J., concurred, "a case alleged by this bill of this nature, that the defendant did by his fraudulent act prevent the agreement from being reduced to writing. I think that there is no allegation on the bill bringing forward a case of fraud. The case alleged is simply this, that there was an agreement, for a sale by the plaintiffs to the defendant for £1000 and the defendant said that he would not sign any agreement. The law has said, that the defendant is not to be sued unless upon an agreement signed by him. Is it a fraud on that law for him to say, I have agreed, but I will not sign an agreement?"

Wood v. *Midgley*, then, definitely established that the mere refusal to sign a writing under the Statute was not fraud; but that decision was entirely negative, and left still undetermined the positive question of what is fraud, in this connection. It would appear that the only authorities directly bearing on this question are a *dictum* of Lord Parker, L.C., in *Montacute* v. *Maxwell*,[2] and the early case of *Cookes et ux.* v. *Mascall and Cookes*.[3]

In *Montacute* v. *Maxwell*, Lord Parker remarked[4] that it would be fraud against which the Court of Chancery would relieve, "if one agreement in writing should be proposed and drawn, and another fraudulently and secretly brought in and executed in lieu of the former".

In *Cookes et ux.* v. *Mascall and Cookes*,[3] the facts were as

[1] (1854) 5 De G. M. & G. 41, 45; 43 E.R. 784, 786.
[2] (1720) 1 P. Wms. 620; 24 E.R. 542; *sub nom. Maxwell* v. *Mountacute*, Prec. Ch. 526; 24 E.R. 235.
[3] (1690) 2 Vern. 200; 23 E.R. 730.
[4] 1 P. Wms. 620; 24 E.R. 542.

follows. A marriage had been arranged between the plaintiff and the defendant Mascall's daughter, and the respective fathers of the betrothed parties entered into negotiations for a marriage settlement. Matters proceeded to the point that articles of agreement were drawn up, but these were never executed. The defendant Mascall, by his answer, denied that any agreement had been arrived at; but the defendant Cookes, on the other hand, swore

"that after the articles were drawn, they were read over and agreed to, and that Mascall promised to meet at another time to execute: that young Cookes [one of the plaintiffs] was afterwards permitted to come to Mascall's house, and in December 1684, married his daughter, Mascall being privy to it, helping to set them forward in the morning and entertaining them, and seemed well pleased with the marriage, upon their return to his house at night".

The case came before the court on a bill brought by the husband and wife to obtain specific performance of the agreement, and it would appear that the court accepted the evidence of the defendant Cookes, as a decree for specific performance was made. The report does not set out the reasons for this decision and it may have proceeded upon any one of the three following grounds, viz. (1) that the marriage was part performance; (2) that the defendant Mascall's omission to sign was fraudulent; or (3) that the defendant Mascall's conduct generally was fraudulent. As to the first two possible grounds, it would seem improbable that the report would have stated the facts of the case so fully, if the decision had turned merely on part performance, or fraud in omitting to sign. Moreover, marriage seems never to have been considered a sufficient part performance of a contract made in consideration thereof.[1] And finally, the facts of the case agree very closely with the facts of the hypothetical case of fraud put by Lord Parker, L.C., in *Maxwell* v. *Montacute*.[2] For these reasons, it is submitted that *Cookes et ux*. v. *Mascall and Cookes*[3]

[1] *Mountacute* v. *Maxwell*, (1720) 1 P. Wms. 618; 24 E.R. 541.

[2] (1720) Prec. Ch. 526; 24 E.R. 235. The passage referred to is quoted *supra*, p. 224.

[3] (1690) 2 Vern. 200; 23 E.R. 720.

was in fact decided on the ground that the defendant Mascall's conduct was tainted with fraud beyond the mere omission to sign. The essential features of *Cookes et ux.* v. *Mascall and Cookes*[1] would appear to have been, first that Mascall deliberately refrained from signing the writing; secondly, that he actively encouraged and induced the plaintiffs to proceed with the marriage; and thirdly, that the plaintiffs duly intermarried and thereby irretrievably altered their position. It is submitted, therefore, that the principle involved in *Cookes et ux.* v. *Mascall and Cookes*[1] may be stated as follows: where a defendant deliberately contrives to avoid signing a writing by actively encouraging and inducing the plaintiff to perform the contract, so that as a result of such encouragement and inducement the plaintiff performs the contract to such an extent or in such respects as irretrievably to alter his position, the defendant will not be allowed to rely on the Statute as a defence.[2]

[1] (1690) 2 Vern. 200; 23 E.R. 720.

[2] The case of *Mallet* v. *Halfpenny*, which was before Sir John Trevor, M.R. (a cousin of the notorious Lord Jeffreys), in 1699, is sometimes cited with reference to the proposition that the Statute does not apply where a person by means of fraud prevents the due execution of a writing. The report of *Mallet* v. *Halfpenny* in 2 Vern. 373; 23 E.R. 836 (*sub nom. Halfpenny* v. *Ballet*) simply sets forth the decree without stating the reasons for it, but an account of the case given by Lord Parker, L.C., in his judgment in *Bawdes* v. *Amhurst*, (1715) Prec. Ch. 402, 403; 24 E.R. 180, 181, would seem to indicate that the Master of the Rolls based his judgment on the ground that the Statute was not to be allowed to shelter a fraud. "My Lord Chancellor", runs the report of Lord Parker's judgment, "...cited the case of *Mallet* v. *Halfpenny*, where the defendant, on a treaty of marriage for his daughter with the plaintiff, signed a writing, comprising the terms of the agreement, and afterwards designing to elude the force thereof, and get loose from his agreement, ordered his daughter to put on a good humour, and get the plaintiff to deliver up that writing, and then to marry him, which she accordingly did, and the defendant stood at the corner of a street to see them go to be married, and afterwards forced the plaintiff to bring his bill in this court to be relieved; and my Lord Chancellor said, he remembered very well, that this cause was heard before the Master of the Rolls, and the plaintiff had a decree; but he said, this was on the point of fraud, which was proved in the cause, and Halfpenny walked backwards and forwards in the court, and bid the Master of the Rolls observe the statute, which he humourously said, *I do, I do.*" See, too, *Welford* v. *Beezely*, (1747) 1 Ves. Sen. 6; 27 E.R. 855, where Lord Hardwicke also treated *Mallet* v. *Halfpenny* as having proceeded on the ground of fraud.

It is to be noted, however, that in *Mallet* v. *Halfpenny*, an agreement had in fact been arrived at between the parties and a writing evidencing it duly

The principle that where the defendant has by fraud prevented the execution of a sufficient writing he will not be allowed to set up the Statute as a defence, is a principle of equity, but it would seem that it is not restricted in its operation to suits in which the plaintiff seeks specific performance, but is equally applicable where the plaintiff is suing for the common law remedy of damages. Prior to the Judicature Act, 1873,[1] those equitable defences and replies which were in their nature of general application were rendered available in common law proceedings by means of writs of injunction directed to the party who had acted fraudulently or unconscionably and restraining him from prosecuting a particular action or setting up a particular defence.[2] Lord Redesdale, in his work on equity pleadings, stated in the following terms the grounds upon which Courts of Equity acted in granting such injunctions.

"Sometimes a party", he wrote,[3] "by fraud, or accident, or otherwise, has an advantage in proceeding in a court of ordinary jurisdiction which must necessarily make that court an instrument of injustice; and it is therefore against conscience that he should use the advantage. In such cases, to prevent a manifest wrong, courts of equity have interposed, by restraining the party whose conscience is thus bound from using the advantage he has improperly gained...." "The courts of equity", continued Lord Redesdale in a subsequent paragraph,[4] "will interfere upon the same grounds to relieve against instruments which destroy, as well as against instruments which create, rights; and

signed. The fraudulent element in the defendant's conduct, therefore, did not consist in preventing the signing of a sufficient writing, but in obtaining that writing out of the plaintiff's possession. At the present time it would seem clear that in such circumstances a plaintiff would be entitled to adduce secondary evidence to prove the contract, merely on the ground of detention of the writing by the defendant, and would not need to concern himself with the question of whether the defendant's action in obtaining possession of the writing was fraudulent. Wigmore, *Treatise on Evidence*, 2nd ed. II, p. 762, para. 1199. It would appear, indeed, that even when *Mallet* v. *Halfpenny* was decided, this had been settled as the law with regard to deeds: Wigmore, *loc. cit.* n. 2; but possibly doubts may have existed, at that time, as to whether a similar principle applied to writings under the Statute.

[1] 36 and 37 Vict. c. 66.

[2] See e.g. *Lloyd* v. *Clark*, (1843) 6 Beav. 309; 49 E.R. 845.

[3] Mitford (Lord Redesdale), *Pleadings in Suits in the Court of Chancery*, 5th ed. p. 149.

[4] *Op. cit.* p. 152.

therefore will prevent a release which has been fraudulently or improperly obtained from being made a defence in an action at law."

Lord Redesdale's statement of the law would appear to be sufficiently wide to cover the principle under discussion, and although there is no express decision on the point, it is submitted that prior to the Judicature Act, 1873, a plaintiff suing at common law on a contract which, by reason of the defendant's fraud in preventing the execution of a writing, did not comply with the Statute, could have had the defendant restrained by injunction from pleading such non-compliance as a defence to the common law action. It is now provided by the Judicature Act, 1925,[1] that

"No cause or proceeding at any time pending in the High Court or the Court of Appeal shall be restrained by prohibition or injunction, but every matter of equity on which an injunction against the prosecution of any such cause or proceeding might formerly have been obtained, whether unconditionally or on any terms or conditions, may be relied on by way of defence thereto...".

Hence, if the foregoing submission is correct, a plaintiff suing for damages for breach of contract may now, without the necessity of instituting separate proceedings, meet a defence of non-compliance with the Statute, by the reply that such non-compliance was brought about by the defendant's own fraud.

[1] 15 & 16 Geo. V, c. 49, s. 41, substantially re-enacting s. 24 (5) of the Judicature Act, 1873 (36 & 37 Vict. c. 66).

CHAPTER VII

THE DOCTRINE OF PART PERFORMANCE

WHERE a party has performed or partly performed his obligations under a contract coming within the Statute but not complying with its requirements, Courts of Equity will sometimes, and notwithstanding the Statute, on grounds of conscience and fair dealing, allow that party to sue for specific performance, and in his suit to adduce parol evidence, of the contract.[1] It has sometimes been said that the basis of this doctrine is the jurisdiction of Courts of Equity to interpose in order to prevent fraud. "In general", said Grant, M.R., in *Buckmaster* v. *Harrop*,[2] "the party seeking the performance must shew a performance on his side; as a reason for the interference of the court in his favour; for the ground, upon which the court acts, is fraud in refusing to perform after performance by the other party."[3]

But although the doctrine was, in its inception,[4] merely an application of the principle that equity would not allow the

[1] *Maddison* v. *Alderson*, (1883) 8 App. Cas. 467.

[2] (1802) 7 Ves. 341, 346; 32 E.R. 139, 141.

[3] Fry, *Specific Performance of Contracts*, 6th ed. p. 269, describes part performance as "but a particular case of fraud".

[4] The earliest cases seem to have proceeded almost wholly on the ground that to refuse relief would be to allow the Statute to cover fraud. See the text, *infra*, p. 234. Reference may be made to *Lester* v. *Foxcroft*, Colles P.C. 108; 1 E.R. 205, decided by the House of Lords in 1700, and except for *Butcher* v. *Stapely*, (1686) 1 Vern. 363; 23 E.R. 524, and perhaps *Hollis* v. *Edwards*, (1683) 1 Vern. 159; 23 E.R. 385, the earliest of these cases. Of *Lester* v. *Foxcroft*, Lord Redesdale, in *Bond* v. *Hopkins*, (1802) 1 Sch. & Lef. 413, 433, spoke as follows: "The first case (apparently) of this kind was *Foxcraft* v. *Lyster*. That case was decided on a principle acted upon in Courts of Law, though not applicable by the modes of proceeding in a Court of Law to the particular case. It was against conscience to suffer the party who had entered and expended his money on the faith of a parol agreement to be treated as a trespasser, and the other party to enjoy the advantages of the money he had laid out. At Law, fraud destroys rights. If I mix my corn with another's, he takes all; but if I induce another to mix his corn with mine, I cannot then insist on having the whole: the law in that case does not give me his corn. The case of *Foxcraft* v. *Lyster*, therefore, I conceive, was decided on clear principle...". See also per Lord Blackburn in *Maddison* v. *Alderson*, (1883) 8 App. Cas. 467, 489.

Statute to be made an instrument of fraud, nevertheless, at the present day, this doctrine has so developed that it must be regarded as a separate head of equity jurisdiction, both more definite in its character, and narrower in its application, than the general principle of fraud.

"That equity [of part performance]", said the Earl of Selborne, L.C., in *Maddison* v. *Alderson*,[1] "has been stated by high authority to rest upon the principle of fraud: 'Courts of Equity will not permit the statute to be made an instrument of fraud'. By this it cannot be meant that equity will relieve against a public statute of general policy in cases admitted to fall within it; and I agree with an observation made by Lord Justice Cotton, in *Britain* v. *Rossiter*,[2] that this summary way of stating the principle (however true it may be when properly understood), is not an adequate explanation, either of the precise grounds, or of the established limits, of the equitable doctrine of part performance...."

The earliest reported case in which relief was given on the ground of part performance by the plaintiff, was *Butcher* v. *Stapely*,[3] which came before Jeffreys, L.C., in 1686. That case, as the Earl of Selborne remarked,[4]

"was a strong case upon its circumstances; for the relief was there granted to a purchaser in possession of land under an unsigned agreement, against a subsequent purchaser (with notice) of the same land from the vendor, the defendant having paid his purchase-money under a signed agreement and having obtained a conveyance of the legal estate". "The Lord Chancellor declared, that inasmuch as possession was delivered according to the agreement, he took the bargain to be executed...", runs Vernon's report.[5]

[1] (1883) 8 App. Cas. at p. 474.

[2] 11 Q.B.D. at p. 130.

[3] (1686) 1 Vern. 363; 23 E.R. 524. See also *Hollis* v. *Edwards*, (1683) 1 Vern. 159; 23 E.R. 385, where Lord Guilford dismissed the plaintiff's bill for specific performance. In that case the plaintiff alleged expenditure upon premises which he stated to be the subject of certain agreements of lease. But it does not clearly appear from the report whether the plaintiff was to be the lessor or the lessee, nor whether any change of possession took place, nor even whether the expenditure was in pursuance of the agreements of lease.

[4] In *Maddison* v. *Alderson*, (1883) 8 App. Cas. 467, 477.

[5] 1 Vern. 365; 23 E.R. 525.

The next case, *Lester* v. *Foxcroft*,[1] was a decision of the House of Lords. The facts, shortly, were that the appellant had orally agreed with the owner of certain lands for a lease thereof, and in pursuance of that agreement had entered into possession of the lands and expended large sums of money in erecting houses thereon. Counsel for the appellant contended, first, that the terms of the oral agreement were clearly proved, and secondly that the appellant's part execution of the agreement entitled him to a decree for specific performance against the alleged lessor's representatives; and the House of Lords presumably adopted this argument, for it made the decree prayed for. Whether, however, the House considered that it was giving effect to any other principle than that of preventing the Statute from being used as a cloak for fraud, may be doubted; especially as it was alleged on behalf of the appellant that the execution of a lease had been prevented by the unfair practices of the respondents (devisees of the alleged lessor) or some of them.[2]

Lester v. *Foxcroft* and *Butcher* v. *Stapely* were followed a few years later in *Pyke* v. *Williams*,[3] a vendor's suit to enforce an agreement for sale and purchase in pursuance of which the vendor had delivered to the defendant possession of the lands comprised in the agreement: in view of this part performance, Wright, L.K., decreed a specific performance. In *Lamas* v. *Bayly*,[4] on the other hand, where the alleged act of part performance consisted in the plaintiff's refraining from purchasing certain lands, it being agreed that the defendant should purchase the lands instead of the plaintiff and should resell portion thereof to the plaintiff at a proportionate price, Lord Cowper, L.C., refused a decree. The grounds of the Lord Chancellor's decision in this case were thus stated in the Registrar's Book: "His Lordship declared, that the circumstances in this case appeared to be too slight to ground the decree for performance of the said agreement".

The next two cases, decisions of Lords Cowper and Maccles-

[1] (1700) Colles P.C. 108; 1 E.R. 205; 2 Wh. & T. L.C. 9th ed. p. 410.
[2] See note 4, p. 230 *supra*.
[3] (1703) 2 Vern. 455; 23 E.R. 891.
[4] (1708) 2 Vern. 627; 23 E.R. 1011.

field, respectively, throw some light on the grounds upon which the doctrine of part performance was supposed at this time to rest. In the first, *Pengall* v. *Ross*,[1] it had been contended that the payment of £100, part of a fine for a lease, was part performance. Lord Cowper, however, declined to admit this contention, and stated in the following terms the ground of his decision and the reasons which induced the court to regard certain acts of part performance as excluding the Statute:

"The Payment of this £100 is not such a Performance of the Agreement on one Part as to decree an Execution on the other: for the Statute of Frauds makes one Sort of Contracts, viz. Personal Contracts good if any Money is paid in Earnest. Now that Statute says, that no Agreement concerning Lands shall be good except it is reduced into Writing; and therefore a parol Agreement, as it is in this Case, cannot be good within the Statute by giving Money in Earnest; for there must be something more than a bare Payment of Money on the one part to induce the Court to decree a Performance on the other Part, either by putting it out of the Party's Power to undo the Thing, or where it would be a prejudice to the Party performing his Part, as beginning to build, or letting the other into Possession, etc., in such Case where the Agreement hath proceeded so far on one Part, the Statute never intended to restrain this Court from decreeing a Performance of the other".[2]

In the second case, *Lockey* v. *Lockey*,[3] Lord Macclesfield explained the grounds for the application of the doctrine to the case of a purchaser, who, having gone into possession, seeks to enforce the agreement against his vendor. Lord Macclesfield remarked that an unwritten agreement relating to land,

"*if executed on one part*, had been always looked upon so far conclusive as to induce the court to decree an execution on the other part, not to destroy or avoid the agreement, so far as it was already carried into execution; and therefore in *Leicester* and *Foxcroft*, could the party who had built upon the ground, if he had enjoyed the houses for several years, have been liable,

[1] (1709) 2 Eq. Ca. Abr. 46; 22 E.R. 40.

[2] Lord Cowper made a decree that the £100 should be refunded. Cf. *Case* 664B, (1680) 1 Freeman 486; 89 E.R. 365.

[3] (1719) Prec. Ch. 518, 519; 24 E.R. 232.

as a wrongdoer, to account for the rents and profits, for want of the agreement's being *reduced into writing*? Most certainly he should not".

It is to be noticed that in none of the foregoing cases is any stress laid upon the act of part performance fulfilling any evidentiary function. The court seems invariably to have been concerned with the moral aspect of the matter; if the Statute should be allowed to interpose, would the plaintiff, by reason of his part performance, be placed in such a position that nothing short of an enforcement of the contract would suffice to do justice between the parties? In other words, the court, in these earlier cases, seems to have been concerned only with preventing the Statute from being used fraudulently to deprive the plaintiff of the fruits of his partly performing the contract on the faith of receiving the benefit of a reciprocal performance from the other party. Courts of Equity considered that such part execution took the case beyond the stage of contract: the acts and deeds of the parties, as distinct from their words and promises, gave birth to rights and duties beyond those arising *ex contractu*. "Equities", such rights and duties were called, and it was these that courts of equity enforced.

"The matter has advanced beyond the stage of contract", said the Earl of Selborne, L.C., in *Maddison* v. *Alderson*;[1] "and the equities which arise out of the stage which it has reached cannot be administered unless the contract is regarded. The choice is between undoing what has been done (which is not always possible, or, if possible, just) and completing what has been left undone."

And a little earlier in his speech, the Earl of Selborne had remarked:[2]

"in a suit founded on such part performance, the defendant is really 'charged' upon the equities resulting from the acts done in execution of the contract, and not (within the meaning of the statute) upon the contract itself. If such equities were excluded, injustice of a kind which the statute cannot be thought to have had in contemplation would follow".

[1] (1883) 8 App. Cas. 467, 476.
[2] *Ib.* 475.

It would appear, however, that, in spite of this broad ground upon which the doctrine of part performance was placed, equity judges felt that even if they did not insist on the written evidence prescribed by the Statute, they should at least be guided by the statutory provisions to the extent of requiring that there should be some evidence of the contract beyond mere oral evidence. This evidence was found in the nature of the act of part performance: it had to be an act of such a nature as of itself to suggest a contract of the kind pleaded. As the Earl of Selborne expressed it,[1] there had to be "some *evidentia rei* to connect the alleged part performance with the alleged agreement".[2]

This requirement of "some *evidentia rei*" was first expressly mentioned in 1739, by Lord Hardwicke, L.C., in *Gunter* v. *Halsey*,[3] the case which may be regarded as the foundation of the modern doctrine of part performance. Lord Hardwicke laid down three conditions which were required to be fulfilled before the court would, on the ground of part performance, dispense with a writing under the Statute. First, he said, "the acts of part performance must have been such as would be a prejudice to the party who had done them, if after that the agreement was to be void". This condition indicates the purpose actuating the judges in the earlier cases of part performance, viz. to prevent

[1] *Ib.* 478.

[2] Cf. the application to suits in courts of equity of periods of limitation adopted by analogy from Statutes of Limitation in terms applying only to actions at common law. *In re Robinson*, [1911] 1 Ch. 502.

The adoption of the requirement of "some *evidentia rei*" was doubtless assisted by the ideas which prevailed, at the time of its adoption, as to the manner in which the Statute was to be construed. "It was thought by very many high authorities", said Lord Blackburn in *Maddison* v. *Alderson*, (1883) 8 App. Cas. at p. 488, "that the statute did not apply when, from the nature of the proof, there could be no risk of perjury. Lord Mansfield intimates such an opinion in *Simon* v. *Motivos*, 1 W. Bl. 599....And there are indications that great equity judges on a similar principle thought that whenever acts had been done which were such as to be consistent only with the existence of a contract, the case was taken out of the mischief of the statute and the only question was the sufficiency of the proof of what the contract was. I so understand some of Lord Hardwicke's remarks in *Gunter* v. *Halsey*, Amb. 586, and *Lacon* v. *Mertins*, 3 Atk. 1." It is submitted, however, that neither *Gunter* v. *Halsey* nor *Lacon* v. *Mertins*, (1743) 26 E.R. 803, justifies Lord Blackburn's *dictum* that the *only* question was the sufficiency of the proof of the contract.

[3] (1739) Amb. 586; 27 E.R. 381.

fraud. Secondly, "as to the acts done in performance they should be such as could have been done with no other view or design than to perform the agreement". It was partly because the alleged acts of part performance in *Gunter* v. *Halsey* failed to satisfy this condition that Lord Hardwicke dismissed the bill in that case, saying "it did not appear but that the acts done by the defendant might be done with other views [than to perform the agreement]". Thirdly, it was necessary that "the terms of the agreement should be certainly proved". It appears that the plaintiff in *Gunter* v. *Halsey* also failed to satisfy this condition.

In cases of part performance occurring subsequently to *Gunter* v. *Halsey*, the courts have been concerned chiefly with the elaboration and application to particular circumstances of the conditions laid down by Lord Hardwicke, and it is therefore proposed to examine the nature and effect of these several conditions. It would seem logical, however, to precede this examination by an inquiry into the extent of the jurisdiction of the court to grant relief in cases of part performance. Thus the following matters arise for consideration: first, (A) the jurisdiction of the court to dispense with a writing under the Statute on the ground of part performance; secondly, the conditions governing the exercise of this jurisdiction, viz. (B) that "the acts of part performance must be such as would be a prejudice to the party who has done them, if after that the agreement was to be void"; (C) that there should be present in the circumstances of the case some *evidentia rei* connecting the alleged part performance with the alleged contract; and (D) that the alleged contract should be certainly proved: thirdly, (E) the question of whether conditions (B) and (C) can be fulfilled by different acts must be considered.

(A) *Jurisdiction of the court in cases of part performance.* The extent of the jurisdiction to grant relief on the ground of part performance did not become a subject of controversy until after the enactment of the *Judicature Act*, 1873.[1] The doctrine of part performance was essentially a creature of the Courts of Equity; the cases in which it had been applied to enable a plaintiff to

[1] 36 & 37 Vict. c. 66.

dispense with a writing all related to the possession, use, or tenure of land;[1] and in all these cases the plaintiff had sought to have his contract specifically enforced. The *Judicature Act* provided, *inter alia*, as follows:[2]

"The said courts [i.e. the High Court and the Court of Appeal] respectively, and every judge thereof, shall recognize and take notice of all equitable estates, titles, and rights, and all equitable duties and liabilities appearing incidentally in the course of any cause or matter, in the same manner in which the Court of Chancery would have recognized and taken notice of the same in any suit or proceeding duly instituted therein before the passing of this Act".

It was further provided by the Judicature Act[3] that the High Court and the Court of Appeal should have jurisdiction to grant all such remedies as any of the parties to any cause or matter appeared to be entitled to in respect of every legal or equitable claim properly brought forward by them respectively. It was argued in *Britain* v. *Rossiter*[4] that these provisions extended the equitable doctrine of part performance so as to render it applicable in a common law action for damages for the breach of a contract of service. This contention, however, was unhesitatingly rejected by the Court of Appeal, who held that the *Judicature Act* had affected procedure only, and not substantive rights.

"I think that the true construction of the Judicature Acts", said Brett, L.J., "is that they confer no new rights; they only confirm the rights which previously were to be found existing in the Courts either of Law or of Equity; if they did more, they would

[1] Per Lord Selborne, L.C., in *Maddison* v. *Alderson*, (1883) 8 App. Cas. 467, 474: "The cases upon this subject...have all, or nearly all, arisen under those words of the 4th section of the Statute of Frauds, which provide that 'no action shall be brought to charge any person upon any contract or sale of lands, tenements, or hereditaments, or any interest in or concerning them, unless the agreement...'". And later in his speech Lord Selborne remarked (p. 480): "The acts of part performance, exemplified in the long series of decided cases in which parol contracts concerning land have been enforced, have been (almost, if not quite, universally) relative to the possession, use, or tenure of the land". An examination of the cases prior to *Maddison* v. *Alderson* bears out Lord Selborne's remarks. See also *Britain* v. *Rossiter*, (1879) 11 Q.B.D. 123.

[2] 36 & 37 Vict. c. 66, s. 24 (4).

[3] *Ib.* sub-s. 7.

[4] (1879) 11 Q.B.D. 123, 129.

alter the rights of parties, whereas in truth they only change the procedure. Before the passing of the Judicature Acts no one could have been charged on this contract either at law or in equity; and if the plaintiff could now enforce this contract, it would be an alteration of the law. I am of opinion that the law remains as it was, and that the plaintiff cannot maintain this action for breach of contract."

Britain v. *Rossiter* established that the doctrine of part performance was not affected by the *Judicature Act*, but was to be restricted to those cases in which it would formerly have been applied by Courts of Equity; and the opinion was apparently expressed by the Court of Appeal that the doctrine had in those courts been restricted to contracts relating to land. Thus Brett, L.J., said[1] that the "doctrine was exercised only as to cases concerning land". It may be doubted, however, whether Brett, L.J., actually meant anything more than that the doctrine applied only to cases in which the court could (assuming there had been a sufficient writing) have granted specific performance, these cases being chiefly cases concerning land.

"This doctrine...", he said, "was never extended to contracts like that before us, because they could not be brought within the jurisdiction of Courts of Equity. Those courts could not entertain suits for specific performance of contracts of service, and therefore a case like the present could not come before them."

It would seem, therefore, that Brett, L.J., in saying that the doctrine of part performance was restricted to contracts relating to land, really meant that it was restricted to cases where the remedy of specific performance would have been available, and that those cases were cases relating to land. But although the remedy of specific performance was chiefly applied in cases concerning land, it was not exclusively restricted to such cases.[2] Brett, L.J.'s, dictum would therefore appear to have been merely an approximation to the true position. Cotton, L.J., expresses an opinion similar to that of Brett, L.J., saying[3] that the doctrine

[1] 11 Q.B.D. 129.

[2] See 2 Wh. & T. L.C. 9th ed. pp. 372, 375 *et seq.*; *ib.* 393, *sub nom. Contracts of Indemnity*.

[3] 11 Q.B.D. at p. 131.

had "always been confined to questions relating to land". He came to this conclusion, however, without considering the cases with any particularity, and after refusing (contrary, it is submitted, to the main current of authorities[1]) to accept as the basis of the doctrine the equitable jurisdiction to interpose in cases of fraud. Thesiger, L.J., contented himself with saying[2] that it had "been held as regards a sale of land, that when there has been an entry by one party to the contract, that is an overt act apparently done under a contract which entitles the court to look at the contract to see to what contract the overt act is really referable". While, however, Thesiger, L.J., held that the Courts of Equity would not have applied the doctrine to a contract of service, he did not, apparently, connect this with the absence of any jurisdiction in those courts to entertain a suit for the specific enforcement of such a contract.

Britain v. *Rossiter*, therefore, could scarcely be regarded, even at the time when it was decided, as a convincing authority in favour of the proposition that the doctrine of part performance was restricted to contracts relating to land. Moreover, it would seem clear that the opinions expressed by the learned Lords Justices were *obiter*. There could be no doubt (as, indeed, the Lords Justices recognized) that the Courts of Equity would not have enforced a contract of service, and it was therefore unnecessary for the court to make any pronouncement regarding the application of the doctrine of part performance to contracts in general. It is not surprising, therefore, to find that *Britain* v. *Rossiter* soon became the subject of adverse criticism. The Earl of Selborne, in the course of his speech in *Maddison* v. *Alderson*,[3] remarked:

"It has been recently decided by the Court of Appeal in *Britain* v. *Rossiter* that the equity of part performance does not extend, and ought not to be extended, to contracts concerning any other subject-matter than land; an opinion which seems to differ from that of Lord Cottenham (see *Hammersley* v. *De Biel*,[4] and *Lassence* v. *Tierney*[5])".

[1] See *infra*, pp. 243 *et seq*.

[2] 11 Q.B.D. at p. 133.

[3] (1883) 8 App. Cas. 467, 474.

[4] 12 Cl. & F. 64 n.; 8 E.R. 1321.

[5] 1 Mac. & G. 572; 41 E.R. 1387.

A few years later the question was exhaustively investigated by Kay, J., in *McManus* v. *Cooke*.[1] Kay, J., considered[2] that "the statement of the doctrine and the grounds on which it rested did not necessarily confine it to agreements for sale or acquisition of an interest in land"; and after reviewing the authorities he came to the conclusion that the restriction alleged to have been established by *Britain* v. *Rossiter* was unsound.

"(1) The doctrine of part performance of a parol agreement", he said,[3] "which enables proof of it to be given notwithstanding the *Statute of Frauds*, though principally applied to the case of contracts for the sale or purchase of land, or for the acquisition of an interest in land has not been confined to those cases. (2) Probably it would be more accurate to say it applies to all cases in which a Court of Equity would entertain a suit for specific performance if the alleged contract had been in writing. (3) The most obvious case of part performance is where the defendant is in possession of land of the plaintiff under the parol agreement. (4) The reason for the rule is that where the defendant has stood by and allowed the plaintiff to fulfil his part of the contract, it would be fraudulent to set up the statute. (5) But this reason applies wherever the defendant has obtained and is in possession of some substantial advantage under a parol agreement which, if in writing, would be such as the court would direct to be specifically performed."

It is submitted that the view of the matter adopted by Kay, J., is both consistent with principle and correct according to the authorities. It receives support from the decision of Chitty, J., in *Lavery* v. *Pursell*,[4] a case in which *McManus* v. *Cooke* was not cited. "Part performance", said Chitty, J., "was an equitable doctrine...applied by the Courts of Equity, and it was applied to those cases where the court would grant specific performance, for instance the case of a sale of land...." Chitty, J., accordingly held that the provisions of the *Judicature Act* did not enable a plaintiff suing for damages for the breach of a partly performed contract not evidenced by writing to rely upon the doctrine. The point was most recently raised in *Elliott* v.

[1] (1887) 35 Ch.D. 681.
[2] *Ib.* 691.
[3] *Ib.* 697.
[4] (1888) 39 Ch.D. 508, 518.

Roberts,[1] a case which very clearly illustrates the empirical nature of the statement that the doctrine of part performance is restricted to contracts relating to land. In *Elliott* v. *Roberts* the contract sued on related to land, but was of such a nature that the remedy of specific performance was not available. It was therefore held by Lush, J., that the doctrine of part performance had no application. In the course of his judgment, Lush, J., stated the effect of *Britain* v. *Rossiter*[2] as read in the light of Kay, J.'s, remarks in *McManus* v. *Cooke*[3] to be as follows: "it is only in cases where the Court of Equity would have entertained a suit for specific performance if the contract alleged had been in writing, that the doctrine of part performance applied". This, it is submitted, is a correct statement of the law.[4]

It has indeed been suggested by a learned writer[5] that it might be more accurate to say that the doctrine applies to all cases in which a Court of Equity would entertain a suit (whether for specific performance or other equitable relief), if the alleged

[1] (1912) 28 T.L.R. 436, 437.

[2] (1879) 11 Q.B.D. 123.

[3] (1887) 35 Ch.D. 681.

[4] This view of the matter was adopted by Fry in his statement of the conditions governing the application of the doctrine of part performance: *Specific Performance of Contracts*, 6th ed. p. 276. Fry's statement was cited with approval by Warrington, L.J., in *Chaproniere* v. *Lambert*, [1917] 2 Ch. 356, 361; and by Romer, J., in *Rawlinson* v. *Ames*, [1925] Ch. 96, 114.

There appears to have been only one actual decision bearing on the question discussed in the text, viz. *Hammersley* v. *De Biel*, 12 Cl. & F. 65 n.; 8 E.R. 1321. The act of part performance relied on in that case was a settlement of an income of £500 per annum made by the plaintiff in favour of his wife. The plaintiff alleged that that settlement was in part performance of a parol contract under which the wife's father was to make a similar settlement, and the action was brought for the enforcement of that obligation. Lord Cottenham, L.C., held that the contract was sufficiently part performed to exclude the Statute. While, however, this decision shews that Lord Cottenham was of opinion that the doctrine of part performance was not restricted to contracts relating to land, it may be doubted whether the acts relied on in that case were in fact sufficient to satisfy the requirement of the doctrine that acts of part performance must be unequivocally referable to some such contract as that alleged. It would seem that a settlement by a husband on his wife might well be explained upon grounds of love and affection, without reference to any sort of contract at all. See p. 252 *infra*. *Hammersley* v. *De Biel* went on appeal to the House of Lords (12 Cl. & F. 45, 8 E.R. 1312), and Lord Cottenham's decision was affirmed, but on other grounds, the question of part performance not being considered.

[5] Fry, *Specific Performance of Contracts*, 6th ed. p. 283.

contract had been evidenced by writing. The case of *Williamson* v. *Lukey*,[1] however, recently decided by the High Court of Australia, is against this suggestion.

In *Williamson* v. *Lukey*, the lessees of a theatre (appellants) orally agreed with a confectioner (respondent) to give him an exclusive right to sell sweets and confectionery in the theatre and its precincts during the continuance of a lease of a shop which the respondent took from the owner of the theatre for a period of more than a year. The respondent exercised his rights under the licence for some time, but subsequently the appellants repudiated the agreement and revoked the licence. It was contended for the respondent that even if the agreement, supposing it to have been in writing, could not have been specifically enforced, yet an injunction might have been issued to restrain the appellants from revoking the licence or admitting others to the theatre to sell sweets; and that therefore the doctrine of part performance would be applicable. The High Court of Australia unanimously decided against the respondent. Of the five judges constituting the court, two, Starke and McTiernan, JJ., expressed no opinion on the point as to whether the doctrine of part performance was applicable to cases other than those in which the remedy of specific performance would have been available had the contract sued on been evidenced in writing. Dixon, J. (with whose judgment Gavan Duffy, C.J., agreed), while resting his judgment on other grounds, seemed to think[2] that the doctrine had no such application. Evatt, J., however, definitely adopted this view as the basis of his judgment. "...I hold", he said,[3] "that the doctrine of part performance does not apply to cases where the only equitable remedy available is that of injunction, and the court refuses to enforce the contract as a whole." Then after referring to the cases of *Maddison* v. *Alderson*[4] and *Britain* v. *Rossiter*,[5] the learned judge continued: "The justification for intervention by the Court of Chancery [in cases of part performance] was, indeed, the vital necessity,

[1] (1931) 45 C.L.R. 282.
[2] *Ib.* pp. 300–301.
[3] *Ib.* p. 308.
[4] (1883)8 App. Cas. 467.
[5] (1879) 11 Q.B.D. 123.

in the interests of justice, of ordering completion of an agreement which had been performed by one party to such an extent that a substantial alteration of position had resulted....But in the case of an application to a Court of Equity for the prevention of the breach of some particular negative stipulation of a contract, the jurisdiction exercised expressly disclaims the right of acting *in personam* so as to secure completion. And the justification for the application of the doctrine of part performance ceases to exist if only a part of the contract within the Statute is enforced. The very name of the doctrine—'*part* performance'—indicates that the object is always to enlarge part performance into complete performance. If a negative stipulation in an agreement within sec. 4 of the Statute were of itself and by itself enforceable in equity, the result would be the procuring of an injunction by one party whilst the defendant in equity would not only *ex concessis* be unable there to enforce the rest of the agreement but would be unable because of the statute to enforce his rights at law".

It would therefore seem that the above-mentioned suggestion that the doctrine of part performance is applicable wherever Courts of Equity would have entertained a suit for any form of relief in respect of the contract (assuming it to have been properly evidenced by writing) is ill-founded.[1]

(B) "*The acts of part performance must be such as would be a prejudice to the party who has done them, if after that the agreement were to be void.*" It seems always to have been regarded as the basis of the doctrine of part performance that the circumstances of the case should be such that it would be a fraud on the plaintiff if the defendant were allowed to succeed in a plea of the Statute. "The ground", said Lord Cranworth, L.C., in *Caton* v. *Caton*,[2] "on which the court holds that part performance takes a con-

[1] Lord Blackburn, in *Maddison* v. *Alderson*, (1883) 8 App. Cas. 467, 489, considered the doctrine of part performance to be restricted to contracts relating to land in which possession of the land should have been given and accepted. He treated the doctrine as constituting an arbitrary exception to the Statute. But if this were so, there would have been no necessity for the elaborate inquiry entered into by Lord Selborne as to whether the alleged acts of part performance in *Maddison* v. *Alderson* were unequivocally referable to the alleged contract. Lord Blackburn's view of the matter receives no support from the judgments of the other Law Lords, and in view of the authorities referred to in the text, it must, it is submitted, be regarded as being unjustifiably narrow.

[2] (1866) L.R. 1 Ch. 137, 148.

tract out of the purview of the *Statute of Frauds* is, that when one of two contracting parties has been induced, or allowed by the other, to alter his position on the faith of the contract, as for instance by taking possession of land, and expending money in building or other like acts, there it would be a fraud in the other party to set up the legal invalidity of the contract on the faith of which he induced, or allowed, the person contracting with him to act, and expend his money." "They [i.e. the acts of part performance]", said Warrington, L.J., in *Chaproniere* v. *Lambert*,[1] "must be such as to render it a fraud in the defendant to take advantage of the contract not being in writing."

It is to be noted, however, that the fraud which the court endeavours to guard against does not consist in the defendant's acting so as to deprive the plaintiff of the benefit of his agreement, for that is a detriment expressly imposed on the plaintiff by the Statute.[2] It consists in the defendant's endeavour to deprive the plaintiff of the benefit of the plaintiff's part execution of the agreement on the faith of the agreement being valid and enforceable. "To take a case out of the statute", said Macdonald, C.B., in *Cooke* v. *Tombs*,[3] "there must be a part execution of the substance of the agreement itself." "It [the act of part performance] must be obligatory", said Lord Brougham in *Thynne* v. *Glengall*,[4] "and what is done must be under the terms of the agreement and by force of the agreement." Accordingly, where the acts relied upon as part performance, although done by the plaintiff on the faith of the validity of the contract, are not also done in pursuance of its terms, they will not constitute a sufficient part performance. Thus, in *Nunn* v. *Fabian*,[5] the plaintiff had spent a considerable sum of money in altering certain premises on the faith of an agreement that he was to have a lease of them; but it was apparently not one of the terms of the lease or the agreement therefor that he should have carried out these alterations. Lord Cranworth, L.C., therefore held

[1] [1917] 2 Ch. 356, 361. See also per Romer, J., in *Rawlinson* v. *Ames*, [1925] Ch. 96, 115.
[2] See p. 225 *supra*.
[3] (1794) 2 Anst. 420, 425; 145 E.R. 922, 924.
[4] (1848) 2 H.L.C. 131, 158; 9 E.R. 1042, 1052.
[5] (1865) L.R. 1 Ch. 35, 40.

that this expenditure did not constitute a sufficient part performance. "Now", said the Lord Chancellor, "I do not think we can exactly call this part performance. The parol agreement was embodied in the lease, which is silent about the alterations."

This principle assists in explaining why the courts have uniformly held that acts done by a plaintiff preparatory to the performance of the contract, such as instructing a solicitor to prepare a lease or conveyance to be granted or made in pursuance of an oral agreement,[1] do not constitute a sufficient part performance. Such acts by themselves cause no detriment to the plaintiff: until he does something towards "the execution of the substance of the agreement" (to borrow the words of Macdonald, C.B.[2]), the detriment to him, if the defendant pleads the Statute, consists merely in the loss of the contract.[3] But it is not until the defendant has stood by and allowed the plaintiff to perform something of the substance of the agreement that it becomes a fraud on his part to plead the Statute. Not until then is the matter "advanced beyond the stage of contract" so that equities arising not only from the contract but also from the acts of the parties, have to be regarded.[4] Thus, in *O'Reilly* v. *Thompson*[5] it was agreed by parol that upon the plaintiff's procuring a release of a right from a third party, the defendant would convey to the plaintiff certain lands. The plaintiff duly procured the release by the payment of a valuable consideration, but it was held by the Court of Exchequer that this act was merely a

[1] *Cooke* v. *Tombs*, (1794) 2 Anst. 420; 145 E.R. 922; *Whitchurch* v. *Bevis*, (1786, 1789) 2 Bro. C.C. 559; 29 E.R. 306; *Whaley* v. *Bagnel*, (1765) 1 Bro. P.C. 345; 1 E.R. 611. See also the cases cited in Fry, *Specific Performance of Contracts*, 6th ed. p. 395.

[2] 2 Anst. 425; 145 E.R. 922; *cit. supra*.

[3] A principle analogous to that under discussion was enunciated by Grant, M.R., in *Buckmaster* v. *Harrop*, (1802) 7 Ves. 341, 346; 32 E.R. 139, 141. "That, without which there would have been no contract," he stated, "cannot be said to be in part performance of the contract." He accordingly held that payment of auction duty, without which the purchaser's bidding would have been void, could not amount to part performance. Cf. *Phillips* v. *Edwards*, (1864) 33 Beav. 440, 444; 55 E.R. 438, 440.

[4] See per Earl of Selborne, L.C., in *Maddison* v. *Alderson*, 8 App. Cas. at p. 476.

[5] (1791) 2 Cox 271; 30 E.R. 126.

preparatory act on the part of the plaintiff and not a part performance of the contract.

"My opinion", said Eyre, C.B.,[1] "inclines that these circumstances are not a sufficient part performance, but they are a condition annexed, and necessary to be fulfilled by the plaintiff to entitle him to call for an execution of the contract. Tender of £42 and lease and delivery of original lease are no part performance, but circumstances of preparation. So this obtaining the lease is no part performance, but merely preparatory. *The detriment to the plaintiff arises from the folly of acting without a written contract.*"[2]

It has been said[3] that, from the general principle that the acts of part performance must be such as to render it a fraud in the defendant to take advantage of the contract not being in writing, flows a subsidiary rule, viz. "that the acts of part performance must in all cases be done by the person asserting the contract with the knowledge of the person sought to be charged that the acts are being done and are being done on the faith of the contract". "For to constitute fraud, there must coincide in one and the same person knowledge of some fact and conduct inequitable having regard to such knowledge." It is submitted, however, that in general the defendant would not be heard to deny knowledge of the plaintiff's action in performing a contract of which the defendant, by his very act of contracting, must have been cognizant.[4] Where, however, the contract, if enforced, would directly affect the property or interests of persons other

[1] (1791) 2 Cox 273; 30 E.R. 127. The italics are mine.

[2] The argument for the defendant in *O'Reilly* v. *Thompson* suggests that what is "preparatory" to the performance of the contract is to be ascertained by considering whether the plaintiff was bound by the contract to do the act in question. "A part performance", runs the argument (p. 273; E.R. 127), "is something which the plaintiff has contracted to do, and here is no *agreement* that the plaintiff shall be *bound* to procure the release; but it is, that *upon his doing so* then that the defendant shall grant the lease." Thus, a purchaser would not be bound by a contract of sale to instruct his solicitor to prepare a conveyance: if he had sufficient skill he might prepare it himself. Hence instructing a solicitor to prepare a conveyance is not considered an act of part performance. This test agrees with the *dictum* of Lord Brougham in *Thynne* v. *Glengall*, (1848) 2 H.L.C. 131, 158; 9 E.R. 1042, 1052 (quoted *supra*, p. 244).

[3] Fry, *Specific Performance of Contracts*, 6th ed. p. 281.

[4] Cf. *Shillibeer* v. *Jarvis*, (1856) 8 De G.M. & G. 79; 44 E.R. 319.

than the defendant or the other contracting party, then it seems that, in the absence of any knowledge on the part of such other persons of the alleged acts of part performance, the court will not apply the doctrine to the detriment of such other persons. Thus it has been decided that where a plaintiff seeks to enforce against a remainderman a parol contract, entered into between the plaintiff and the tenant for life, acts of part performance which would have bound the tenant for life will not bind the remainderman unless it can be shewn that he permitted the acts of the plaintiff with a knowledge of the contract entered into by the tenant for life.[1]

"The reason", said Stuart, V.-C., in *Trotman* v. *Flesher*,[2] "why a parol agreement in part performed is taken out of the operation of the Statute of Frauds has no application where the lease is to bind the persons entitled in remainder. A man who permits expenditure on the faith of his parol agreement is considered guilty of fraud in taking advantage of its not being in writing. But the remainderman who has entered into no agreement, written or parol, and done no act on the faith of which the other party could have relied, is guilty of no fraud, and cannot be bound....In the present case the decree of specific performance is asked at the Bar only against the tenants for life. It would be impossible to make such a decree in this case without affecting the interests of the remainderman."

Inasmuch as the basis of the doctrine of part performance is fraud, it follows that the acts of part performance must be acts of the plaintiff. If the defendant, after partly performing the contract, chooses to forego the benefit of his performance, this is no fraud on the plaintiff, but the defendant's own loss.[3]

It is to be noted, however, that acts may sometimes have a bilateral effect. Thus, where the alleged part performance is change of possession of land, that can operate both in favour of a vendor or lessor putting the purchaser or lessee into possession,[4] and of the purchaser or lessee accepting such possession.[5]

[1] See Fry, *Specific Performance of Contracts*, 6th ed. p. 281.

[2] (1861) 3 Giff. 1, 9; 66 E.R. 297, 301.

[3] Per Grant, M.R., in *Buckmaster* v. *Harrop*, (1802) 7 Ves. 341, 346; 32 E.R. 139, 141.

[4] E.g. *Smallwood* v. *Sheppards*, [1895] 2 Q.B. 627.

[5] E.g. *Surcome* v. *Pinniger*, (1853) 3 De G.M. & G. 571; 43 E.R. 224.

Change of possession of land is, indeed, much the most usual form of part performance, and it may perhaps be asked how it satisfies the principle that the doctrine of part performance depends on fraud. In the earlier cases, entry into possession by a purchaser or lessee was said to satisfy the requirement in question, because it was thought that if the contract were not regarded, the purchaser or lessee would be rendered liable to answer as a trespasser.

"I take it", said Lord Redesdale in *Clinan* v. *Cooke*,[1] "that nothing is considered as a part performance which does not put the party into a situation that is a fraud upon him, unless the agreement is performed: for instance, if upon a parol agreement, a man is admitted into possession, he is made a trespasser, and is liable to answer as a trespasser if there be no agreement. This is put strongly in the case of *Foxcraft* v. *Lister*[2]....Then for the purpose of defending himself against a charge which might otherwise be made against him, such evidence was admissible, and if it was admissible for such purpose, there is no reason why it should not be admissible throughout."

The grounds upon which *delivery* of possession came to be regarded as sufficient part performance do not appear anywhere to be clearly stated; but presumably the courts had regard to the detriment to the plaintiff involved in his yielding up possession to the defendant.

At the present time it would seem that where the act of part performance is change of possession of land, the importance of the element of fraud has dwindled almost to vanishing point. A subsidiary rule, it is submitted, has been evolved, to the effect that where the contract is one which would have been specifically enforced if it had been in writing,[3] change of possession of land will constitute a sufficient part performance; and this regardless of any question of fraud as between the contracting parties.[4]

[1] (1802) 1 Sch. & Lef. 22, 41.

[2] Cited, Prec. Ch. 519; 2 Vern. 456; vid. 1 Colles P.C. 108.

[3] As *Elliott* v. *Roberts*, (1912) 28 T.L.R. 436, shews, a contract affecting land may sometimes be of such a nature that the remedy of specific performance is not available; and in that event there is no room for the doctrine of part performance. See p. 241 *supra*.

[4] Of course, where the contract would affect the property or interests of third parties, other considerations may arise: *Trotman* v. *Flesher*, (1861) 3 Giff. 1, 9; 66 E.R. 297, 301. *Vide supra*, p. 247.

"But a promise", said Malins, V.-C., in *Ungley* v. *Ungley*,[1] "followed by possession, is taken out of the operation of the Statute....I should say, therefore, that if *A.* is about to marry, and proves a promise on behalf of the intended wife's father that he will give him a house on his marriage, that is a void contract, because it is not in writing; but *if that promise is followed upon the marriage by possession, that simple fact, if it be for an hour only, ought, in my opinion, as being a part performance of the promise, to take the case out of the Statute of Frauds*, and the party who has got the contract thus perfected by part performance is in just as good a situation as if he had a contract in writing by the father saying that, 'in consideration of the marriage, I will give or settle upon you a house'."

In *Brough* v. *Nettleton*,[2] the plaintiff agreed with the defendant for the lease of a house; and it was one of the terms of the agreement that the plaintiff might, at any time during the tenancy, purchase the house at a named sum. Possession was given and taken, and rent paid and accepted; and in due course the plaintiff exercised the option to purchase, but the defendant refused to go on with the deal. In the subsequent proceedings the defendant pleaded the Statute, but P. O. Lawrence, J., held that there was sufficient part performance to take the case out of the Statute.

"The defendant", he said, "allowed the plaintiff to enter into possession of the house, well knowing that he was doing so on the faith of the verbal agreement which had been come to between them. The defendant had at that time in his possession a document signed by the plaintiff in which the terms of that agreement were fully set forth, so there could have been no doubt in his mind either as to the exact terms or as to the belief of the plaintiff. In these circumstances I am clearly of opinion that the taking of possession of the house by the plaintiff constitutes an act of part performance of the agreement, and that the defendant is precluded from setting up the statute."

It is submitted that in *Brough* v. *Nettleton* the only detriment to the plaintiff if the defence had prevailed would have been the loss of his contract: but it does not appear that he would have

[1] (1876) 4 Ch.D. 73, 76. The italics are mine.
[2] [1921] 2 Ch. 25, 28.

been subject to any other loss. Certainly it would not have been open to the defendant to have sued him in trespass, as the defendant had accepted rent. Accordingly, even if the oral agreement had been disregarded, the plaintiff could have defended any proceedings for trespass by pleading the tenancy from year to year, which, if no other tenancy be made out, the law will imply from the payment and receipt of rent.[1]

(C) "*There must be present in the circumstances of the case some evidentia rei connecting the alleged part performance with the alleged contract.*" Not only must the nature of the part performance be such that it would be a fraud on the plaintiff if the agreement were not specifically enforced, but the circumstances of the part performance must be such as unequivocally to indicate the existence of some such contract as that alleged. "It is said", remarked Lord Hardwicke, L.C., in *Lacon* v. *Mertins*,[2] "it must be such an act done, as appears to the Court would not have been done, unless on account of the agreement; and to be sure this is right." This principle is commonly expressed in the cases by saying that the part performance must be *unequivocally referable* to the contract sought to be enforced.

"In order to amount to part-performance", said Plumer, M.R., in *Morphett* v. *Jones*,[3] "an act must be unequivocally referrible to the agreement; and the ground on which courts of equity have allowed such acts to exclude the application of the statute, is fraud. A party who has permitted another to perform acts on the faith of an agreement, shall not insist that the agreement is bad, and that he is entitled to treat both acts as if it had never existed. That is the principle, but the acts must be referrible to the contract."

It has been suggested[4] that it is enough that the part performance should indicate the existence of *some* contract, and be consistent with the contract alleged. But this view of the matter, although at first sight supported by *dicta* in one or two of the

[1] See Redman, *Landlord and Tenant*, 8th ed. p. 16.
[2] (1743) 3 Atk. 1, 4.
[3] (1818) 1 Sw. 172, 181; 36 E.R. 344, 348.
[4] Fry, *Specific Performance of Contracts*, 6th ed. p. 278.

earlier cases,[1] seems inconsistent with *Maddison* v. *Alderson*,[2] the leading case on the subject, and with the main current of authorities. The principle of *Maddison* v. *Alderson* seems to have been accurately stated by the Earl of Selborne, L.C., in these words: "All the authorities shew that the acts relied upon as part performance must be unequivocally, and in their own nature, referable to some such agreement as that alleged".

In *Maddison* v. *Alderson* the appellant alleged that a contract had been entered into between her late master and herself to the effect that if she would continue to serve him as housekeeper for the remainder of his life, he would leave her a life estate in certain lands. The act of part performance relied upon by the appellant was *continuing* in the deceased's service. The House of Lords seems to have decided the appeal partly on the notion that inasmuch as the appellant merely *continued* to serve, her case was analogous to that of the tenant who has continued in possession after the expiration of his tenancy, and without paying a different rent.[3] It may be doubted, however, whether the parallel so drawn was really justifiable. In the case of the tenant holding over, the law already imposes a construction on his act and im-

[1] For example, per Wigram, V.-C., in *Dale* v. *Hamilton*, (1846) 5 Ha. 369, 381; 67 E.R. 955, 960: "It is, in general, of the essence of such an act that the court shall, by reason of the act itself, without knowing whether there was an agreement or not, find the parties unequivocally in a position different from that which, according to their legal rights, they would be in if there were no contract. Of this a common example is the delivery of possession. One man, without being amenable to the charge of trespass, is found in the possession of another man's land. Such a state of things is considered as shewing unequivocally that some contract has taken place between the litigant parties; and it has, therefore, on that specific ground been admitted to be an act of part-performance". When, however, these words are considered in the light of the example of part performance given by the learned Vice-Chancellor, it would appear that he did not intend to state the proposition as widely as his language would *prima facie* indicate. Change of possession of land implies a contract, but it is a contract relating to the land: some such contract as a sale, lease, or settlement of the land.

See also per Grant, M.R., in *Frame* v. *Dawson*, (1807) 14 Ves. 386, 388; 33 E.R. 569. In this case, the alleged act of part performance was not necessarily referable to any sort of contract, so that there was no occasion for the Master of the Rolls to consider with any degree of particularity the evidentiary effect which an act must produce in order to be a sufficient part performance.

[2] (1883) 8 App. Cas. 467, 479.

[3] Per Earl of Selborne, *ib.* 481.

plies from the holding over a tenancy at will,[1] or, upon payment of rent, a tenancy from year to year.[2] Moreover, it has since been held that where one entered pending negotiations for a lease, but before an agreement had been reached, and continued in possession after an agreement had been arrived at, such continuance in possession was a good part performance.[3] Another ground suggested[4] for the House's decision in *Maddison* v. *Alderson* was that the alleged part performance was not unequivocally referable to any contract, inasmuch as the appellant might possibly have remained with the deceased for other reasons than those of contract—gratuitously, for example. But it is submitted that change of possession is as much open to this construction as the appellant's continuance in the deceased's service: the person receiving possession may be doing so as the result of a gift, or as a mere licensee. Nevertheless, change of possession is in general a sufficient part performance. It is submitted that the true ground of the decision in *Maddison* v. *Alderson* was that the alleged acts of part performance, although consistent with the contract pleaded by the appellant, were not necessarily referable to it. Continuance in another's service does not necessarily relate to or indicate a contract affecting that other's land.

"But, though her long service is consistent with her present case", said Lord O'Hagan,[5] "it is not demonstrative of any contract to give her the life estate she claims. She might unquestionably have remained with her master, in the enjoyment of some present comforts and the expectation of some future provision, though no such contract had been ever dreamt of. There have not been wanting recorded cases in which time and care have been bestowed by one person upon another, even from a vague anticipation that the affection and gratitude so created would, in the long run, ensure some indefinite reward. And legal tribunals have refused in those cases to turn courtesy into contract and compel any payment although such service

[1] Redman, *Landlord and Tenant*, 8th ed. p. 3. [2] *Ib.* p. 8.

[3] *Hodson* v. *Heuland*, [1896] 2 Ch. 428; see also *Biss* v. *Hygate*, [1918] 2 K.B. 314.

[4] Per Lord O'Hagan, 8 App. Cas. 486.

[5] *Ib.* 485. The italics are mine. See also per Earl of Selborne, L.C., *ib.* 481.

had been performed. In such circumstances, and even where there may have been a general undertaking to afford a suitable acknowledgment, *there would be no ground for inferring a contract for the conveyance or devise of landed estate to the person rendering the service*, however valuable it might have been, and however clear might be the right to remuneration for it in another way, the rendering of it not being necessarily referable to any such contract."[1]

If, then, the principle is that the acts of part performance must be unequivocally referable to some such contract as that alleged, two questions arise: first, as to how this unequivocal

[1] Lord Redesdale, indeed, seems to have thought that the part performance must be of such a nature as unequivocally to point to the very contract alleged, and to no other. On this principle he held, in *Lindsay* v. *Lynch*, (1804) 2 Sch. & Lef. 1, that a part performance by payment of rent was not sufficient to enable the plaintiff to prove a lease for three lives when the defendant admitted a lease for one life. "For, what is the ground", asked Lord Redesdale (p. 7), "on which a plaintiff is allowed to give parol evidence of an agreement? its appearing clearly that *that* very agreement was in part executed. Now here, it is beyond doubt; it is admitted by the defendant, that there was an agreement for a lease for one life; and payment of rent, which is the only circumstance of part execution, is perfectly consistent with that agreement; and being so, there is no case to admit proof of a further agreement." This view of the matter, however, would clearly appear to be wrong. It would be impossible to reconcile with it the undoubted fact that change of possession of land will constitute sufficient part performance to enable proof to be given either of an agreement for sale, or for a lease, or for a settlement of the land. Cf. *Daniels* v. *Trefusis*, [1914] 1 Ch. 788; *Brough* v. *Nettleton*, [1921] 2 Ch. 25; and *Ungley* v. *Ungley*, (1876) 4 Ch.D. 73. Moreover, it is apparent from general considerations that such a proposition must be unsound, for in the nature of things no act of part performance could be so eloquent as to point unequivocally to one particular contract and no other. If, indeed, the act of part performance were required to possess this evidentiary character, there would be no call for the admission of parol evidence of the terms of the contract. Yet it is precisely that such evidence may be rendered admissible that part performance is alleged and proved. See per Lord O'Hagan, *Maddison* v. *Alderson*, 8 App. Cas. at p. 483.

The proposition that the act of part performance must be unequivocally referable to some such agreement as that alleged has been accepted and is supported by the more recent authorities. Thus, in *Rawlinson* v. *Ames*, [1925] Ch. 96, Romer, J., expressly approved the following statement of the principle: "the acts of part performance must be such as not only to be referable to a contract such as that alleged, but to be referable to no other title". See Fry, *Specific Performance of Contracts*, 6th ed. p. 276. After consideration, he held that, in *Rawlinson* v. *Ames*, the alleged acts of part performance were in fact "referable only to a contract such as that alleged" (at p. 114). See also per Warrington, L.J., in *Chaproniere* v. *Lambert*, [1917] 2 Ch. 356, 361; and *Humphreys* v. *Green*, (1882) 10 Q.B.D. 148, 155.

reference occurs; and secondly, as to the precise significance of "some such contract". It is submitted that an unequivocal reference, within the meaning of the rule, occurs only where the act of part performance visibly relates to or affects the subject-matter which the contract relates to or affects; and that the phrase "some such contract" means a contract relating to or affecting that subject-matter.

In the first place, the part performance must affect or relate to the subject-matter of the contract.

"The Lord Chancellor", said Lord FitzGerald, in *Maddison* v. *Alderson*,[1] "has well laid down that the acts relied on as performance to take the case out of the statute must be unequivocally and in their own nature referable to some such agreement as that alleged, and I may add must necessarily relate to and affect the land the subject of that agreement."

It is only by affecting or relating to a particular subject-matter that dumb acts can indicate the existence of a contract of a particular class; and clearly the contract which such acts would indicate is a contract affecting the subject-matter in question.

"That general principle is stated in the following terms", said Baggallay, L.J., in *Humphreys* v. *Green*,[2] quoting from the judgment he had delivered for the Court of Appeal in *Alderson* v. *Maddison*:[3]—'Now, it is a well-recognised rule, that if in any particular case the acts of part performance of a parol agreement as to an interest in land are to be held sufficient to exclude the operation of the Statute of Frauds, they must be such as are unequivocally referable to the agreement; in other words, there must be a necessary connection between the acts of part performance and the interest in the land which is the alleged subject-matter of the agreement; it is not sufficient that the acts are consistent with the existence of such an agreement, or that they suggest or indicate the existence of some agreement, unless such agreement has reference to the subject-matter.'"

The "necessary connection" between the act of part performance and the subject-matter is to be found in the act *visibly* affecting or relating to that subject-matter. Accordingly it has

[1] 8 App. Cas. at p. 491.
[2] (1882) 10 Q.B.D. 148, 154.
[3] (1881) 7 Q.B.D. 174, 178.

been laid down that payment of purchase money is no part performance: for whatever the payer's intention, it does not appear from the act of payment that it relates to the thing purchased.

"The best explanation...", said the Earl of Selborne, in *Maddison* v. *Alderson*,[1] "seems to be, that the payment of money is an equivocal act, not (in itself), until the connection is established by parol testimony, indicative of a contract concerning land."

Thus, in *Ex parte Broderick*,[2] one since adjudicated bankrupt was indebted to a banking company and orally promised to give them security when they should require it. Subsequently the deeds to a property, in which the bank manager and the bankrupt were each entitled to a one-fifth share, came into the possession of the bank manager; he later told the bankrupt that he had possession of the deeds, and that he held the bankrupt's one-fifth share for the bank. The bankrupt expressed his assent. The equitable mortgage alleged by the bank to have been so created was attacked by the trustee in bankruptcy. There was no writing evidencing the agreement to give security, and the bank accordingly contended that the contract was partly performed. The Court of Appeal (affirming the decision of the Queen's Bench Division) rejected this contention, and held that the conversation between the bankrupt and the bank manager, not being followed by any act which altered the legal position of the parties, was not a sufficient part performance of the oral promise to exclude the Statute.

"I take that proposition", said Lord Esher, M.R., "to amount to this—that where there is a mere oral promise to do something, and nothing takes place afterwards but the speaking of more words by the parties—when nothing more is done in fact—there is no part performance which can exclude the application of the Statute of Frauds."

[1] 8 App. Cas. at p. 479. As to the submission that the act of part performance must *visibly* affect the subject-matter of the contract, cf. the statement by the Earl of Selborne (at p. 479) and Lord FitzGerald (at p. 491) that the act must be "in its own nature referable" to some such agreement as that alleged.

[2] (1887) 18 Q.B.D. 766, 769.

The foregoing propositions may be tested with reference to the act of part performance *par excellence*, change of possession of land. Change of possession of land is a visible act, and it clearly relates to or affects the land in such a manner as to indicate a contract affecting that land. Accordingly it constitutes a sufficient part performance of a contract for the sale, lease or settlement of the land,[1] for a contract affecting the land is *some such contract* as any one of these.

The part performance may, indeed, be of a composite nature: it may consist of some act (positive or negative in character), which visibly affects the subject-matter of the contract, but does not unequivocally imply a contract; and this act may be qualified[2] by some further act, only to be accounted for on the footing of a contract. Thus continuance in possession by a tenant after the expiration of his lease is no part performance of a contract for a new lease;[3] but if coupled with payment of a different rent the case is otherwise.[4] There is now a part performance unequivocally indicating the existence of a new contract affecting the land which is the subject-matter of the alleged contract.

It follows from the foregoing considerations, that even if a contract be one which in its own nature could be specifically enforced, yet it may not be susceptible of part performance within the meaning of the rule.

> "There was no part performance in the case before us such as has been defined as necessary", said Lord FitzGerald in *Maddison* v. *Alderson*,[5] "and I may add that the peculiar character of the alleged agreement does not admit of such a part performance by the defendant as could affect the operation of the statute."

In such a case, even if the plaintiff has wholly performed the obligations imposed on him by the contract, he will not be

[1] *Daniels* v. *Trefusis*, [1914] 1 Ch. 788; *Brough* v. *Nettleton*, [1921] 2 Ch. 25; *Ungley* v. *Ungley*, (1876) 4 Ch.D. 73.

[2] "Qualified": see per Earl of Selborne, 8 App. Cas. at p. 480.

[3] Per Lord Loughborough, L.C., in *Wills* v. *Stradling*, (1797) 3 Ves. 378, 381; 30 E.R. 1063, 1065.

[4] *Nunn* v. *Fabian*, (1865) L.R. 1 Ch. 35; *Miller and Aldworth* v. *Sharp*, [1899] 1 Ch. 622.

[5] 8 App. Cas. at p. 491.

allowed to prove the contract by parol.[1] This may be so (i) because the contract relates to a subject-matter incapable of being affected in the manner necessary to comply with the doctrine of part performance, or (ii) because, although the contract relates to a subject-matter which could be affected in such a manner, yet the acts to be performed by the plaintiff under the contract either do not relate to or affect the subject-matter in question or are equivocal in their nature.

(i) *Contract relating to subject-matter incapable of being visibly affected in such a manner as to comply with doctrine.* The distinction between subject-matters which can be visibly affected in such a manner that a contract relating to them is unequivocally indicated, and those which cannot be so affected, does not exactly correspond with the distinction between corporeal and incorporeal things.[2] It is not necessary that the subject-matter shall be a corporeal thing—a *res quae tangi potest*—but it must be a thing which can be visibly affected by the acts of the plaintiff. Thus, in *McManus* v. *Cooke*,[3] it was held that an easement was capable of being so affected that an agreement for its grant could be partly performed within the meaning of the rule. In that case the plaintiff, as a result of alterations mutually carried out by the plaintiff and the defendant on their adjoining premises, was openly receiving light over the defendant's property when the defendant constructed a skylight of his own in such a position as to obstruct the plaintiff's skylight. The plaintiff thereupon brought an action for the specific performance of an agreement to give him an easement of light. Kay, J., thus summed up the position:[4]

"I find the defendant in possession of an easement of light over the plaintiff's land by reason of the plaintiff having taken down and re-erected at a less height a boundary wall partly on the defendant's and partly on the plaintiff's land. By the same act the defendant has been put in possession of a larger space on his side of the wall, the new wall erected being much thinner than the old one. These acts could not have been done by the plaintiff and

[1] *Ib.*

[2] Salmond, *Jurisprudence*, 8th ed. p. 281.

[3] (1887) 35 Ch.D. 681.

[4] *Ib.* at p. 697.

these advantages could not have been obtained by the defendant without some agreement between them."

(ii) *Acts to be performed by plaintiff not affecting subject-matter, or equivocal in their nature.* In *Maddison* v. *Alderson*[1] the acts to be performed, and in fact performed, by the appellant did not in any way relate to or affect the land which she alleged that the deceased had contracted to devise to her. Hence it was said by Lord FitzGerald that the contract in that case was incapable of part performance.

Moreover, although an act may visibly affect the subject-matter of the contract, it may be equivocal in its effect. Thus, if the subject-matter of the contract is the property of the plaintiff, his acts in regard to that property may well be accounted for on the supposition that he was desirous of improving his own property. For example, it would not be a part performance of a contract for the sale of a house, that the vendor, being the owner of the land, built the house thereon, in order to put himself in a position to perform the contract.[2]

An act may also be equivocal from its negative nature. Thus, continuance in possession by a tenant after the expiration of his lease is an equivocal act where it is sought to establish a contract for a new lease.[3] Another instance is given by Lord Cranworth, L.C., in the course of his judgment in *Caton* v. *Caton*.[4]

"I must further observe", said the Lord Chancellor, "that the nature of the alleged agreement was such as hardly to admit, even on the part of the party to be charged, of anything like part performance. As a will is necessarily until the last moment of life revocable, a contract to make any specified bequest, even when a will having that effect has been duly prepared and executed, is in truth a contract of a negative nature—a contract not to vary what has been so prepared and executed. I do not see how there can be part performance of such a contract."

(D) "*The alleged agreement should be certainly proved.*"

[1] 8 App. Cas. 467, 491.

[2] Per Kekewich, J., in *Dickinson* v. *Barrow*, [1904] 2 Ch. 339, 343; per Romer, J., in *Rawlinson* v. *Ames*, [1925] Ch. 96, 114.

[3] Per Lord Loughborough, L.C., in *Wills* v. *Stradling*, (1797) 3 Ves. 378, 381; 30 E.R. 1063, 1065.

[4] (1866) L.R. 1 Ch. 137, 148.

"There must be proper parol evidence of the contract which is let in by the acts of part performance", said Romer, J., in *Rawlinson* v. *Ames*.[1] Proof of an act or acts of part performance is not proof of the contract; such proof merely opens the door to let in parol evidence to establish the terms of the contract in the ordinary way. "The effect of the removal of the barrier set up by the statute", said P. O. Lawrence, J., in *Brough* v. *Nettleton*,[2] "in my judgment is to open the door to parol evidence of the whole agreement...."

The rule under discussion does not, however, mean that the standard of proof should be higher in the case where the evidence is admitted on account of a part performance than in any other case.[3] It simply means that the plaintiff has the burden of proving his contract to discharge, and he must discharge it by adducing such evidence as will, taken in conjunction with the part performance, satisfy the court that he has made out his case. Thus in *Maddison* v. *Alderson*[4] the existence and terms of the contract sued upon were determined partly on the verdict of a jury, and partly by inference from the jury's finding. In *Smallwood* v. *Sheppards*,[5] an appeal from a County Court, a Divisional Court (Wright and Kennedy, JJ.) ascertained the terms of the contract sued upon by inference from the facts stated in the County Court judge's notes of evidence. And it has been laid down that if the defendant admits the contract but pleads the Statute, this admission will suffice to prove the contract, upon the plaintiff's first making out a sufficient part performance.[6] In short, the courts, in deciding whether the con-

[1] [1925] Ch. 96, 114, quoting from Fry, *Specific Performance of Contracts*, 6th ed. p. 276.

[2] [1921] 2 Ch. 25, 28.

[3] Lord Cottenham, L.C., indeed, seems to have thought that the fact of part performance should even, if anything, warrant the courts in adopting a standard of proof lower than usual, in deciding whether the plaintiff has adequately made out his contract. *Mundy* v. *Jolliffe*, (1839) 5 My. & Cr. 167, 177; 41 E.R. 334, 338.

[4] (1883) 8 App. Cas. 467; see report of case before Stephen, J. (*sub nom.* *Alderson* v. *Maddison*), 5 Ex.D. 293.

[5] [1895] 2 Q.B. 627, 629.

[6] Per Lord Eldon, L.C., in *Cooth* v. *Jackson*, (1801) 6 Ves. 12, 37; 31 E.R. 913, 926.

tract is properly proved, will accept all relevant and otherwise admissible evidence, and will determine the matter in the ordinary way upon the just weight and effect which they consider should be attached to such evidence.

(E) *Must condition as to fraud, and condition as to "some evidentia rei" be fulfilled by the same acts?* It has been shewn above that to satisfy the doctrine of part performance it must appear that a refusal to enforce the contract would be a fraud on the plaintiff; and secondly that the circumstances of the part performance must be such as unequivocally to indicate the existence of some such contract as that alleged. Is it necessary, however, that these two functions should be discharged by the same act or acts? It is submitted that the answer to this question is, "No". Clearly, to satisfy the first requirement it must appear that the acts relied upon have been done by the plaintiff on the faith of the contract; and it has been shewn above[1] that they must also have been done in pursuance of it. But, on principle, there would seem to be no reason why the necessary *evidentia rei* should not be provided by acts which are not those of the plaintiff, nor yet done in pursuance of the contract.

This, indeed, seems to have been the opinion of Lord Hardwicke. After stating, in *Gunter* v. *Halsey*,[2] the general conditions of the doctrine of part performance, and that the acts of part performance must be such as could be done with no other view or design than to perform the agreement alleged, he said that in that case "it did not appear but that the acts done by *the defendant* might be done with other views". Lord Hardwicke, therefore, was willing to admit that the evidentiary condition could be satisfied by acts of the defendant. It was recognized by Lord Cranworth, L.C., in *Caton* v. *Caton*[3] that acts, although done by the defendant, might afford strong evidence of the existence of the contract alleged; and in *Nunn* v. *Fabian*,[4] that acts, although not done in pursuance of the contract, might yet afford convincing evidence of the existence of such a contract.

[1] *Supra*, p. 244.
[2] (1739) Amb. 586; 27 E.R. 381. The italics in the passage quoted are mine.
[3] (1866) L.R. 1 Ch. 137, 148.
[4] (1865) L.R. 1 Ch. 35, 40.

In 1904, Kekewich, J., in *Dickinson* v. *Barrow*,[1] actually decided that the evidentiary requirements of the doctrine of part performance could be discharged by acts of the defendant not done in pursuance of the contract. The contract in that case was that the plaintiffs should build on a plot of land belonging to them a house, and should sell the house and land, complete, to the defendant. The plaintiff built the house, but that act, although sufficient to satisfy the condition of the doctrine of part performance as to fraud, was not unequivocally referable to some such contract as that alleged. But, in addition, the defendant had frequently visited the house during the course of its erection, had inspected the work, and had from time to time suggested minor alterations. This conduct, Kekewich, J., held, was consistent only with the existence of such a contract as that alleged, and hence he accepted it as satisfying the evidentiary requirements of the doctrine.[2]

In view of the foregoing authorities, therefore, it is submitted that so long as an act is unequivocally referable to some such contract as that alleged, it is immaterial, for the purpose of the evidentiary requirements of the doctrine of part performance, that it is not the act of the plaintiff, or that it was not done in pursuance of the contract.[3]

[1] [1904] 2 Ch. 339.

[2] See also *Rawlinson* v. *Ames*, [1925] Ch. 96. In *Hohler* v. *Aston*, [1920] 2 Ch. 420, Sargant, J., held that an act of a third party, in the circumstances of that case, was sufficient to satisfy the requirement under discussion.

[3] The discussion of part performance given in the text has been chiefly directed to the general principles of the doctrine. The various acts which have from time to time been held to be sufficient part performance are very fully considered and discussed in Fry, *Specific Performance of Contracts*, 6th ed. pp. 276–302, and it seems unnecessary again to traverse material which has already been so well and authoritatively dealt with. See also *White and Tudor's L.C.* 9th ed. II, pp. 410 *et seq.*, *sub nom. Lester* v. *Foxcroft and others.*

CHAPTER VIII

THE EQUITABLE JURISDICTION TO RECTIFY DOCUMENTS IN ITS APPLICATION TO WRITINGS UNDER THE STATUTE

IN certain cases a party may, on the ground that the writing purporting to evidence his contract by mistake fails properly to set forth all the terms of that contract, apply to the court for the rectification of such writing and also, if necessary, for the specific enforcement of the contract as evidenced by the writing when it has been rectified.

The rectification of documents which by mistake do not express the true intention of the parties has long been a settled head of equity jurisdiction.

"No doubt", said Lord Hardwicke, in 1749,[1] "but this court has jurisdiction to relieve in respect of a plain mistake in contracts in writing as well as against frauds in contracts; so that if reduced into writing contrary to the intent of the parties, on proper proof that would be rectified. But the plaintiff comes to do this in the harshest case that can happen: of a policy, after the event and loss happened, to vary the contract so as to turn the loss on the insurer, who otherwise, it is admitted, cannot be charged; however, if the case is so strong as to require it, the court ought to do it."

There was formerly much controversy as to whether the admission of extrinsic evidence to support a suit for the rectification of a writing purporting to evidence a contract under the Statute was not contrary both to the common law rule which

[1] *Henkle* v. *Royal Exchange Assurance Co.*, (1749) 1 Ves. Sen. 317, 318; 27 E.R. 1055. See also *Thomas* v. *Davis*, (1757) 1 Dick. 301; 21 E.R. 284; *Mortimer* v. *Shortall*, (1842) 2 Dr. & War. 363; Mitford (Lord Redesdale), *Pleadings in Suits in the Court of Chancery*, 5th ed. (1847), pp. 150, 151; Judicature Act, 1873, s. 34 (now Judicature Act, 1925, s. 56): "There shall be assigned...to the Chancery Division...(3)....The rectification, or setting aside, or cancellation of deeds or other written instruments". And see Fry, *Specific Performance of Contracts*, 6th ed. p. 371.

excludes extrinsic evidence to add to, vary or contradict documents,[1] and to the Statute itself.

So far as regards the common law rule, the very fact that the jurisdiction to rectify existed would seem to shew that that rule could have no application where it was sought to admit parol evidence merely to establish that the case was such that the court could exercise that jurisdiction. The admissibility of evidence in cases coming within this jurisdiction would appear to be subject to the same considerations as the admissibility of evidence in cases where it is sought to shew that the plaintiff is acting unconscionably in endeavouring to impose on the defendant a contract differing from that to which the defendant actually agreed:[2] neither in the one class of cases nor in the other would it have been compatible with the jurisdiction of the court to have followed the common law rule.

"A court of equity", wrote Story,[3] "would be of little value, if it could suppress only positive frauds, and leave mutual mistakes, innocently made, to work intolerable mischiefs, contrary to the intention of parties. It would be to allow an act originating in innocence, to operate ultimately as a fraud, by enabling the party, who receives the benefit of the mistake, to resist the claims of justice, under the shelter of a rule framed to promote it. In a practical view, there would be as much mischief done by refusing relief in such cases, as there would be introduced by allowing parol evidence in all cases to vary written contracts."

Nevertheless, it would appear to have been laid down by Grant, M.R., in *Woollam* v. *Hearn*,[4] that, because of the above-mentioned common law rule, parol evidence to prove that by mutual mistake a writing failed to express the real agreement between the parties, could not be admitted where the plaintiff sought rectification of the writing and specific performance of the contract. In *Woollam* v. *Hearn* the plaintiff set out in her bill that she had entered into an agreement for a lease at a certain rent, but that by mistake the writing contained a higher rent than the parties had agreed upon; and she prayed for the specific

[1] See p. 149 *supra*. [2] See p. 166 *supra*.
[3] *Equity Jurisprudence*, 2nd English ed. p. 94.
[4] (1802) 7 Ves. 211; 32 E.R. 86; 2 Wh. & T. L.C. 9th ed. p. 464.

performance of the actual agreement. After stating the rule of common law rejecting extrinsic evidence, the Master of the Rolls remarked on the evidence tendered by the plaintiff,[1] that it was offered "first, to falsify the written agreement; and then to substitute in its place a parol agreement, to be executed by the court...". And later he said:[2] "But this is evidence to vary an agreement in a material part; and having varied it to procure it to be executed in another form. There is nothing to shew that it ought to be done, and my opinion being that it ought not, I must dismiss the bill...". It is to be observed of this case, however, that the plaintiff prayed simply for the specific performance of an alleged agreement, and failed to produce a writing sufficient to support her case: it does not appear that a prayer for rectification was included in the bill.[3]

The same remark seems applicable to *Davies* v. *Fitton*,[4] which came before Sir Edward Sugden (afterwards Lord St Leonards), when he was Lord Chancellor of Ireland. In that case the bill prayed for the rectification of a conveyance made in pursuance of a written agreement which by mutual mistake omitted one of the terms which the parties had agreed upon. The Lord Chancellor held that to grant such relief would, in effect, be to rectify the written agreement and then to enforce it specifically; and this, he considered, could not be done. "I cannot", he said, "decree a specific performance with the variation of a new term, no matter how inconsiderable that term may be—as for instance, the payment of taxes—nor how clearly that term may be proved by parol evidence; the court cannot receive that evidence." *Woollam* v. *Hearn* and *Davies* v. *Fitton* were expressly followed by Farwell, J., in *May* v. *Platt*,[5] a case in which the facts were similar to those in *Davies* v. *Fitton*.

In each of these cases, the attention of the court appears to have been directed chiefly to the specific performance sought by the plaintiff: the objection to admitting the evidence of mistake was not that the court had no jurisdiction to rectify, but

[1] (1802) 7 Ves. 219; 32 E.R. 89. [2] *Ib.* 221; E.R. 90.
[3] See per Neville, J., in *Thompson* v. *Hickman*, [1907] 1 Ch. 550, 561.
[4] (1842) 2 Dr. & War. 225, 232. [5] [1900] 1 Ch. 616.

rather that it could not enforce, with a parol variation, a contract evidenced by writing. Where, however, the bill prayed for rectification, and not specific performance, it would seem clear that parol evidence to prove mistake would be admitted.[1] Moreover, there would appear to have been nothing to prevent a plaintiff who had in one suit had the writing evidencing his contract rectified, from then instituting another suit to have the contract specifically enforced. Indeed, it is a little difficult to see why both forms of relief could not have been separately claimed in the same bill.[2]

The Judicature Act, 1873,[3] provided as follows:

"The High Court of Justice and the Court of Appeal respectively, in the exercise of the jurisdiction vested in them by this Act in every cause or matter pending before them respectively, shall have power to grant, and shall grant, either absolutely or on such reasonable terms and conditions as to them shall seem just, all such remedies whatsoever as any of the parties thereto may appear to be entitled to in respect of any and every legal or equitable claim properly brought forward by them respectively in such cause or matter; so that, as far as possible, all matters so in controversy between the said parties respectively may be completely and finally determined, and all multiplicity of legal proceedings concerning any of such matters avoided".

Fry, in the second and subsequent editions of his work on *Specific Performance of Contracts*,[4] expressed the opinion that this provision of the Judicature Act finally settled the "vexed question" of the court's jurisdiction in this connection, and

[1] *Mortimer* v. *Shortall*, (1842) 2 Dr. & War. 363.

[2] Lord Redesdale (Mitford, *Pleadings in Suits in the Court of Chancery*, 5th ed.) does not refer to any rule which would have prevented such a course from being followed, nor does he indicate any technical objection to a plaintiff suing first for rectification, and in a subsequent suit for specific performance. "Every bill", he wrote (*op. cit.* p. 8), "must have for its object one or more of the grounds upon which the jurisdiction of the court is founded." This statement seems to imply that claims for several forms of relief could be joined in the one bill. Williams, *Vendor and Purchaser*, 3rd ed. II, p. 774, expresses a similar opinion. See also *Hodgkinson* v. *Wyatt*, (1846) 9 Beav. 566; 50 E.R. 462; and *Stedman* v. *Collett*, (1854) 17 Beav. 608; 51 E.R. 1171.

[3] 36 & 37 Vict. c. 66, s. 24 (7); substantially re-enacted as s. 43 of the Supreme Court of Judicature (Consolidation) Act, 1925.

[4] See 6th ed. p. 381.

enabled the High Court to entertain an action in which the plaintiff sought both rectification and specific performance. The grounds upon which Fry based this opinion are not, however, quite clear. As Stirling, L.J., pointed out in *The James Westoll*,[1] the Judicature Act merely enabled the High Court "to give effect to all the remedies which the parties were, in the language of the Act, entitled to—that is to say, as could have been given by any court which was made a member of the High Court by the Judicature Act"; but the act did not confer any new jurisdiction. Hence, unless it were accepted that before the Judicature Act a party could first have preferred a bill to obtain rectification and could then have preferred a second bill claiming specific enforcement, it would not appear that the Judicature Act affected the position.

But whatever may have been the position before the Judicature Act, North, J., in *Olley* v. *Fisher*,[2] which came before him in 1886, accepted Fry's conclusions. This decision was followed, some years later, by Kay, J., in *Shrewsbury and Talbot Cab Co.* v. *Shaw*.[3] In *May* v. *Platt*,[4] on the other hand, Farwell, J., adhered to the doctrine of *Davies* v. *Fitton*;[5] and subsequently Neville, J., in *Thompson* v. *Hickman*,[6] held himself to be bound by *Davies* v. *Fitton*[5] and *May* v. *Platt*.[4] In the course of his judgment, however, Neville, J., very clearly pointed out the difficulties involved in these cases.

"I feel considerable difficulty, however", he said, "in following the reasoning upon which they appear to be based. The doctrine of *Woollam* v. *Hearn*[7] appears to me to have no bearing upon a case of rectification. Specific performance comes under a head of equitable jurisdiction quite distinct from rectification. The former is based upon the inadequacy of the remedy appointed in certain cases by the common law, and from the nature of the case involves a contravention of its rules. To refuse rectification, therefore, on the ground that to grant it would offend against a rule of law appears to me to strike at the root of equitable jurisdiction in the matter....It is to be observed that the rule in

[1] [1905] P. 47, 51.
[2] (1886) 34 Ch.D. 367.
[3] (1890) 89 L.T. Jo. 274.
[4] [1900] 1 Ch. 616.
[5] (1842) 2 Dr. & War. 225.
[6] [1907] 1 Ch. 550, 561.
[7] (1802) 7 Ves. 211.

question, which excludes parol evidence to contradict a written agreement, applies with even greater force to a deed."

This controversy has now, it is submitted, been set at rest by the recent case of *Craddock Bros.* v. *Hunt*,[1] a decision of the Court of Appeal (Lord Sterndale, M.R., and Warrington, L.J.; Younger, L.J., dissenting), affirming a judgment of P. O. Lawrence, J. The facts of *Craddock Bros.* v. *Hunt* were as follows. The parties had agreed for the sale and purchase of certain land, but owing to a mistake, common to both of them, in the reducing of the contract to writing, the writing failed to express the true bargain; and the mistake was later embodied in the deed of conveyance. It was held, both by P. O. Lawrence, J., and the Court of Appeal, that the court had jurisdiction in the one proceeding to rectify the writing so as to express the true contract between the parties and then to enforce the contract specifically. Lord Sterndale, M.R., after discussing the authorities referred to above, remarked:[2]

"In these circumstances I think I am at liberty, at any rate since the Judicature Act, 1873, to express my opinion that rectification can be granted of a written agreement on parol evidence of mutual mistake, although that agreement is complete in itself, and has been carried out by a more formal document based upon it. I think the contrary view is based upon an insufficient consideration of the result of rectification. After rectification the written agreement does not continue to exist with a parol variation; it is to be read as if it had been originally drawn in its rectified form: *Johnson* v. *Bragge*,[3] and it is that written document, and that alone, of which specific performance is decreed".[4]

Although, however, it be allowed that the writing evidencing a contract can in general be rectified by the court upon parol evidence of a mutual mistake, it may be asked whether the Statute will not exclude such evidence in the case of contracts coming within its provisions. "Rectification", it was said in

1 [1922] 2 Ch. 809; [1923] 2 Ch. 136.

2 [1923] 2 Ch. 151.

3 [1901] 1 Ch. 28, 37.

4 See also per Warrington, L.J., [1923] 2 Ch. 159, 160. Younger, L.J., disagreed: see *ib.* 166, 167. The decision in *Craddock Bros.* v. *Hunt* was approved by the Judicial Committee in *United States* v. *Motor Trucks, Ltd.* [1924] A.C. 196, 201–202.

the American case of *Glass* v. *Hulbert*,[1] "by making the contract include obligations or subject-matter, to which its written terms will not apply, is a direct enforcement of the oral agreement, as much in conflict with the Statute of Frauds, as if there were no writing at all." It is well settled now, however, that the view of the matter expressed in this passage is not the law of England; but for a time it seemed possible that English law might have adopted that view. Thus *Woollam* v. *Hearn*[2] appears to have proceeded partly on the ground of the Statute. "Thinking, as I do", said Grant, M.R., in that case, "that the Statute has been already too much broken in upon by supposed equitable exceptions, I shall not go farther in receiving and giving effect to parol evidence, than I am forced by precedent." In *Attorney-General* v. *Sitwell*,[3] Alderson, B., remarked, *obiter*, in regard to an information and bill claiming both rectification and specific performance: "I confess I should have had great difficulty in holding that this could be done; because I cannot help feeling that, in the case of an executory agreement, first to reform and then to decree an execution of it would be virtually to repeal the Statute of Frauds".

On the other hand, the case of *Thomas* v. *Davis*[4] was a clear decision that the Statute formed no bar to the admission of parol evidence to support a suit for rectification. This was followed by Cozens-Hardy, J., in *Johnson* v. *Bragge*.[5] In the course of his judgment in that case, Cozens-Hardy, J., remarked:

"Now the plea of the Statute of Frauds somewhat surprises me, for the books are full of cases in which marriage settlements and conveyances of land have been rectified on parol evidence. But I was told that the Statute of Frauds had not been pleaded in those cases, although it might have been. The reason why the Statute of Frauds was not pleaded in modern cases is because it was settled at least a century and a half ago that parol evidence is admissible in an action to rectify a mistake in a marriage settlement, notwithstanding the Statute of Frauds: an action of

1 (1869) 102 Mass. 24, 35.
2 (1802) 7 Ves. 211, 219; 32 E.R. 86, 89.
3 (1835) 1 Y. & C. Ex. 559, 583; 160 E.R. 228, 238.
4 (1757) 1 Dick. 301, 303; 21 E.R. 284.
5 [1901] 1 Ch. 28, 36.

that kind not being one seeking 'to charge any person upon any agreement made upon consideration of marriage' within the meaning of s. 4".

The question was again raised in *Craddock Bros.* v. *Hunt*[1] and there Lord Sterndale, M.R., and Warrington, L.J., both held that the Statute did not apply to a suit to rectify a writing, and formed no bar to the subsequent enforcement of the contract. The ground of their decision was that once a writing had been rectified, it was to be taken as having always existed in its rectified form. "It seems to me", said Warrington, L.J.,[2] "that on principle, if an instrument of whatever nature is rectified it ought to be treated as if the necessary alteration had actually been made with the pen and had been part of the document at the date of its completion."

The point was last before the courts in the recent case of *United States* v. *Motor Trucks, Ltd.*[3] In that case, the writing, by mistake, omitted to refer to certain lands forming part of the subject-matter of the contract; and the Judicial Committee, reversing the decision of the Appellate Division of the Supreme Court of Ontario, held that the mistake might be rectified in spite of the Statute, and specific performance be granted. The Earl of Birkenhead, who delivered the judgment of the Committee, thus disposed of the contention that the Statute formed a bar to the admission of parol evidence to prove the mistake.

"It was further suggested", he said, "that the present action involved an attempt to enforce a parol contract inconsistently with the principle of the Statute of Frauds. It is, however, well settled by a series of familiar authorities that the Statute of Frauds is not allowed by any court administering the doctrines of equity to become an instrument for enabling sharp practice to be committed. And indeed the power of the court to rectify mutual mistake implies that this power may be exercised notwithstanding that the true agreement of the parties has not been expressed in writing....The statute, in fact, only provides that no agreement not in writing and not duly signed shall be sued on; but when the written instrument is rectified there is a writing

1 [1922] 2 Ch. 809; [1923] 2 Ch. 136.
2 [1923] 2 Ch. 160.
3 [1924] A.C. 196, 200.

which satisfies the statute, the jurisdiction of the court to rectify being outside the prohibition of the statute."

It may therefore be taken as settled, that in a proper case, the court will rectify a mistake in a writing evidencing a contract under the Statute, notwithstanding the common law rule of evidence referred to above, and in spite of the provisions of the Statute itself. It remains to consider the conditions on which this relief will be granted. These conditions were concisely stated by Warrington, L.J., in the course of his judgment in *Craddock Bros.* v. *Hunt.*[1] He said:

"The jurisdiction of Courts of Equity in this respect is to bring the written document executed in pursuance of an antecedent agreement into conformity with that agreement. The conditions to its exercise are that there must be an antecedent contract and the common intention of embodying or giving effect to the whole of the contract by the writing, and there must be clear evidence that the document by common mistake failed to embody such contract and either contained provisions not agreed upon or omitted something that was agreed upon, or otherwise departed from its terms".

The conditions enumerated by the learned Lord Justice may be considered in their order. The first is that there must be an antecedent contract. The jurisdiction of the court in this respect is to rectify mistakes in the written evidence of the contract, and not to make a contract where the parties have made none. "Nor does the rule", said the Earl of Birkenhead,[2] "make any inroad upon another principle, that the plaintiff must show first that there was an actually concluded agreement antecedent to the instrument which is sought to be rectified...."[3] The point is well illustrated by the case of *Mackenzie* v. *Coulson.*[4] There the plaintiffs, who were underwriters, claimed the rectification of a policy of marine insurance by the insertion of a clause to the effect that the insurance was "free of particular average", in

[1] [1923] 2 Ch. 136, 159.

[2] *United States* v. *Motor Trucks, Ltd.* [1924] A.C. 196, 200.

[3] See also per Gordon, J., in *Jackson* v. *Stopford,* [1923] 2 I.R. 1, 4; and per O'Connor, M.R., p. 10.

[4] (1869) L.R. 8 Eq. 368, 375.

lieu of a clause making the plaintiffs liable for "average recoverable as customary". It was alleged that the true agreement was contained in an insurance "slip", but that by mistake the policy had not been drawn conformably with it. As to the slip, however, James, V.-C., held that it was merely an offer and no evidence of a contract. "Repeated authorities", he said, "have decided that I am not at liberty even to look at that slip as evidence of a contract. I am bound by law to hold that it did not amount to a contract of any kind." The policy itself, therefore, was the contract, and the Vice-Chancellor held that he had no jurisdiction to rectify this.

"Courts of Equity", he said, "do not rectify contracts; they may and do rectify instruments purporting to have been made in pursuance of the terms of contracts. But it is always necessary for a plaintiff to shew that there was an actual concluded contract antecedent to the instrument which is sought to be rectified; and that such contract is inaccurately represented in the instrument."

The second condition is that there must be a common intention to embody the whole contract in the writing. Two results flow from this condition. First of all, the court has no jurisdiction to rectify any writing which the parties deliberately intended should not completely or properly state their contract. Thus in *Irnham* v. *Child*,[1] where there was a contract for an annuity and the parties to it intentionally omitted a proviso for redemption, thinking it would make the transaction usurious, Lord Thurlow, L.C., refused to rectify the deed. Lord Eldon, L.C., in a subsequent case[2] stated as follows the ground of Lord Thurlow's decision:

'*Lord Irnham* v. *Child* went upon an indisputably clear principle; that the parties did not mean to insert in the agreement a provision for redemption; because they were all of one mind, that it would be usurious; and they desired the court, not to do what they intended, for the insertion of that provision was directly contrary to their intention, but they desired to be put in the same situation, as if they had been better informed, and

[1] (1781) 1 Bro. C.C. 92; 28 E.R. 1006.
[2] *Townshend* v. *Stangroom*, (1801) 6 Ves. 328, 332; 31 E.R. 1076, 1078.

consequently had a contrary intention. The answer is, they admit, it was not to be in the deed; and why was the court to insert it; where two risks had occurred to the parties: the danger of usury, and the danger of trusting to the honour of the party".[1]

In the second place, it would seem that where the case is under the Statute, and the writing relied upon is not one which was *mutually* intended by the parties to evidence their contract, the doctrine of rectification can have no application. Thus it is submitted that it would not apply to a mere letter, or a receipt, or an invoice or any similar informal and unilateral document. If, in a case under the Statute, the plaintiff relies upon such a document to constitute a writing, and it is incomplete or erroneous, his action must fail.[2]

The third condition mentioned by Warrington, L.J., is that by *common mistake* the writing must fail to embody the antecedent contract.

"I agree with the proposition", said Sir Edward Sugden in *Mortimer* v. *Shortall*,[3] "as laid down by the defendant's counsel, that I must be satisfied that there was a mistake on both sides, for I cannot otherwise rectify this lease. A mistake on one side might be a ground for rescinding a contract, but never could be relied on as a reason for taking from a man, what he thought he was to get under his agreement."

The case is one of common mistake where the contract, by inadvertence or accident, is erroneously or incompletely stated in the document which the parties have mutually accepted as the evidence of their contract.[4]

[1] See also *Portmore* v. *Morris*, (1787) 2 Bro. C.C. 219; 29 E.R. 122.

[2] *Supra*, pp. 153 *et seq.*

[3] (1842) 2 Dr. & War. 363, 372. See also *Blay* v. *Pollard and Morris*, [1930] 1 K.B. 628, 633 (per Scrutton, L.J.), and 636 (per Greer, L.J.).

[4] Per Lord Sterndale, M.R., in *Craddock Bros.* v. *Hunt*, [1923] 2 Ch. 136, 150: "I have already said that the vendors, if the yard were sold separately, instructed the auctioneer to sell the whole yard let to Greenstone for 6*s*. a week, that Stephen Craddock [one of the co-purchasers] instructed the auctioneer to buy the whole yard, that the auctioneer understood those instructions, and that, when it was knocked down, the auctioneer intended to buy for the one party and sell for the other the whole yard. The memorandum signed by one of the vendors shews that he so understood the transaction. The contract was wrongly drawn so as not to include the brown land by a careless blunder on the part of Mr Stirk, and accepted by Mr George Crad-

It is sometimes said that *Garrard* v. *Frankel*,[1] *Harris* v. *Pepperell*[2] (both before Lord Romilly, M.R.), and *Paget* v. *Marshall*[3] (before Bacon, V.-C.), have established an exception to the rule that mistake must be mutual before the court can grant rectification. These cases have, however, been the subject of adverse criticism,[4] and it would seem that they can only be supported on the ground that the conduct of the party seeking to take advantage of the other's mistake was fraudulent.

"I have always understood the law to be", said Farwell, J., in *May* v. *Platt*,[5] "that in order to obtain rectification there must be a mistake common to both parties, and if the mistake is only unilateral, there must be fraud or misrepresentation amounting to fraud. It is true that Lord Romilly in *Harris* v. *Pepperell*[2] and *Garrard* v. *Frankel*,[1] and perhaps Bacon, V.-C., in *Paget* v. *Marshall*,[3] appear to have shrunk from stigmatizing the defendant's conduct in terms as fraud, but they treated it as equivalent to fraud, and in my opinion would have had no jurisdiction to grant the relief that they did in the absence of fraud."[6]

The fourth and last of the conditions laid down by Warrington, L.J., to be satisfied by a plaintiff seeking rectification is that there must be clear evidence of the mistake. The evidence must be such as to leave no fair and reasonable doubt as to the mistake and the terms of the real contract,[7] but it need not be uncontradicted evidence.

dock [the other co-purchaser] as carrying out what he believed to be the bargain. It seems to me to be as clear a case of mutual mistake as could occur...". See also per Malins, V.-C., in *Clark* v. *Girdwood*, (1877) 7 Ch.D. 9, 16–19.

[1] (1862) 30 Beav. 445; 54 E.R. 961.

[2] (1867) L.R. 5 Eq. 1.

[3] (1884) 28 Ch.D. 255.

[4] Williams, *Vendor and Purchaser*, 3rd ed. II, p. 782.

[5] [1900] 1 Ch. 616, 623.

[6] See, as to these cases, the elaborate discussion in Williams, *Vendor and Purchaser*, 3rd ed. II, pp. 779–787. In Fry, *Specific Performance of Contracts*, 6th ed. p. 373, the effect of the cases in question is stated to be as follows: "The error of the plaintiff alone may, however, where (but, it is conceived, only where) there has been fraud or conduct equivalent to fraud on the part of the defendant, be a ground for putting the defendant to elect between having the transaction annulled altogether or submitting to the rectification of the deed in accordance with the plaintiff's intention". This passage was approved by Scrutton, L.J., in *Blay* v. *Pollard and Morris*, [1930] 1 K.B. 628, 633.

[7] Per Lord Chelmsford, L.C., in *Fowler* v. *Fowler*, (1859) 3 De G. & J. 250, 264–265; 45 E.R. 97, 103.

"Now is the evidence conclusive?" inquired Sir Edward Sugden in *Mortimer* v. *Shortall*.[1] "I must be certain that there has been a mistake, and that the mistake is such as ought to be corrected. I do not mean to say, that the evidence must be all one way, or that there must not be any conflict; there must, however, be such a preponderance as will satisfy my mind."

[1] (1842) 2 Dr. & War. 363, 371.

CHAPTER IX

PLEADING THE STATUTE

It has never been considered necessary that a plaintiff, suing on a contract under the Statute, should allege in his pleading that the requirements of the Statute have been complied with.[1] Non-compliance with the Statute is a matter of defence to be raised by the defendant if he sees fit. The court will not of its own motion take notice of such non-compliance, and if the defendant does not claim the benefit of the Statute in the appropriate manner, he will be taken to have waived the defence which it would have afforded him.[2]

The manner in which the defence of the Statute must be raised is determined by the rules regulating the procedure of the court in which the action is being prosecuted. Prior to the Judicature Acts and Rules of Court established thereby, the defence of the Statute was in common law courts[3] raised by

[1] The principle is that "With respect to acts valid at common law, but regulated as to the mode of performance by statute,—it is sufficient to use such certainty of allegation, as was sufficient before the statute". Stephen, *Principles of Pleading*, 5th ed. (1843) 410; 6th ed. (1860) 287. Thus in *Field* v. *Hutchinson*, (1839) 1 Beav. 599; 48 E.R. 1073, the plaintiff alleged an agreement within the Statute, without stating whether the requirements of the Statute had been satisfied. The defendant demurred, but Lord Langdale, M.R., overruled the demurrer, remarking: "It is said that it does not appear, from the record, that the agreement was signed in the manner required by the Statute of Frauds. It is not distinctly alleged on the record, but the statements are quite consistent with there being a sufficient signature by the party to be charged". See also *Rist* v. *Hobson*, (1824) 1 Sim. & St. 543; 57 E.R. 215.

[2] Per Lord Eldon, L.C., in *Cooth* v. *Jackson*, (1801) 6 Ves. 12, 39; 31 E.R. 913, 927; "if he [the defendant] does not say anything about the statute, then he must be taken to renounce the benefit of it...". See also per Lord Cranworth, L.C., in *Ridgway* v. *Wharton*, (1854) 3 De G.M. & G. 677, 689; 43 E.R. 266, 271. The principle seems to be *quilibet potest renunciare juri pro se introducto*. See Broom, *Legal Maxims*, 9th ed. p. 452. See also per Earl Cairns, L.C., in *Dawkins* v. *Penrhyn*, (1878) 4 App. Cas. 51, 58; and per Kekewich, J., in *James* v. *Smith*, [1891] 1 Ch. 384, 389.

[3] At common law it was not permissible to raise a defence of the Statute by demurrer: per Mellish, L.J., *Catling* v. *King*, (1877) 5 Ch.D. 660, 662. In

special plea or plea of the general issue, and in Courts of Equity by demurrer, plea or answer, or plea and answer, according to the circumstances. In the common law courts it was usually unnecessary to plead the Statute specially, a plea of the general issue (*non assumpsit*)[1] being sufficient to enable the defendant to take advantage of the Statute at the hearing.[2] In the equity courts, however, a contrary rule prevailed, and a defendant relying on the Statute had expressly to plead or to claim by his answer the benefit of it.[3] The same principle seems to have applied where the defence was raised on demurrer.[4]

There was at one time much controversy in the Courts of Equity as to whether a defendant who admitted the contract could at the same time avail himself of the defence of the Statute. It was early settled that a simple admission of the contract by the defendant took the case out of the Statute, the reason given in the authorities being that the admission took the case out of the mischief which the Statute was designed to remedy.[5] Where, therefore, the defendant admitted the contract and at the same time sought to set up the Statute, the courts at first held that by such admission the defendant had entirely excluded the application of the Statute to the case.[6] But, as it was

Courts of Equity, however, a contrary rule prevailed, and where it clearly appeared on the face of the plaintiff's bill that his suit was defeasible for non-compliance with the Statute, the defendant might demur: *Field* v. *Hutchinson*, (1839) 1 Beav. 599; 48 E.R. 1073; *Wood* v. *Midgley*, (1854) 5 De M. & G. 41; 43 E.R. 784.

[1] See Stephen, *Principles of Pleading*, 5th ed. pp. 169, 172; 6th ed. pp. 144, 145.

[2] See *Leaf* v. *Tuton*, (1842) 10 M. & W. 393; 152 E.R. 523; *Buttemere* v. *Hayes*, (1839) 5 M. & W. 456; 151 E.R. 193; *Eastwood* v. *Kenyon*, (1840) 11 A. & E. 438; 113 E.R. 482; Bullen and Leake, *Precedents of Pleadings*, 3rd ed. (1869), p. 467.

[3] *Skinner* v. *McDouall*, (1848) 2 De G. & Sm. 265; 64 E.R. 120; *Heys* v. *Astley*, (1863) 4 De G.J. & S. 34; 46 E.R. 827. Cf. per Lord Cranworth, L.C., in *Ridgway* v. *Wharton*, (1854) 3 De G.M. & G. 677, 689; 43 E.R. 266, 271.

[4] See per Earl Cairns, L.C., in *Dawkins* v. *Lord Penrhyn*, (1878) 4 App. Cas. 51, 58.

[5] *Gunter* v. *Halsey*, (1739) Amb. 586; 27 E.R. 381; *Attorney-General* v. *Day*, (1749) 1 Ves. Sen. 218, 221; 27 E.R. 992, 994; *Limondson* v. *Sweed*, (1711) Gilb. Rep. 35; 25 E.R. 25; *Spurrier* v. *Fitzgerald*, (1801) 6 Ves. 548, 556; 31 E.R. 1189, 1193.

[6] *Child* v. *Godolphin*, (1723) Dick. 39, 42; 21 E.R. 181, 182; *Lacon* v. *Mertins*, (1743) 3 Atk. 1, 3; 26 E.R. 803, 804.

usually necessary for the defendant to answer on oath to the allegations in the plaintiff's bill,[1] it is plain that this view of the matter virtually amounted to a denial to a party sued in a Court of Equity, of the advantages of the Statutory defence. Accordingly, though not without considerable doubt and hesitation,[2] the earlier cases and *dicta* were at last overruled, and the rule became established that provided a defendant raised the defence of the Statute in a proper manner, it was immaterial that at the same time he confessed the fact of the agreement. The Statute nevertheless protected him.[3]

Modern procedure. At the present time the manner in which the defence of the Statute must be raised is prescribed by the Rules of the Supreme Court. With reference to the Statute, the effect of these rules is substantially to reproduce the procedure which prevailed in the Courts of Equity prior to the Judicature Acts. By Order XIX, rule 17, the procedure which obtained at Common Law, whereby the defendant might plead the general issue, is abrogated, and he must now "deal specifically with each allegation of fact of which he does not admit the truth, except damages".

By Order XIX, rule 15, the defendant is required "to raise by his pleading all matters which show the action not to be maintainable, and all such grounds of defence, as if not raised would take the plaintiff by surprise, as, for instance, Statute of Frauds". The effect of this rule is to require that the Statute shall be expressly pleaded. The degree of certainty in pleading required by this rule has been considered in several cases. In 1890, Kekewich, J., held in *James* v. *Smith*,[4] that it was unnecessary for the defendant to specify which of the sections of the Statute

[1] See *Cooth* v. *Jackson*, (1801) 6 Ves. 12, 39; 31 E.R. 913, 927; *Walters* v. *Morgan*, (1792) 2 Cox 369; 30 E.R. 169.

[2] See per Lord Loughborough, L.C., as late as 1798, in *Moore* v. *Edwards*, 4 Ves. 23, 24; 31 E.R. 12, 13; and per Lord Thurlow, L.C., in *Whitchurch* v. *Bevis*, (1786) Dick. 664; 21 E.R. 430. The point had already been treated as settled in the Court of Exchequer: *Walters* v. *Morgan*, (1782) 2 Cox 369; 30 E.R. 169.

[3] *Walters* v. *Morgan* (*supra*); *Cooth* v. *Jackson*, (1801) 6 Ves. 12, 39; 31 E.R. 913, 927; *Blagden* v. *Bradbear*, (1806) 12 Ves. 466, 471; 33 E.R. 176, 178.

[4] [1891] 1 Ch. 384, 389.

of Frauds he relied upon; but that if he pleaded a particular section he was bound by such pleading. In *James* v. *Smith* the defendant had pleaded s. 4 of the Statute of Frauds, whereas he should have pleaded s. 7. At the trial leave to amend was sought, but Kekewich, J., refused to grant the application. In *In re Robinson's Settlement*,[1] however, it was pointed out by Buckley, L.J., that it is in the discretion of the court in such a case to allow an amendment on terms protecting the plaintiff from injustice and surprise. But the courts do not appear to favour a defence based on the Statute, and it would seem that they will not, save in exceptional circumstances, exercise this discretion to enable a defendant to raise such a defence by amending his defence during the trial.[2]

In *North* v. *Loomes*,[3] Younger, J., held that a general plea of the Statute was to be construed with reference to the case pleaded by the plaintiff, taken in conjunction with any allegations of fact pleaded by the defendant. Accordingly he decided that where a plaintiff produced, at the trial, a writing proving the contract as pleaded, it was not then open to the defendant to give evidence to show that the contract in fact contained a term not stated in the writing and not alleged in the pleadings of either plaintiff or defendant. If a defendant intends to rely on such an omission to support a plea of the Statute he should allege in his statement of defence the term so omitted.

It was decided by the House of Lords in *Brunning* v. *Oldham*[4] that if the plaintiff, after pleading a contract which he alleges to be in writing, proceeds at the trial to prove by parol evidence a contract which is not the alleged contract in writing, the defendant, although he has not already pleaded the defence of the Statute, will be allowed to amend his pleadings to raise such defence.

[1] [1912] 1 Ch. 717, 727.

[2] See per Younger, J., in *North* v. *Loomes*, [1919] 1 Ch. 378, 384. Since the rule now represented by Ord. XIX, r. 15 was first made, many of the provisions of the Statute of Frauds then existing have been repealed. For the most part, however, these repealed provisions have been replaced by enactments to substantially the same effect, and it is conceived that the rule would be held to include these new enactments within its scope.

[3] [1919] 1 Ch. 378, 383.

[4] (1896) 75 L.T. 602.

Where a defendant who might have pleaded the Statute omits to do so, he and his privies will be estopped from pleading the Statute in any subsequent action on the same contract by the same plaintiff or his privies.[1] An estoppel, however, like the Statute, must, under Order XIX, rule 15, be specially pleaded or it will be deemed to be waived.[2] A plaintiff, therefore, proposing to rely upon estoppel by *res judicata* to meet a defence of the Statute, must expressly plead such estoppel in his reply.

By Order XIX, rule 20, it is provided that a bare denial of a contract in any pleading is to be construed only as a denial in fact of the express contract, or of the matters of fact from which the same may be implied by law, and not as a denial of the legality or sufficiency in law of such contract, whether with reference to the Statute, or otherwise. And by Order XIX, rule 13, it is provided that allegations not denied or stated to be not admitted, shall be taken to be admitted. Hence if a defendant in an action in which the Statute might be pleaded does not expressly deny the contract in fact, and also plead the Statute, he will be taken to admit both the existence of the contract and its compliance with the Statute. If, however, the defendant wishes to plead the Statute while at the same time admitting the fact of the contract, it would seem clear from Order XIX, rule 15, considered in the light of the former Chancery practice, that he may do so.

[1] *Humphries* v. *Humphries*, [1910] 2 K.B. 531 (C.A.). Phipson, *Law of Evidence*, 7th ed. pp. 398 *et seq.*

[2] Roscoe's *Evidence in Civil Actions*, 19th ed. I, p. 168; *Annual Practice*, 1932, p. 355.

CONCLUSION

As abundantly appears from the foregoing pages, the body of law which has developed around the Statute is both large and complex, and the steady tendency of the courts has been, where possible, to save contracts from the effects of non-compliance with the Statutory requirements. This tendency may readily be discerned in the restrictive manner in which the courts have construed the definitions of contracts not to be performed within a year,[1] and contracts to answer for the debt default or miscarriages of another.[2] It is clearly exhibited in the development of the authenticated signature fiction,[3] the relaxation of the rules regulating the use of several documents to make one writing,[4] the application of the common law principle of quasi-contract to contracts not complying with the Statute,[5] the application to writings under the Statute of the equitable jurisdiction to rectify documents,[6] and the operation in regard to the Statute of the equitable principles as to fraud[7] and part performance.[8] The effect of the cases may, it is submitted, be accurately summed up by saying that to a large extent the courts have practically repealed the Statute. Lord Moulton (then Fletcher Moulton, L.J.), in his judgment in *Hanau* v. *Ehrlich*,[9] expressed the position very vividly.

"In my opinion", he said, "little is left of the statute. The courts are bound by decisions which they may well think out of harmony both with the spirit and the letter of the enactment. For instance, in very early decisions the courts, influenced by the fear that the statute would otherwise work injustice, decided that a contract was to be performed within a year if one of the contracting parties could perform his part within a year. The result is that a contract which cannot be completely performed within twenty years must be treated as a contract to be performed within a year, if on one side it can be so performed."

[1] P. 28 *supra*.
[2] P. 5 *supra*.
[3] P. 82 *supra*.
[4] P. 127 *supra*.
[5] P. 212 *supra*.
[6] P. 262 *supra*.
[7] P. 221 *supra*.
[8] P. 230 *supra*.
[9] [1911] 2 K.B. 1056, 1066.

Although, however, the Statute has to a great extent been nullified by the courts, the processes by which the courts have achieved this result have of necessity brought in their train many complexities and over-refined distinctions. The distinction which has been drawn between a contract for an indefinite period and one for a definite period exceeding a year, but determinable within the year, may be instanced.[1] Other examples are the rules which have been developed with regard to signature,[2] the doctrine of part performance,[3] the distinction between a subsequent agreement producing an implied rescission and a subsequent agreement amounting merely to a variation,[4] and the distinction between a contract of guarantee and a contract of indemnity.[5]

In view of these considerations it may well be asked whether the Statute should not be repealed, or if not repealed, extensively modified. The complexity and bulk of the law with which the Statute has become surrounded would certainly indicate that at the very least some sort of restatement and amendment of that law is called for. But there are further considerations to be taken into account, and these indicate that amendment and restatement would be but an inadequate remedy: the Statute has, in truth, outlived its usefulness, and should, it is submitted, be entirely repealed.

In the first place, the Statute, as has been shewn above,[6] was designed to afford a remedy for deficiencies which existed in the procedure of trial by jury at the time when the Statute was passed, accentuated as those deficiencies were by the imperfections existing in the law of evidence at that period. But nowadays, with the development of the device of granting a new trial where a jury returns a verdict against the weight of evidence and the development and improvement of the law of evidence, especially by the abrogation of the rules which formerly rendered the parties to an action incompetent as witnesses,[7] the defects in the law which led to the enactment of the Statute have long since ceased to exist.

[1] P. 32 *supra*. [2] P. 81 *supra*. [3] P. 230 *supra*.
[4] P. 179 *supra*. [5] P. 13, *supra*. [6] Introd. pp. xxx, xxxi.
[7] See Holdsworth, *History of English Law*, VI, pp. 388, 389.

Moreover, juries are, at the present day, frequently required to pronounce upon evidence and arguments of the most complex nature. And if, in the generality of cases, the jury is nowadays a satisfactory and adequate tribunal, capable of pronouncing upon any evidence which is admissible under the general law of evidence, it seems impossible to justify a rule which, in particular cases presenting no special features of difficulty, arbitrarily rejects all evidence except such as is embodied in signed writings.[1]

The effect of the Statute has, indeed, long been simply to restrict the freedom of contract, and that it has such an effect is by itself a most serious indictment of it. The fundamental importance of preserving unimpaired the freedom of contract was emphatically stated by Jessel, M.R., in a case[2] in which it was contended that a particular contract was void as being contrary to public policy. The following passage from the judgment of the Master of the Rolls may be quoted:

"...if there is one thing which more than another public policy requires, it is that men of full age and competent understanding shall have the utmost liberty of contracting, and that their contracts when entered into freely and voluntarily shall be held sacred and shall be enforced by Courts of Justice".

Contract is the creature of the mutual agreement of the parties; and it is conceived that in general the parties may be trusted to secure that their contracts are evidenced in a satisfactory and adequate manner. The penalty of having their contract declared void for uncertainty should be a sufficient incentive to induce the parties to attend to this aspect of the matter. It is no sufficient argument for the retention of the Statute to say that the provision of written evidence simplifies the task of the court. In cases such as actions on contracts, where in general the parties

[1] The New Procedure Rules (Rules of Supreme Court, Ord. XXXVIII A) which came into operation on May 24, 1932, render less necessary than ever any such safeguard as the Statute purports to provide, for by virtue of these Rules, it will henceforth be in the discretion of the judge whether actions on contracts shall be tried before a jury. The Rules are restricted to actions proceeding in the Central Registry and the Manchester and Liverpool Registries.

[2] *Printing and Numerical Registering Co.* v. *Sampson*, (1875) L.R. 19 Eq. 462, 465.

and others concerned are available to give their personal testimony, it should be the duty of the courts, as being the instruments by which the Crown gives effect to the Royal declaration *nulli negabimus justitiam*, to hear the evidence adduced, whether oral or written, and to pronounce upon it. The case for the repeal of the Statute seems, indeed, to be unanswerable.[1]

[1] See Holdsworth, *History of English Law*, VI, p. 396 and Pollock, L.Q.R. XIX, p. 247. The view that the Statute should be repealed is at the present day generally accepted both in legal and commercial circles. Holdsworth, *loc. cit.*

INDEX

A

E

F

U

V

W

Y

For EU product safety concerns, contact us at Calle de José Abascal, 56–1°, 28003 Madrid, Spain or eugpsr@cambridge.org.

www.ingramcontent.com/pod-product-compliance
Ingram Content Group UK Ltd.
Pitfield, Milton Keynes, MK11 3LW, UK
UKHW040226290926
15471UKWH00001B/20
* 9 7 8 1 1 0 7 6 7 3 7 7 9 *